Forming a Nation

the story of Canada and Canadians

Book 2

RODERICK STEWART

NEIL McLEAN

Gage Educational Publishing Limited

ISBN 0-7715-8521-7
1 2 3 4 5 6 7 8 9 10   BP   82 81 80 79 78
Written, printed, and bound in Canada

THE GAGE CANADIAN STUDIES SERIES:

FORMING A NATION: The Story of Canada and Canadians, Book 1 by Roderick Stewart and Neil McLean

FORMING A NATION: The Story of Canada and Canadians, Book 2 by Roderick Stewart and Neil McLean

THE PEOPLE WE ARE: Canada's Multicultural Society by Dean Wood and Robert Remnant

FORGING A DESTINY: Canada Since 1945 by E. A. Mitchner, M. B. Demaine, J. P. Raymond, and R. A. Frise

PREFACE

FORMING A NATION: The Story of Canada and Canadians, Book 2 offers a study of Canadians, their challenges and achievements, from 1867 to 1945. This core book presents topics in such a way that students can examine them not as isolated events but as parts of a larger, ongoing process. It can be used for chronological and thematic studies.

Prime objectives of this book are to develop:

- a knowledge of Canada's multicultural tradition. The emphasis is not on the *immigrations* but on the people, the *immigrants* — their backgrounds, problems, and adjustments.
- an appreciation that Canadian unity is based on a recognition of cultural diversity.
- an appreciation of the Canadian experience. It may sometimes parallel, sometimes merge with, sometimes diverge from the American experience — but it is uniquely our own.
- a knowledge of Canada's post-Confederation expansion from sea to sea.
- an understanding of the social, political, and economic strands that are interwoven in the story of Canada.
- an appreciation of the changes in Canadian society through political reform, technology, labor movements, and other social forces.
- an awareness of values through time.
- an ability to distinguish fact from fiction.
- an ability to differentiate between prejudice and point of view.

The historical approach is developed through the application of the kinds of questions, viewpoints, and techniques a trained social scientist uses. The Study sections in this book have been designed to develop skills in collecting, selecting, analysing, interpreting, and evaluating information.

Last, but not least, history comes alive through the many illustrations in this book. There are sketches, paintings, engravings, and photographs that provide "visual proof" of the people and events of our past.

CONTENTS

LIST OF MAPS AND DIAGRAMS

A WORD TO THE READER

Several special features have been included in this book to help you locate, bring together, and understand details of Canadian history in the period 1867-1945.

Marginal notes. These appear in the margin beside the person or event being discussed. They have been included as "handy helps" to assist review, supply extra information, or refer you to more material on the same topic elsewhere in the book.

Study sections. These appear at the end of each chapter. Their purpose is to help you recall and analyse information, summarize material, promote discussion, make judgments, and do research using sources outside this book.

Indexes. There are two indexes, on pages 310-314. One lists proper names, so that you can find information on personalities and places. The other lists major topics, so that you can locate the pages in the book that deal with a particular subject.

unit 1

Immigration and Settlement

CHAPTER I

Confederation: the early years

"Monday, 1st Dominion Day! The first day of July, in the year of our Lord 1867, is the Birth Day of the Dominion of Canada. Nova Scotia has entered today into a new state of things, having now entered into a partnership, forever, with New Brunswick and the Canadas. The booming of the cannon early this morning announced the Birth of the New Dominion and the ringing of the Church Bells proclaimed the gladness . . . ." So Adolphus Goetz of Lunenburg, Nova Scotia, remembered Confederation in his diary.

In Ottawa, the day had started shortly after midnight, with an artillery salute of 101 guns, the pealing of all the church bells, and a huge bonfire. Saint John, New Brunswick, marked "this greatest of all modern marriages" with a 21-gun salute at four o'clock in the morning. The batteries of Fort Henry near Kingston, Ontario, boomed out their greeting as well. And throughout the new Dominion, Canadians attended church services to pray for the nation's welfare.

By the middle of the day, Canadians had made their way to town halls, to local parks, or to city squares, to hear the proclamation of the British North America Act (BNA Act). With pomp and ceremony, the new Dominion was proclaimed; military bands played "God Save The Queen"; and the people raised three cheers for Queen Victoria and Confederation.

THE NEW NATION

Canada's Population, 1867

British	60%
French	30%
Other	10%

Many Canadians living today would be surprised if they returned in time to that Canada of 1867. The new nation was tiny, stretching in a narrow corridor from Cape Breton Island in the east to Lake Superior in the west. Its total population was only about 3 300 000 people — fewer than in Canada's two largest cities today. There were only a few cities — Halifax and Saint John, Quebec City and Montreal, Kingston and Toronto. Some of the larger towns had become the home of industries. But most of the people lived on the land; Canada was mainly a country of farms and villages.

Almost half of Canada's people lived in Ontario. In this mostly English-speaking province, most of the good farmland had already been taken up. Throughout Ontario place names give evidence of where settlers came from. Around Toronto, names like York, Scarborough,

N.F.B. Photothèque, Photo by John Hus, November 1973

North America's oil industry was born in Ontario. Here, at what was later called Oil Springs, James M. Williams of London, Ontario, built a refinery to process surface deposits of bitumen, an almost solid form of petroleum. From this he obtained a foul-smelling, brightly burning lamp fuel that sold for $1 a gallon. In 1858, he dug down 15 metres and found free-flowing petroleum.

Pickering, and Whitby come directly from a map of northeastern England. In western Ontario, names from northern Ireland abound — Belfast, Dungannon, Donegal, Newry, and Dundalk. And in tiny villages and large towns can be found the Scots names — Seaforth, Kincardine, Lochalsh, Kintail, and Tobermory. But while English-speaking peoples from the British Isles were in the majority, there were pockets of peoples of other origins. Near Windsor, there was a small group of French-speaking Canadians. In Kent County, near Chatham, was established a settlement of former black slaves, now "freemen and citizens of Canada." In Waterloo County was a large concentration of people of German origin. These were the Pennsylvania Dutch — Mennonites who had trekked north from the United States in search of fertile farmland. Many immigrants from Germany had joined these original settlers, and the place names reflected their roots — Berlin, Breslau, Wallenstein, Heidelberg, and Baden.

In the midst of the settled rural communities in the south and the frontier clearings of Huron and Bruce counties, a new Ontario was beginning to take shape. In addition to the flour and saw mills of earlier

The German word for "German" is "Deutsch."

Berlin was renamed Kitchener in 1916.

This photograph of Quebec City's harbor was taken about 1867. Prior to this time, the harbor had been a forest of masts and rigging as several hundred ships lay anchored in the St. Lawrence River, waiting their turn to dock. But in the late 1850s, the channel farther up the river was deepened and widened, and Montreal replaced Quebec City as the port of call for large cargo vessels.

George Brown, 1818-1880

days there were new industries: leather tanneries, producing the raw materials for shoe factories; furniture factories, using the hardwoods of southern Ontario to produce sturdy home furnishings; and iron mills, providing the raw materials for a growing agricultural implement industry. Led by men like George Brown, the owner of the Toronto *Globe*, Ontario was growing up and out. Its farmers wanted new lands to cultivate; its industrialists and businessmen, new markets. Ontario saw opportunities in the Confederation of 1867 and intended to take advantage of them.

In the Province of Quebec, the picture was different. Of Quebec's total population of a little over one million, about 750 000 people were French-speaking. Most of them lived in rural communities, away from towns and cities where industry and commerce were developing. In these centres, the proportion of English-speaking residents was much higher than in the general population of the province.

By the terms of the British North America Act, French Canadians maintained the rights needed to guarantee the survival of their culture in Quebec. Control of education was to remain in the hands of the provinces, and French was designated an official language both federally (in Parliament, federal courts, and publications of the federal government) and in the Province of Quebec (in the legislature, courts, and provincial government publications). But whether these rights would really guarantee the survival of Quebec as a "French island in the

Education is dealt with in Section 93 of the BNA Act. See p. 117.

4

English-speaking sea of North America" was another question.

In 1871, 41 per cent of the 60 000 residents of Quebec City were English-speaking. And Quebec City, the centre of traditional Quebec, was watching its economy decline. Iron ships were replacing wooden ones, and Quebec City's biggest industry, shipbuilding, faltered. Moreover, the new steamships could plough their way up the St. Lawrence as far as the port of Montreal, much farther than the sailing ships, which generally berthed at Quebec. Montreal was quickly replacing Quebec City as the centre of the province's commerce. By 1871, the old settlement of Ville Marie had become the largest city in Canada, as well as the transportation, trading, and banking centre of the Dominion. And Montreal had become more than half English-speaking.

The outlook for many French-speaking Québecois was bleak. They could stay on their small farms, but this meant a hard, hand-to-mouth existence, worsened by debts and outdated farming methods. For those who wanted bigger farms, a lack of roads made it impossible to get to new settlement areas like the Eastern Townships. An individual or family might move to the developing industrial centres, but this often meant exchanging rural poverty for urban poverty. Moreover, many industrial employers were Anglophones, so a move to an industrial town would probably mean a loss of traditional cultural values.

In spite of the probable loss of their heritage, however, large numbers of Québecois *had* left the limited farming situation of their homeland for jobs in the mill towns of New England. "The flood of emigrants from the Province of Quebec," it was said, "overcame all obstacles, swept over all dams." Confederation, political leaders like Georges Etienne Cartier hoped, would provide opportunities for Québecois and stop the draining away of Canadien blood.

In the Maritime Provinces, there was much less enthusiasm than in Ontario and Quebec about the possibilities of Confederation. And even after it accepted Confederation, New Brunswick still looked not inland

Nature offered the Province of New Brunswick great opportunities to engage in shipbuilding and shipping. There were stands of black birch, hackmatack, spruce, and yellow and red pine. There were rivers to carry the timber to shipyards near the sea. And there were protected harbors to shelter vessels engaged in an extensive coastal trade.

ARCTIC OCEAN

GREENLAND
(Denmark)

ALASKA
(U.S.A.)

THE

NORTH-WESTERN

PACIFIC OCEAN

British
Columbia

TERRITORY

Hudson
Bay

RUPERT'S

LAND

Newfoundland

49°N

QUEBEC

P.E.I.

UNITED STATES OF AMERICA

ONTARIO

Ottawa

N.S.

N.B.

ATLANTIC
OCEAN

0   500
km

CANADA IN 1867

to Canada, but outward to the sea. At Saint John, for example, shipyards continued to build sailing ships for commerce and the fisheries. The fertile soils of the province were still almost totally covered with heavy forest — profitable for the lumber trade, but a major obstacle to settlement. Only in the Saint John River Valley had good-sized communities developed. Even here, where Loyalists from the American colonies had been joined by a trickle of immigrants from the British Isles, settlement was restricted by landlords who failed to provide the roads necessary for expansion.

If New Brunswick was at best cool to Confederation, its neighbor, Nova Scotia, was hotly opposed. As early as 1865, the "Grand Old Man of Nova Scotia," reformer Joseph Howe, had begun his fight against union with Canada. In a series of articles called the "Botheration Let-

*Joseph Howe,
1804-1873*

6

Joseph Howe, "The Tribune of Nova Scotia" as he was sometimes called, had a long and brilliant career as a journalist and politician. As editor of the Nova-scotian and as a member of the Legislative Assembly, Howe fought for improvements in government, education, agriculture, railways, mail service, fisheries, etc. After the negotiation of the financial terms of Confederation, Howe described his province as having been sold for "eighty cents per head, the price of a Nova Scotian as well as a sheep!"

ters," he had preached against Confederation and gained the support of many Nova Scotians. The people of the province suspected, perhaps rightly so, that the benefits of Confederation would go to Ontario and Quebec. Besides, did Nova Scotia really need Canada? In the 1860s, the province was the centre of important shipbuilding and shipping industries, and its prosperity was linked not with the interior of North America, but with the sea. One famous Haligonian, Samuel Cunard, had led the way in North Atlantic shipping in the 1840s and 1850s, and his fleet was still the best afloat. Yarmouth was still one of the most important shipbuilding centres on the Atlantic. Could being Canadian really improve life in Nova Scotia?

An immediate answer to this question came in the first elections held after Confederation. In the provincial election, thirty-six of thirty-eight members elected were opposed to the union with Canada. In elections for the House of Commons, seventeen of the eighteen members of Parliament for Nova Scotia ridings were anti-Confederationists. Armed with this massive support, Joseph Howe sailed for London to convince the British government that Nova Scotia should be released from its ties with Canada.

Howe's mission was unsuccessful. The British government refused to let Nova Scotia leave Confederation. Howe had little choice but to accept this decision and return home. He did manage to get some benefits for his province, however. The Dominion government agreed to take over some of the province's debt and to increase the annual subsidy Nova Scotia would receive under the terms of Confederation.

The course of Confederation was not to be decided only by the provinces of Canada. Factors operating far beyond the boundaries of the new nation were to affect its future. Of these factors, three were particularly important: the state of the British Empire; the expansion of Canada's neighbor, the United States; and the future of North American colonies and territories that belonged to Great Britain.

In 1867, Great Britain was reaching a turning point. For more than half a century, Britain had been the workshop of the world. Its manufactured products — cotton goods, china and porcelain, cutlery, glassware, iron rails, locomotives, machine tools — had found markets everywhere. The Industrial Revolution had begun in Britain, and the British enjoyed a fifty-year head start on all the other manufacturing nations in the world. But, by the time of Confederation, industries were beginning to grow in Europe and the United States, and British manufacturers began to encounter some competition. Great Britain began to look for sure markets. It found them — not in the Dominion of Canada or in the colonies of North America, with their small populations, but in other parts of the British Empire, like India, where tens of millions of people could provide large markets for British goods.

From the British point of view, therefore, Confederation could be viewed as a tidying-up of colonial affairs. It was a way of freeing Britain from responsibility for its colonies in North America, which would allow the British government to concentrate on issues of greater importance to Great Britain.

Tidying up in North America involved relations with Canada's southern neighbor. The United States had just suffered through a Civil War, which had resulted in the defeat of the southern, agricultural states. The northern states could now pursue their vision of North America — a vast, continental market, in which the industrial and financial centres of the northeastern United States would develop and control territories from Mexico all the way to the Arctic Ocean. The United States had already taken over territories south of the 49th parallel, from the Atlantic Ocean to the Pacific. What was to be the future of the remaining British territories in North America — Newfoundland and Prince Edward Island; British Columbia and the hundreds of thousands of hectares of Arctic and subarctic lands? And what was to become of Rupert's Land, the historic region owned by the Hudson's Bay Company?

Canadians, like Americans, also had a vision for the future of the northern half of North America. During the Confederation discussions in London, the "Kingdom of Canada" had been rejected as a title for the new nation. Premier Tilley of New Brunswick suggested another name, a name he took from the Old Testament (72nd Psalm):

> In His days shall the righteous flourish, and
> abundance of peace so long as the moon endureth;
> He shall have dominion also from sea to sea, and
> from the river to the ends of the earth.

The term "Dominion of Canada" meant a territory under the "dominion" of the British Crown. However, it could also be interpreted as the promise of a dominion that would stretch far beyond the boundaries of the Confederation of 1867 — from the Atlantic to the Pacific, and from the 49th parallel to the Arctic Ocean.

 Canada's first prime minister, Sir John A. Macdonald, was a practical politician. For some of his opponents, he was perhaps too practical, too clever, too much of a politician to ever be a statesman. At first he had accepted the idea of Confederation as a practical solution to the political problems in the Province of Canada. But then, once Confederation had

John A. Macdonald, 1815-1891

Left: A carving of Sir Samuel Leonard Tilley (1818-1896), druggist-turned-politician, who became a strong supporter of, and tireless worker for, Confederation. It was Tilley's speeches on the necessity of Confederation that convinced many a New Brunswicker to vote for the Conservatives.

Right: In 1867, John Alexander Macdonald was fifty-two years old, tired and worn down by years of political battles and the strain of helping to put Confederation together. However, his dream was not yet fully realized. He was destined to spend a further twenty-four years extending Confederation to create a Dominion from sea to sea.

New Brunswick Museum   The Public Archives of Canada, C 5327

N.F.B. Photothèque, Photo by George Hunter, 1966

Until the twentieth century, settlement in Newfoundland was mostly confined to the harbors and coves along a 3700-kilometre coastline. People earned their living from the sea, and the ocean was often the only means of communication between settlements. Newfoundland was Britain's oldest colony. It was formally claimed for Queen Elizabeth I of England by Sir Humphrey Gilbert in 1583 in the harbor of St. John's.

been achieved, he began to see a larger Canada. Macdonald's challenge was to make real that vision of a dominion from sea to sea.

EXTENDING CONFEDERATION

This territory has had three names: North-Western Territory, 1869; North-West Territories, 1875; Northwest Territories, 1905.

Newfoundland feared increased taxes and the breaking of ties with Great Britain.

The first six years of Confederation witnessed an almost unbelievable extension of Canadian territory. By 1873, Canada was almost eight times the size it had been in 1867. Newfoundland, Rupert's Land, the "North-Western Territory," British Columbia, and Prince Edward Island — all were sought as members of the new Dominion.

Newfoundland had sent delegates to the Quebec Conference in 1864, and, in 1865, had elected a government sympathetic to union with the other British colonies. Still, Newfoundlanders remained hesitant about union. So July 1, 1867, came and went, without the island colony's joining Confederation. However, negotiations continued, and seemed to promise positive results. In May of 1869, Newfoundland delegates were in Ottawa agreeing on the terms of union, and in June, Macdonald was writing a colleague that Newfoundland was to join Confederation. Then, in November 1869, the people of the colony voted heavily against their pro-Confederation government, and the idea of union was dropped. Eighty years were to pass before Newfoundland became Canada's tenth province.

The same Macdonald letter that described the Newfoundland situation also mentioned an agreement reached with the British government, by which Canada had "quietly and almost without observation annexed all the country between here and the Rocky Mountains." Imagine what that means. In today's terms, it would amount to Canada, "quietly and almost without observation," annexing the entire land masses of the United States, Mexico, and Central America! This was imperialism on a grand scale; the drama of Canadian empire was about to unfold.

What was "all the country between here and the Rocky Mountains"? Was Macdonald referring to what many Canadians called the "Northwest" — all the territory to the west and the north of Canada? Or was he referring to a specific region in the Northwest? One region is Canada's Precambrian Shield, the huge U-shaped mass of ancient rock that surrounds Hudson Bay and stretches northward into the Arctic Ocean. Another is the immense drainage basin of the Mackenzie River, whose waters drain into the Arctic Ocean. The third region, sometimes described as that part of North America's Great Plains that lies north of the 49th parallel, can be defined as the land through which flow the Saskatchewan, Assiniboine, Souris and Red rivers. This is the region most Canadians call the "prairies," and this is the region Macdonald was thinking about when he spoke of the "country between here and the Rocky Mountains."

The old Province of Canada had been thinking about expansion into the Northwest for a long time. People in Montreal and Toronto were just as able and just as ready to plan continental expansion as people in New York City or Philadelphia or Washington. In the 1840s and 1850s, in response to this interest, governments sent out scientific expeditions to investigate the lands beyond the Great Lakes. In 1857, the British government sent out one of the most famous expeditions. Under the leadership of Captain John Palliser, a party of "Gentlemen, Scotch half-breeds, French half-breeds, Americans, Canadians and one coloured man, Dan Williams" criss-crossed the prairies. Their travels took them from Fort Garry, on the Red River, into the Rocky Mountains. Palliser reported on the climatic conditions, on the wild life, and on the best ways to reach agreement with the Indian tribes in the area and to establish law and order. As far as he was concerned, there was agricultural potential in a "Fertile Belt" in the watersheds of the North Saskatchewan and Assiniboine rivers. However, the open prairies, where there was uncertain rainfall and a general lack of water and wood, were of little value: ". . . wherever we struck out on the broad prairie we generally found the soil worthless, except here and there in small swamps."

That same year, the government of the Province of Canada also sent an exploring party west. It included Simon Dawson, the man who laid out the Dawson Road north of Lake Superior, and Professor Henry Youle Hind of Toronto's Trinity College. Professor Hind's report on western prospects was more favorable than Palliser's. Because they were interested in westward expansion, Canadian politicians were more prepared to accept Hind's report.

The politicians reflected the hopes of the people of Canada West,

A member of the expedition was knocked senseless by a kicking horse in one of the passes in the Rocky Mountains.

This open prairie, which became known as Palliser's Triangle, is now the bread-basket of Canada.

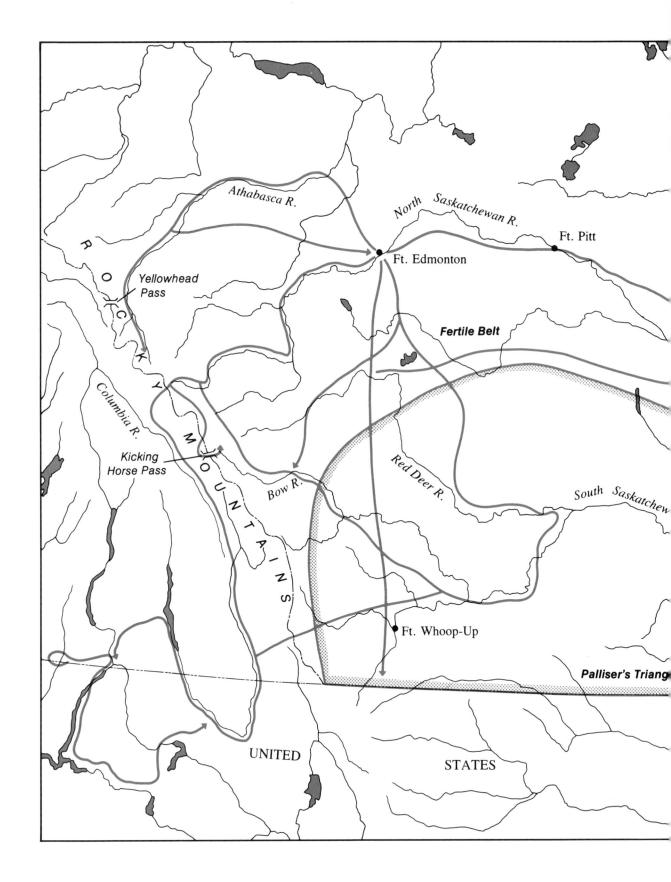

Athabasca R.

North Saskatchewan R.

Ft. Pitt

R
O
C
K
Y

Yellowhead
Pass

Ft. Edmonton

Fertile Belt

Columbia R.

M
O
U
N
T
A
I
N
S

Kicking
Horse Pass

Bow R.

Red Deer R.

South Saskatchew

Ft. Whoop-Up

Palliser's Triang

UNITED

STATES

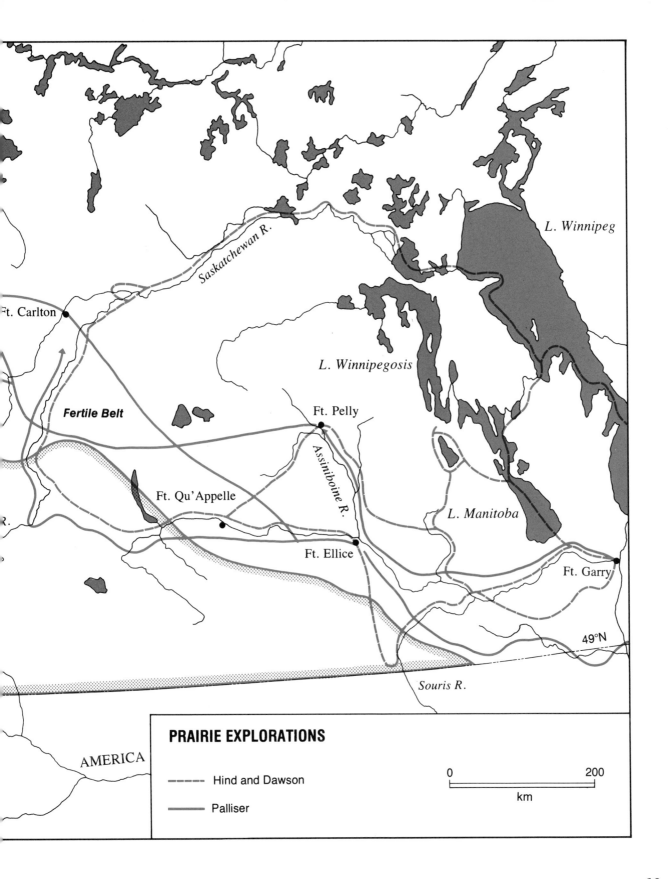

L. Winnipeg

Saskatchewan R.

Ft. Carlton

L. Winnipegosis

Fertile Belt

Ft. Pelly

Assiniboine R.

Ft. Qu'Appelle

L. Manitoba

Ft. Ellice

Ft. Garry

49°N

Souris R.

AMERICA

PRAIRIE EXPLORATIONS

- - - - - Hind and Dawson

——— Palliser

0   200
km

particularly the farmers in present-day southern Ontario. These Anglophone Canadians saw at least two opportunities in the Northwest. First, in spite of the mosquitos in summer and the blizzards in winter, the Northwest promised farmland that would be easy to clear. Canada West was running out of good land, and the little that was left was wooded. While there might be only thirty or thirty-five trees to a hectare (an area a little larger than a Canadian football field), the trees were gigantic hardwoods — maple, black walnut, and cherry — sometimes almost two metres in diameter at the base! Weeks and months of dangerous, backbreaking work went into chopping down these trees and removing their stumps. As well, in many parts of Canada West, thousands of troublesome rocks, from small stones to huge boulders, had to be picked up or blasted into smaller pieces with dynamite so they could be hauled away. Stone fences still mark the boundaries of many fields in Ontario, evidence of the long hours and sore backs that went into preparing fields for cultivation.

By the Act of Union, Canada East and Canada West were joined to form the Province of Canada.

The people of Ontario also hoped that the Northwest would help them achieve a political goal: the domination of English Protestant Ontario over French Catholic Quebec. The Act of Union of 1841 had originally been an advantage for Canada West, because, in spite of its smaller population, it was to have equal representation with Canada East, which was predominantly French. In the 1840s and 1850s, however, the situation changed. Immigrants swelled the population of Canada West until it surpassed that of Canada East. But the same old representation rule remained in effect, and to stay in power, governments needed support in both Canadas. The Reformers in Canada West had been furious that the Conservatives were able to hold on to power simply because of the support of French Catholics in Canada East.

Even before Confederation, Canada West had exerted political influence in the affairs of the Northwest. In 1859, the fur monopoly of the Hudson's Bay Company had not been renewed, partly as a result of the arguments against renewal by the government of the Province of Canada. Also in 1859, two journalists from Canada West, William Buckingham and William Coldwell, established a newspaper called the *Nor'Wester* in the Red River colony, to promote Canada West's desire to annex the Northwest. In 1863, the London bankers of the Province of Canada's Grand Trunk Railway formed the International Financial Society and bought control of the Hudson's Bay Company. And in the BNA Act, the Canada West representatives insisted on a clause (146) that provided for the admission of "Rupert's Land and the North-Western Territory, or either of them into the Union."

For details on the Grand Trunk Railway, see pp. 40-45.

After Confederation, Ontario pressure for expansion into the Northwest grew steadily. In the Northwest, there would be agricultural opportunities for Ontario farmers and commercial opportunities for Ontario businessmen. The Northwest would also give Ontario an opportunity to establish once and for all its domination over Quebec, and so

In 1852, when this water color of John Palliser was painted, he had already visited the Great Plains of North America. In 1847-1848, he wandered about the lands bordering the headwaters of the Missouri River, sometimes in company with traders working for the American Fur Company, sometimes on his own. He learned to run buffalo, stalk antelope, track elk and deer, and shoot wolves and grizzly bears.

For several centuries, the fur trade was Canada's greatest industry. This photograph, taken in the 1890s, shows one independent trader sorting about $35 000 worth of beaver, fox, mink, and other pelts.

start Confederation off on the "right" political foot. This point of view was pressed by George Brown, who wanted to see religion, particularly the Catholic religion of so many French Canadians, removed as a factor in Canadian politics. He believed that the Church should have no influence on politics; with the expansion of Ontario into the Northwest, the influence of the French Canadians would be reduced, and the Catholic Church would have a much less significant role to play in Canadian politics.

Canada West had not been the only outsider interested in Rupert's Land and the North-Western Territory. Americans were taking an interest in the Red River colony. Minnesota became a state in 1858, and some people in St. Paul, the state capital, thought it natural and right that the Red River settlement should become part of the United States. Proof of the natural ties between Minnesota and the Red River settlement was reinforced in 1859, when the Hudson's Bay Company began to ship supplies to the depot of Fort Garry down the Red River from St. Paul instead of via York Factory on Hudson Bay. In 1862, the Minnesota legislature suggested that the United States should annex what was termed "Saskatchewan." Two American agents in the Red River colony, James Wickes Taylor and Enos Stutzman, continued this agitation for annexation. In 1866, Taylor was the moving force behind a bill introduced into the U.S. Congress for the admission of all British territories, including "Selkirk," into the American Union!

Selkirk was Taylor's name for the Red River area. The first settlement here was founded by Lord Selkirk in 1812.

16

THE NORTHWEST

Two steamrollers, Canadian and American, seemed ready to roll into the Northwest. But what about the people who lived there? How did they feel about the situation? In the Red River district, there was a good-sized settlement of about 11 700 people who were vitally concerned about the future of *their* Northwest.

The Census of 1871 provides useful figures on Canada's original peoples about the time of Confederation. The total estimated population of approximately 146 000 Indians and Inuit was located regionally as follows:

Maritimes	4 000
Ontario and Quebec	26 000
British Columbia	82 000
Rupert's Land and the North-Western Territory	34 000

The peoples of the North-Western Territory and Rupert's Land included the Cree of the Precambrian Shield, the Inuit of the North, the Athapaskan-speaking peoples of the Mackenzie River drainage basin, and the people of the Plains — Cree, Assiniboine, and the Blackfoot Confederacy of Blackfeet, Piegan, Blood, and Sarcee.

A painting of the junction of the Red and Assiniboine rivers in 1867. On the far left is one edge of Upper Fort Garry, built by the Hudson's Bay Company in the 1830s on the site of the future city of Winnipeg. On the other side of the Red River are the buildings of a Roman Catholic mission, the beginnings of a Francophone settlement that later became the city of St. Boniface.

Courtesy of the Hudson's Bay Company

These people included about 500 Indians; 1500 settlers (descendants of the original Kildonan Scottish settlers); a few Hudson's Bay Company employees; a handful of recently arrived immigrants from Canada; and approximately 4000 English-speaking Métis and about 5700 French-speaking Métis.

In the half century before the 1860s two different lifestyles had developed in the Red River settlement. Generally speaking, the children of Indian mothers and English or Scottish fathers learned English and sometimes went to the British Isles or the Province of Canada for their education. These English Métis farmed or got jobs with the Hudson's Bay Company as clerks or factors (senior administrators at HBC depots). Their culture and way of life followed that of their fathers, and was much the same as that of Englishmen or Scots. Although some of the children of Indian mothers and French fathers — French Métis or *bois-brûlés* — followed a farming life like many English Métis, most of them pursued different occupations. The most free-spirited were probably the HBC tripmen. With nicknames like "Whitefish," "Badger," or "Bull," they manned the York boats of the Company's "brigades," carrying supplies to the interior depots and posts in the

The word "Métis" refers to people of mixed Indian and European descent. Sometimes the term "bois-brûlés" was used for French Métis.

The boats were so called because they were first built at York Factory on Hudson Bay.

No nails were used in the construction of the Red River cart; it was held together by thongs made from buffalo hide. No grease could be used to lubricate the wheels because of the ever-present prairie dust. The result was a screeching and wailing of wood on wood, which could be heard for long distances.

In the nineteenth century, the only way to get through the vast forest belt north and west of the prairies was by following certain waterways. Here, a trader's scow runs a set of rapids on the Slave River, which leads to the fur-rich lands bordering Canada's longest and largest river: the Mackenzie.

spring and returning with loads of furs in October. When the Company began to import its supplies from St. Paul, some of these tripmen became carters — wagon-drivers who took Red River carts filled with supplies and provisions to and from prairie posts.

The chief occupation of the French Métis was the buffalo hunt, the annual expedition to the Plains for pemmican and buffalo robes. Begun as hunting trips by individuals, it had gradually developed into a large-scale, well-planned organization that involved a large proportion of the *bois-brûlé* community. Each individual was responsible for his own equipment — ponies, guns, ammunition, and Red River cart. The need for organization and discipline was fulfilled through the democratic election of hunt officers: the president or "chief" of the hunt, his councillors, and hunt "captains." In a sense, the buffalo hunt *was* the Métis nation — a whole society on the move, including family groups, elected officials, and priests, who held religious devotions on the Sabbath, when no hunting was allowed.

This free-spirited frontier society was quite different from the agricultural and partly industrialized society of eastern North America. But changes were coming to the Red River settlement. The great buffalo herds had not yet been destroyed, but "free traders," operating without the restraint of Hudson's Bay Company rules and regulations, were stripping the country of all the furs they could lay their hands on. Pressure for annexation was coming from Minnesota and from Canada.

The first use of Red River carts was to bring back meat from the Métis buffalo hunt.

19

Bright young Métis like James Ross and Louis Riel went away to school in Toronto or Montreal, saw for themselves the changing outside world, and began to wonder about the future of their homeland and its people.

There had been proposals in the early 1860s that the Red River settlement become a Crown colony, with its own government, to replace the old HBC-sponsored Council of Assiniboia. But the British government did not accept the Crown colony proposal. It preferred to wait until it could hand over responsibility for the entire Northwest to the Dominion of Canada. Soon after Confederation, this was what happened. After years of discussion and argument, the Dominion government, backed by the British government, negotiated with the Hudson's Bay Company the terms under which Canada would take over Rupert's Land. By late 1869, all the legal preparations had been completed. The date of transfer of ownership to Canada was set for December 1st, 1869, although this would not be a legal takeover date until the deed of surrender was actually signed by HBC officials in London.

Official Canadian activity in the region had begun in 1868. Partly to develop a link between Canada and the Northwest, and partly to provide jobs, a Canadian construction party had been sent west to begin a road between St. Boniface and the Lake of the Woods. Unofficial activity had also begun; Canadian settlers were moving in, not so much to the Red River settlement itself as to an area farther west around Portage la Prairie. All these activities made the Métis suspicious. Moreover, there appeared to be an effort to tamper with Métis land claims. Métis farms generally followed the Quebec pattern of land division — narrow strips stretching back from the riverfront. These farms provided a little grain and hay for winter feed for livestock. A Canadian government party, sent to survey the Red River settlement, began to lay it out not in narrow strips but in square or rectangular blocks, like those in Ontario. When the Métis protested, Colonel J. S. Dennis, the leader of the party, stopped the surveys inside the settlement. But suspicion remained.

The activities of a tiny group of Canadians in the settlement, led by John Christian Schultz, increased the suspicion. Schultz and his friends gave everyone the impression that when Canada took over, things were going to change. Upset by uncertainty and suspicion, some Métis decided to act to protect themselves. On October 11, 1869, a group of Métis confronted and stopped Canadian surveyors who were laying out the base line for the settlement. This was no spur-of-the-moment act. Rather, it was a planned demonstration to show the Canadian government that the residents of the Red River area would have to be consulted on any arrangements that would be made for their colony.

One group of Métis led by Louis Riel began to emerge as the only really effective political force within the settlement. They did not represent all the Métis; even some of the *bois-brûlés* were not willing to accept Riel's leadership. But his supporters represented a legitimate Red River organization — the buffalo hunt — taking action according

In return for giving up its ownership of Rupert's Land, the HBC was to receive from Canada: £300 000 (about $1 500 000); 1/20 of the land within the Fertile Belt; continued ownership of blocks of land around HBC posts; and the right to continue trading activities.

Louis Riel, 1844-1885

This photograph of Louis Riel was taken about 1875. Riel's family was among the earliest settlers in the Red River region. His grandmother, Marie-Anne Gaboury, was the first French-Canadian woman to settle in Western Canada. Her voyageur husband, Jean-Baptiste Lagimodière, acted at one time as a courier for Lord Selkirk, the founder of the Red River colony of Assiniboia.

to the traditions of the settlement. Their leader, though still only twenty-five, commanded respect among his people. Riel's father had been something of a leader in his time, and Riel himself had been chosen as a possible candidate for the priesthood and had gone to Montreal for his education. When he returned to the Red River in 1868, he seemed to have developed a political sense and a desire to serve his people.

In mid-October, the National Committee of the Métis (*Comité National des Métis*) was formed, with John Bruce as president, although

PUBLIC NOTICE TO THE INHAB-ITANTS OF RUPERTSLAND.

The President and Representatives of the French-speaking population of Rupert's Land in Council, ("the Invaders of our rights being now expelled") already aware of your sympathy, do extend the hand of friendship to you our friendly fellow Inhabitants, and in doing so invite you to send twelve Representatives from the following places, viz.

St. John's 1, St. Margret's 1, Headingly 1, St. James 1, St. Mary's 1, Kildonan 1, St. Paul's 1, St. Andrew's 1, St. Clement's 1, St. Peter's 1, Town of Winnipeg 2 in order to form one body with the above Council consisting of twelve members to consider the present political state of this Country, and to adopt such measures as may be deemed best for the future welfare of the same.

A meeting of the above Council will be held in the Court House at Fort Garry on Tuesday the 16th day of November at which the invited Representatives will attend.

Winnipeg Nov. 6th 1869.

By order of the President,
LOUIS RIEL,
SECY.

Provincial Archives of Manitoba

Louis Riel did not consider his seizure of Fort Garry an act of rebellion. His aim was to force the Dominion government to negotiate, with all the settlers, terms of entry into Confederation. Riel was particularly anxious to get the support of the English-speaking settlers. Thus, in November, 1869, after occupying Fort Garry, he issued this announcement in the name of John Bruce, president of the "Comité National des Métis."

22

Riel, the secretary, was the real leader. A challenge to this Committee came very soon. The government of Canada was to take over Hudson's Bay Company territories on December 1, 1869; in order to provide for the administration of the area, Ottawa had passed an Act for the Temporary Government of Rupert's Land. By this Act, the Honorable William McDougall, Canadian minister of public works, was appointed lieutenant-governor. McDougall had long favored annexation of the Northwest and was the minister who had sent out the road and survey parties. In fact, McDougall was actually at Pembina, just across the border in the United States, ready to enter Rupert's Land. There, he received several appeals from Schultz and his companions to come to Red River and display the authority of Canada by announcing the impending takeover.

McDougall crossed the border, but was met by a party of armed Métis and turned back. Their aims were simple: they wished to prevent the Canadians in the settlement from using McDougall's presence as an excuse for seizing power, and they wanted the Dominion government to negotiate with them the terms on which Rupert's Land would be added to Canada. But these aims were not known, or were misunderstood or ignored. In Ontario, people made up their minds that the Métis action was illegal, and illegal action of this sort deserved only one name. The movement of the Red River people to protect their interests was considered a rebellion in spite of the fact that Canada did not yet legally own Rupert's Land, and that McDougall, when he crossed the border at Pembina, had no authority whatsoever to take over.

Riel meanwhile moved to strengthen his position in the settlement. On November 2, his men took over the HBC depot of Fort Garry, the strategic centre of Red River. On November 6, he invited representatives of the English-speaking people in the settlement to join with French Métis in a discussion about the future of the region. Throughout November, the Red River settlement experienced a period of intense debate and argument.

Then, on December 1, William McDougall appeared on the scene once again. He had been encouraged by the Canadians in the settlement to announce the takeover proclamation personally, and this was the official date that had been agreed on for the transfer. So, stepping over the border from Pembina on a dark night and speaking to an empty plain, McDougall read the proclamation by which Rupert's Land became part of Canada and he became its governor. As it turned out, this act was both illegal and foolish.

The transfer of Rupert's Land had been stalled by Ottawa. On November 19, the Company *had* signed an agreement with Canada and the transfer *was* to have taken effect on December 1, but Prime Minister Macdonald had decided to postpone the takeover. He wanted things to quiet down before Canada took over the colony. His motives were understandable. Why accept control over, and responsibility for, a

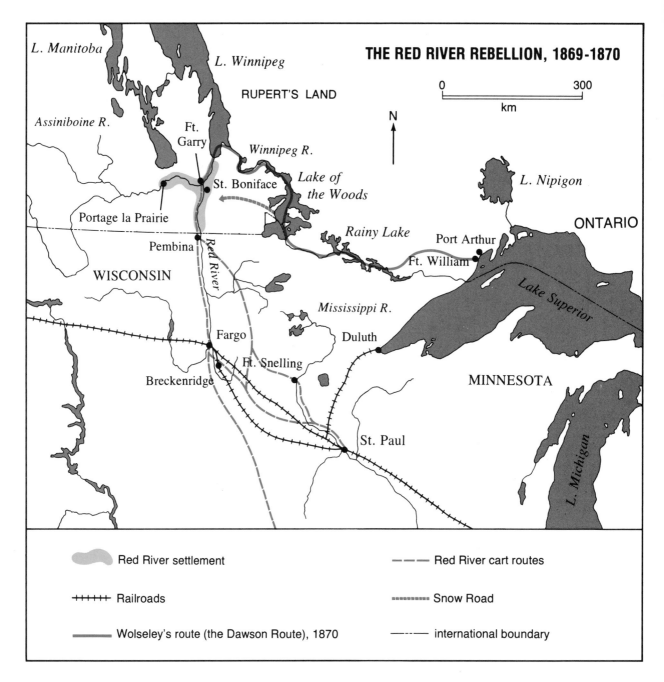

THE RED RIVER REBELLION, 1869-1870

L. Manitoba

L. Winnipeg

RUPERT'S LAND

Assiniboine R.

Ft. Garry

Winnipeg R.

St. Boniface

Lake of the Woods

L. Nipigon

Portage la Prairie

Pembina

Red River

Rainy Lake

Port Arthur

Ft. William

ONTARIO

WISCONSIN

Mississippi R.

Duluth

Lake Superior

Fargo

Ft. Snelling

Breckenridge

MINNESOTA

St. Paul

L. Michigan

N

0   300
km

Red River settlement

Railroads

Wolseley's route (the Dawson Route), 1870

Red River cart routes

Snow Road

international boundary

region that could only cause trouble for his government? In a letter to McDougall, Macdonald had pointed out that if McDougall were unable to assert his authority, and if the people of the colony were to form "a government . . . for the protection of life and property," the United States would find such a situation "very convenient." Better to leave the responsibility in the laps of the Hudson's Bay Company and the British government.

What Macdonald's government *did* do was to send commissioners to the West to find out what the people of Red River wanted. (Six months earlier, such a commission of inquiry might have worked out terms that would have avoided confusion and turmoil for everyone!) The commissioners were Colonel Charles de Salaberry, who had been a member of Professor Hind's party; Father Jean-Baptiste Thibault, who had served for many years as the pastor of St. François-Xavier parish in the Northwest; and Donald Smith, a senior officer in the Hudson's Bay Company, who had a special commission to "take steps . . . for effecting the peaceable transfer of the country and the government [of Rupert's Land] from the Hudson's Bay authorities to the Government of the Dominion."

Meanwhile, the situation in the Red River settlement was becoming more complicated. McDougall, acting quite illegally, appointed Colonel Dennis deputy-governor, and Dennis began to organize a force to oppose Riel. On December 8, the Métis leader issued the "Declaration of the People of Rupert's Land," in which he proclaimed the establishment of what he called a "Provisional Government." Riel became president of that government on December 27, the same day Donald Smith arrived in Red River. During the first three months of 1870, developments in the colony see-sawed back and forth, sometimes favoring one side, sometimes the other. They can be viewed as two separate but related streams — one political, the other military and physical.

Politically, Riel's aim was to get the backing of all the people of the settlement — not just the armed Métis of the buffalo hunt, but the

Donald Smith,
1820-1914
For more information
on Donald Smith,
see Chapter 3.

Hudson's Bay Company

In this painting, Donald Smith is explaining his task as "Special Commissioner" to a large crowd of Red River residents. Smith and his fellow commissioners had no authority to negotiate; their job was to persuade, not bargain. Smith addressed two meetings at Fort Garry. On each occasion, several hundred French and English Métis and Scots settlers stood for several hours in the biting wind, listening to Smith's explanation of Ottawa's intentions. After these meetings a convention was held, at which a List of Rights was drawn up, and, at Smith's suggestion, delegates were picked to go to Ottawa to discuss union with Canada.

25

French Métis farmers and traders, the English Métis, and the English-speaking settlers in Kildonan, in St. Andrew's, and in Portage la Prairie. Donald Smith worked at reducing Riel's influence, in the hopes of creating a stronger bargaining position for Canada. In the end, Riel was moderately successful. A List of Rights was drawn up, and delegates set out for Ottawa at the end of March to present it to the Canadian government. By the end of April, Riel's provisional government had begun to reorganize and to make laws for the territory, which they called "Assiniboia."

The other stream — the military/physical one — led to disaster and tragedy. A group of men, led by John Schultz, decided to challenge Riel. Riel's men anticipated the challenge, surrounded Schultz and his men in Schultz's house, and placed them in cells at Fort Garry on December 7. Late in January, Schultz and some of the other prisoners, one of whom was called Thomas Scott, escaped. Together with other supporters, they planned a raid to free their comrades still in Fort Garry. On the night of February 14, a party from nearby villages, under Schultz, and another party from Portage la Prairie, under a Captain Boulton, met near Kildonan. The next day, however, they were nearly all taken prisoner by Riel's men.

The Métis response to this second challenge was court-martial proceedings. Two men — Captain Boulton and Thomas Scott — were tried by a court, much like the ones the Métis used to deal with troublemakers on their buffalo hunts. Both men were condemned to death, although Donald Smith got Riel to persuade his colleagues to spare Captain Boulton's life. But there was no saving Thomas Scott, whose crime was "insubordination and striking the guards." Ambroise Lépine, the senior member of the court-martial, passed the death sentence on him. Scott was shot by a firing squad at Fort Garry on March 4, in Riel's words, in order to "make Canada respect us."

Death made Scott a hero and a martyr. In life, Scott had been a thoroughly unattractive character, a man who got attention as a workman on the Dawson Road by bullying and hard drinking. When he was a prisoner of the Métis, he refused offers of freedom if he took an oath of loyalty to Riel's provisional government; perhaps more important, he continually subjected his guards to insults and curses.

This person-to-person confrontation between Scott and his guards illustrates, perhaps better than anything else, the conflict that lay at the root of Red River politics in 1869-1870. Scott came from Ontario, and he brought with him to the Northwest a belief in the superiority of his own "civilization" and contempt for "half-breeds." The Métis naturally responded with proud anger. The people of Ontario never understood, perhaps they never even tried to understand, the pride of the Métis. Scott's execution aroused in the people of Ontario an anger of their own. Scott's death had the same effect in that province as dropping a lighted match into a barrel of gasoline. The majority of the inhabitants were

At twelve o'clock on March 4th, 1870, Thomas Scott was taken outside the walls of Fort Garry. In the presence of about two hundred people, he was made to kneel before a firing squad. The first volley of rifle fire only wounded him, and a member of the squad stepped forward and finished him off with a revolver shot.

Protestants, and many men in Ontario — including Thomas Scott — belonged to an organization known as the Orange Lodge. Irish immigrants brought their religious differences with them into Canada, and the strong Orange Lodge in Ontario continued the anti-Catholic sentiments of the past. These sentiments were an important part of Ontario's attitudes toward the Métis, most of whom were devout Roman Catholics.

In spite of Scott's death, arrangements for the political settlement of Rupert's Land continued. Three delegates from the colony travelled to Ottawa to meet the Canadian government, and by May 12, 1870, the Manitoba Act had been passed into law. Many of its provisions were taken from the very List of Rights drawn up by Riel. These included a guarantee that, as in Quebec, both the French and the English languages would have official status; provision for a provincial Legislative

The Orange Lodge, founded in Ireland in 1795, took its name from the Protestant King of England, William of Orange.

27

This cartoon, called "The Situation," shows Macdonald's deep distrust of Riel. Macdonald suspected that Riel had sent delegates to Ottawa to draw attention away from secret arrangements he was making to get United States help in establishing Assiniboia as an independent republic.

Council and Assembly; a guarantee that all existing land claims and occupancies would be respected; the provision of 566 560 hectares of land for the unmarried children of Métis families; and a guarantee of denominational (church-operated) schools for the province. Manitoba was also to have representation in the Canadian Senate and in the House of Commons.

When Manitoba became a province on July 15, 1870, however, it was not the province the Métis had hoped to create. Symbolically, the Canadian government chose to call the province not Assiniboia, the long-standing name of the Red River region, but Manitoba, a name associated with the heavily Canadian settlement around Portage la Prairie. The new province was tiny — "postage-stamp size" some called it — and only a fraction of the whole Northwest. Moreover, the Dominion government kept control of the management and sale of public lands in Manitoba, which was not the case in the older provinces. In other words, Manitoba was part-province, part-colony.

The thorniest question at the time of the creation of Manitoba was what to do about Louis Riel. Would Canadians — notably those in Ontario — accept the Métis leader as a politician who had looked after the interests of his people and a man who might well have a further role to play in Manitoban and Canadian politics? Should Riel be given amnesty for his actions, particularly for the execution of Thomas Scott? Or should he be branded a rebel and a criminal and dealt with accordingly?

Ontario definitely wanted to see the "rebel" punished. Faced with Ontario's feelings, Macdonald decided to send the military to the West, supposedly to keep law and order, but, in Ontario minds, to bring justice to Riel and the Métis. A force under Colonel Garnet Wolseley, a British officer who had served in all parts of the Empire, set out across the Dawson Route north of Lake Superior. For the British troops under Wolseley's command, the expedition was just another in a series of regular duties all over the British Empire. Among the Ontario volunteers in the two Canadian battalions, however, there was a definite belief that they were going west to avenge the murder of Thomas Scott.

Inevitably, there were those in Quebec who began to react to Ontario's efforts to take over the Northwest. The Société Saint Jean Baptiste became a rallying point for those opposed to the efforts of the Orange Lodge. Founded in 1834 as a patriotic organization for French Canadians, the Société began to take up Riel's cause, not because of any deep understanding of the situation in the Northwest, but because Riel was Catholic and French-speaking.

The deepening split in the nation showed up in Canada's House of Commons. In 1873 and 1874, Riel was actually elected as the Member of Parliament for Provencher in Manitoba. Because he still risked arrest in Ontario, however, Riel never took part in any Commons debates. The House debated whether or not Riel should be expelled, and the vote went against him. The important thing about that vote is that the Members of Parliament did not vote according to party policies. Instead, the Commons split, for the first time, along French-English lines — English-speaking members voting to expel Riel, French-speaking members voting to have him keep his seat. The annexation of

Feeling in Ontario ran so high that two of the Red River delegates to Ottawa were arrested by the provincial government.

St. John the Baptist is the patron saint of French Canadians.

A hunting party of bois-brûlés. An historian wrote of them: "No one who ever saw [one of] these plains hunters come into Fort Garry, after the season's work on the Saskatchewan [River] could fail to see that he was a person in exceedingly comfortable material circumstances. . . . he had any number of [Red River] carts . . . laden with . . . buffalo meat, marrow-fat, beaver-tail, etc., while he also had a goodly supply of furs that would bring handsome prices."

29

the Northwest, which might have provided Canadians with an opportunity to build something together, turned instead into something that drove Canadians farther apart.

And what of Riel himself? He left the Red River settlement, spent some time in Montreal, and then lived for some years in the western United States. But Canada had not heard the last of Louis Riel. He would later make another startling appearance on the stage of Canadian history, an appearance that was to have a profound effect on the future development of the Dominion.

CONFEDERATION EXPANDS FARTHER IN THE WEST

Territorially, the addition of Rupert's Land and the North-Western Territory brought Canada's western boundary to the Rocky Mountains (and its northern boundary to the Arctic Ocean). This meant that a Canada from sea to sea was within the realm of practical possibility. For across the mountains lay the British colony of British Columbia, where there were indications of interest in Confederation with Canada.

In the middle of the nineteenth century, there were four distinct parts to North America's North Pacific coast. In 1846, British and American claims had been resolved by creating two different political realms — the future British colonies of Vancouver Island and British Columbia to the north of the 49th parallel, the future American states of Washington and Oregon to the south of that parallel of latitude. Farther south still lay California, grabbed from Mexico by the United States in 1848. Far to the north lay Alaska, its shores explored by many mariners, including Royal Navy captains James Cook and George Vancouver. In the year of Confederation, Russia sold its claim to Alaska to the United States for $7 200 000.

So, after 1867, British Columbia found itself between American territory on its southern and northern flanks. With American transcontinental railroads almost ready to link the Atlantic with the Pacific, and with American prospectors and merchants moving into the colony, a number of British Columbia's inhabitants expected to become part of the United States. Indeed, some of them actively supported a movement to have the United States annex the colony. But they met with stiff opposition.

Taking the lead in proposing Confederation with Canada was one of Canada's most interesting historical characters, a man who preferred to be known as Amor De Cosmos, meaning "Lover of the Universe." He was born plain William Alexander Smith in Nova Scotia, but he left his native province to seek a career elsewhere. After crossing the United States by wagon train, he made a living for a while as a photographer in California. British Columbia's gold rush attracted De Cosmos north, and, in Victoria, he became the owner-editor of a newspaper called *The British Colonist*. In his very first issue, De Cosmos described the basic

The claims were settled by the Oregon Treaty of 1846.

Amor De Cosmos, 1825-1897

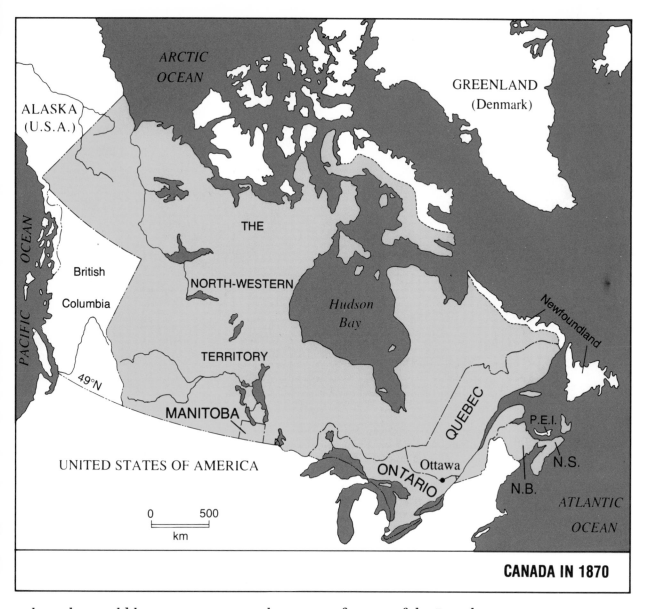

policies he would later support as a politician: unification of the British colonies in North America; the creation of communication lines to link them; and responsible government for British Columbia based on the British parliamentary model.

De Cosmos's call for responsible government brought him into conflict with Governor James Douglas, who, at that time, was both a public official and an employee of the privately-owned Hudson's Bay Company. Douglas tried to squelch De Cosmos by imposing a licence fee of $3000 for publishing *The British Colonist*, but De Cosmos organized a successful subscription campaign. Not only did he get the money to pay the enormous licence fee, he also got many more people to read his editorial attacks on what he called the "Family-Company-Compact." In

James Douglas,
1803-1877

31

Left: Governor James Douglas, "Old Square Toes" as some of his staff privately called him, demanded hard work and long hours. A great believer in rules and regulations, Douglas governed his colonists almost as sternly as he did the members of his own family.

Right: The careers of Amor De Cosmos and his fellow Nova Scotian, Joseph Howe, are curiously similar. They both began their political careers with newspapers they owned and edited. They both fought for responsible government in their respective provinces. Each man supported the idea of Confederation, and each was a provincial representative in Ottawa.

1863, De Cosmos became a full-time politician and began his campaign to have Vancouver Island united with the colony on the mainland. On January 27, 1865, he finally introduced a resolution into the Vancouver Island House of Assembly for just such a union. The following year, the Crown Colony of British Columbia was established.

When news of Confederation arrived, De Cosmos immediately started to work for union with Canada. In 1867, he pushed a resolution through the British Columbia Legislative Council for union with the new nation in the east. He made a special journey to Ontario to let Canadians know that he and his supporters wanted British Columbia to join Canada. And he established the Confederation League, with several branches in southern British Columbia, to promote the idea of union. In his blunt fashion, De Cosmos told anybody who would listen that the aim of the Confederation League was "to effect Confederation as speedily as possible and secure representative institutions for the colony and thus get rid of the present one-man government, with its huge staff of overpaid and do-nothing officials."

British Columbia's union with Canada, however, was stalled by several factors. The British government wanted to see the Canada-Rupert's Land-North-Western Territory arrangements completed, and in British Columbia itself, Lieutenant-Governor Seymour was not enthusiastic about union. When Seymour died, Prime Minister Macdonald arranged for the appointment of Anthony Musgrave as the new governor of British Columbia. As governor of Newfoundland, Musgrave had worked hard on behalf of the island's proposed entry into Confederation, and Macdonald expected that Musgrave would also encourage British Columbia to join Canada. Sure enough, with Musgrave's co-operation, the Legislative Council of British Columbia agreed on the terms it required, and in 1870 three delegates from the colony began negotiations with Ottawa. The colony's terms included the following points: first, Canada would take over British Columbia's public debt; second, Canada would undertake a program of public works in the colony; and, perhaps most importantly of all, Canada would begin a railway to the Pacific within three years.

British Columbians must have been a little surprised at Canada's quick, and generous, agreement. Through the efforts of Sir Georges Étienne Cartier, Macdonald's partner and acting prime minister during Sir John's illness, the Canadian House of Commons agreed to all the major terms and more. They not only promised to build a railway to the Pacific, but to start it within *two* years and *complete it within ten*. British Columbia accepted the terms quickly. On July 20, 1871, the colony became Canada's sixth province.

Georges Etienne Cartier, 1814-1873

Macdonald had suffered a severe gallstone attack, which nearly killed him.

THE WASHINGTON TREATY OF 1871

In late 1870, while the new Province of Manitoba was being organized and British Columbia was considering Confederation, in the East an international situation was developing. A large number of problems had arisen between the United States and Great Britain, some of which involved Canada. Before Confederation, this would have been simply a matter of British and American representatives discussing all questions, including those which affected Canada. Now, however, Canada had a new status — not yet a completely independent country, but something more than a grouping of colonies with something to say on their own behalf. And in the discussions between Great Britain and the Americans, Canada wanted to see at least some of its own concerns looked after.

One of the questions had to do with the Fenian raids of the 1860s. Some Canadians had suffered losses as a result of these raids. The Dominion wanted compensation from the United States, because Americans had done next to nothing to prevent the Fenians from

The Fenians were anti-British Irish Americans who made raids into British North America.

CANADA IN 1871

In the early nineteenth century, most leading nations began to accept the idea that each nation had the right to control its "territorial seas" out to 3 miles (5 km) from shore — slightly more than the range of existing cannon.

attacking from bases in the United States. Another problem had to do with the east coast fisheries. While the Reciprocity Treaty between the United States and the British North American colonies was in effect, from 1854 to 1866, Americans had permitted Canadian products to enter the United States without high tariffs. In return, Americans had been permitted to fish inside the five-kilometre limit anywhere on the east coast of Canada. By 1866, the situation had changed. The United States was angered by British actions during the Civil War, so Americans refused to renew the Reciprocity Treaty. American fishermen lost their fishing rights as a result and were required to pay for fishing licences. When the licence fees were raised, they refused to pay — but continued to fish. The Dominion had to control this foreign fishing in Canadian waters if it was to protect the livelihoods of Canadian fishermen.

The British approached the negotiations as an imperial power, a nation with many different interests to consider and safeguard. The North American situation had to be balanced against more pressing problems elsewhere in the world. So the Parliament in Westminster wanted North American affairs settled quickly and was prepared to go a long way to reach agreement with the United States. After the Civil War, with the southern states secure within the union, some Americans began to look for ways to ensure their domination of all of North America. So the United States sought some way of forcing Great Britain to reduce its strength and influence in North America. They needed a bargaining point – and they found it in the *Alabama* claims. (The *Alabama* was a warship which the Confederacy, the southern states, had had built in Britain during the Civil War.) The United States claimed that the *Alabama* had caused great damage, which had prolonged the American Civil War. It claimed that the British should pay for all the damage that the *Alabama* had caused. Some Americans even argued that fair compensation for the *Alabama* claims would be the transfer of the Dominion of Canada from Britain to the United States.

This was the international situation that faced John A. Macdonald in 1870-1871. He was aware of an American eagerness to take over the entire continent, and he knew that Britain was distracted by problems elsewhere in the world. So should he agree to an exclusively British delegation to the Washington talks, which might sell out Canadian interests for the sake of a speedy agreement? Or should he himself go to Washington as a member of the British delegation, in order to ensure that the Canadian point of view would be heard? Sir John A. decided he had to go in person.

During the treaty negotiations in March and April 1871, the American government tried to bring all kinds of pressure to bear on the British to get them out of North America. Canadian interests and participation were belittled; in a speech delivered in late 1870, President Grant had described Canada as a "semi-independent but irresponsible agent" of British interests, which made "narrow but inconsistent claims." On the other side of the conference table, the British negotiators resented the interference of a Dominion in matters of the Empire. They expected Macdonald, as a "colonial," to follow British policy and not to try to influence it. Indeed, as the negotiations developed, there was more argument and real conflict between the British commissioners and Macdonald than there was between the British and the Americans.

In the end, there was little in the Washington Treaty of 1871 for Macdonald to be proud of. Increasing British pressure had forced the Canadian prime minister into a corner. The British commissioners regularly sent secret telegrams off to London to complain about Macdonald's behavior; they themselves were outraged, however, when Macdonald sent his views, through the Canadian Governor General,

One of Britain's problems was Russia's decision to rebuild its fleet in the Black Sea, which would threaten British trade lines through the Mediterranean to the East.

35

Lord Lisgar, to the British Foreign Office. About the only concession that Macdonald was able to win from the British Commissioners was that the conditions of the Treaty that applied to Canada would have to be accepted by the Canadian Parliament. In other words, they had to be approved or rejected by Canadians.

The Treaty was no triumph for Canada, nor for Britain. Great Britain agreed to permit Americans to continue fishing in Canadian waters; the United States refused to discuss anything but the *Alabama* claims. Americans won the right to free navigation on the St. Lawrence and on Canadian canals forever; Canadians received navigation rights on Lake Michigan and on the Yukon, Porcupine, and Stikine rivers only for the life of the Treaty. The Canadian claim for compensation for Fenian raid damages was disregarded. The only really useful item for Canada arose out of a private deal with the British. To make up for their reluctance to press Canada's Fenian raid claims, the British agreed to provide loans for Canadian public works, such as roads and railways, amounting, in all, to £2 500 000.

Coming as they did so soon after Confederation, the problems that arose during the Treaty of Washington negotiations pointed up very

To many of his opponents, John Alexander Macdonald was a clownish figure, an impression that seemed to be confirmed by his liking for crumpled clothes and a fondness for making outrageous jokes. It has been recorded that "his pranks were the street-corner gossip and family joke of the nation." However, as a practical politician, "Old Tomorrow" had very few equals. He excelled not only in delaying awkward decisions but also in deflecting attention from those that turned out badly.

clearly the weaknesses of the new nation. Without strong military or economic power of its own, Canada had to rely on an alliance with Great Britain to guarantee its independence from the United States. This alliance, in turn, required that Canada make concessions; Canada could not press Britain too hard, at least not if it expected British support.

As it turned out, the Washington Treaty was not a complete disaster for Canada. The British came to share Canadian feelings about the expansionist aims of Americans. The British realized that they needed Canadian support for their bargaining position, and they were more than ever prepared to guarantee Canada's loans. For Canada, loans for public works meant support for railways, and support for railways meant that Canada could start on the rail link between eastern Canada and the Pacific.

CONFEDERATION EXPANDS IN THE EAST

Railways played a rather surprising role when Canada's seventh province, Prince Edward Island, joined Confederation.

After the British took over the island from the French, its agricultural lands were granted to a relatively small number of landlords, who ran the island as if it were their personal possession. Four main groups of settlers — Acadian-French, American-English, Scots, and Irish — gradually moved in to occupy the landlord-controlled farms. Prince Edward Island had participated in the original discussions for Confederation (the Charlottetown Conference). However, two unresolved questions had led to its rejection of union in 1867: representation in the Canadian Parliament, and buying out its absentee landlords, who happily spent in Britain the money earned by their tenant farmers. The price of $800 000 to buy out the owners had been the sticking point. But, in the 1870s, both Canada and Prince Edward Island softened their positions. The Canadian government wanted to bring the island's fisheries under the control of the Dominion; the islanders found that their new, narrow-gauge railway had run them into far greater debt than they expected. The stage was set for negotiations to be reopened. In November, 1872, Lieutenant-Governor Sir William Robinson wrote to the new Governor General of Canada, Lord Dufferin, and terms were soon reached. The Dominion agreed to pay the $800 000 to get rid of the landlords and to provide $50 per person to reduce the railway debt. In addition, Canada promised to provide year-round transportation between the island and the mainland.

Thus, on July 1, 1873, six years after Adolphus Goetz's ecstatic recording of the "Birth Day of the Dominion of Canada," Prince Edward Island became the seventh province.

*   *   *

A Dominion from sea to sea had been partially created. There was, after

all a huge, unpopulated gap between Manitoba and British Columbia. But at least Sir John A. Macdonald's government had achieved the original purpose of Confederation, the preservation of the British colonies as a separate entity within North America. Still, Macdonald's success was marred by personal sorrow and political catastrophe. Cartier, his trusted colleague and Francophone partner, had died in London in 1873. And Macdonald was being accused of bribery and corruption. Railways were at the centre of the political storm, and the winds of the Pacific Scandal were about to blast away Macdonald's government.

STUDY 1

1. You are living in British North America at the time of Confederation. Your cousin in Europe has read about the new nation, Canada, and wants to know more about it. Write a letter describing how Canada is organized, how the people live, and what the features of the provinces are. Tell your cousin what you think of the whole idea.

2. How many Senators for each of Canada's provinces at Confederation did the BNA Act provide for? How many Members of Parliament? For what reasons do you think the provinces were given different representation in the two houses? What problems might this arrangement solve? What problems might it create?

3. What interest did (a) Great Britain and (b) the United States have in Canada in 1867?

4. On a map of North America, find the junction of the Red and Assiniboine rivers. (What city has grown there?) How far is this point from (a) Canada's east coast, (b) its west coast, (c) its north coast, and (d) the Gulf of Mexico? What conclusion can you draw about the continental importance of this location? On a sketch map of North America, show with broad arrows the direction of interest in this location. Write a paragraph on the actions and motives of the interested groups.

5. Describe the lifestyles of the Red River people in the 1860s.

6. What factors contributed to the conflict in the Red River settlement from 1869 to 1871? Which was most important? Why?

7. Debate this resolution: "That the key event in the Red River troubles of 1869-1870 was the execution of Thomas Scott."

8. Review the history of the language rights of French Canadians, from the Quebec Act of 1774 to the Manitoba Act of 1870.

9. Start a file on "Canada-U.S. Relations," with the Treaty of Washington, 1871, as your first entry. Your entries should include such details as date, event, important personalities, terms of treaties, etc. As you record individual entries, be on the lookout for factors and issues that occur repeatedly.

10. Explain how British Columbia became part of Canada. Why was it important for Canada that British Columbia become a province within Confederation?

11. Explain why, in the 1870s, Prince Edward Island joined Confederation and Newfoundland did not.

12. Compare Canada in 1873 with Canada in 1867 under these headings: population; percentage of population (a) English-speaking, (b) French-speaking, (c) other; land area; length of coastline; number of provinces; number of MPs and Senators; percentage of British North America outside of Canada.

CHAPTER 2

Railways and Politics

High above the Ottawa River rise our Parliament Buildings, the centre of national political life in Canada. In the House of Commons — the Green Chamber — the stained glass windows with their provincial floral emblems bear witness to the fact that Canada is a federal state. In the Senate of Canada — the Red Chamber — the large mural paintings record outstanding incidents in our history. The corridors of the Centre Block are lined with portraits of prime ministers and speakers of both Houses — a truly "national" gallery of Canadian statesmen. And in the entrance halls and Parliamentary Library, wood and limestone sculpture adds a distinctly Canadian touch to the dignified and impressive setting.

Just off the Centre Block's main corridor, to the right, is a large room. This is Committee Room Number One — the Railway Committee Room. It is most appropriate that this is the largest committee room of all. For railways, which helped to bind our country together "from sea to sea," have also been at the heart of much of our politics.

THE GRAND TRUNK

In the late 1840s and 1850s, it would have been difficult to say where railroad business stopped, and where politics started. Sir Allan Mac-Nab, as chairman of the Railway Commission of the Province of Canada, helped Sir Allan MacNab, as president of the Great Western Railway, to get government money to actually build his railway. "Railroads," said Sir Allan, "are my politics." Joseph Howe, champion of responsible government, was also commissioner-in-chief of the Railway Board of Nova Scotia. He pushed through the Halifax-Truro-Pictou line in 1854. Sir Francis Hincks was an important force behind the organization of the Grand Trunk Railway. He became premier of the Province of Canada in 1851, but he had to resign after embarrassing questions were asked about how he had come to own 1008 shares in the Grand Trunk Railway. And Sir Georges Etienne Cartier, the leader of the Conservatives in Canada East, was chief lawyer for the Grand Trunk.

The old Grand Trunk Railway was quite an undertaking. The company worked out a very complicated set of deals with other railway companies, so as to join its own routes with other charters to create one grand scheme: from opposite Quebec City, at Lévis, constructing a line to Trois Pistoles and eventually to the New Brunswick border; acquiring

New Brunswick Museum

In nineteenth-century Canada, a lot of railway companies started out as independent operations and ended up as part of some other company. One such was the New Brunswick and Canada Railway (N.B. and C.R.), for which this locomotive was built in 1858. The N.B. and C.R., a local operation in southeastern New Brunswick, was absorbed by the New Brunswick Railway. It, in turn, was taken over by the Canadian Pacific Railway when it expanded into the Maritime Provinces in the 1890s.

control over the Montreal-Kingston and Kingston-Toronto sections; buying or leasing sections of Alexander Galt's St. Lawrence and Atlantic Railroad; acquiring the charter to build a railway from Quebec City to Richmond, Quebec. Then, west of Toronto, the scheme hit a snag. Sir Allan MacNab was not satisfied with the price the Grand Trunk offered for his Great Western Railway (Niagara-Hamilton-Windsor). The Grand Trunk then turned to Gzowski and Company. This group, composed of Sir Casimir Gzowski, David Macpherson, Luther Holton, and Alexander Galt (again! he was a true railway "promoter"), held the charter for a rail line from Toronto to Guelph to Sarnia, Ontario. On paper, a very impressive railroad had been put together — a railroad that stretched from the Atlantic Ocean to the heart of the continent.

The work in the 1850s proceeded quickly. By 1853, the St. Lawrence and Atlantic from Portland, Maine, to Montreal was complete. In 1854, the Quebec-Richmond line was ready for service. On October 27, 1856, the first train from Montreal arrived in Toronto. In 1860, the great Victoria Bridge over the St. Lawrence at Montreal was completed. The Grand Trunk could now boast of a line running from Portland, Maine, through Montreal and Toronto, and on to Sarnia. Another line from Rivière-du-Loup through Lévis joined the main line at Montreal. And one day, the Grand Trunk would reach all the way to Chicago in the American Midwest.

Chicago as the terminus of the Grand Trunk reflects the thinking of its promoters and backers. The scheme may have been put together by Canadians, but its scope went beyond national boundaries to win for Canadians the profits to be gained from North American business. As an international rather than a purely Canadian line, it was in competition with other North American lines, particularly those that started in New York City. These ran up the Hudson River Valley and then turned west to the Niagara River. Sir Allan MacNab's Great Western Railway became important at this point, because it could join Niagara (Buffalo) in the east with Windsor (Detroit) in the west. If the United States railroads acquired the Great Western, they would then have a direct route

The Grand Trunk bought out the Great Western in 1882.

41

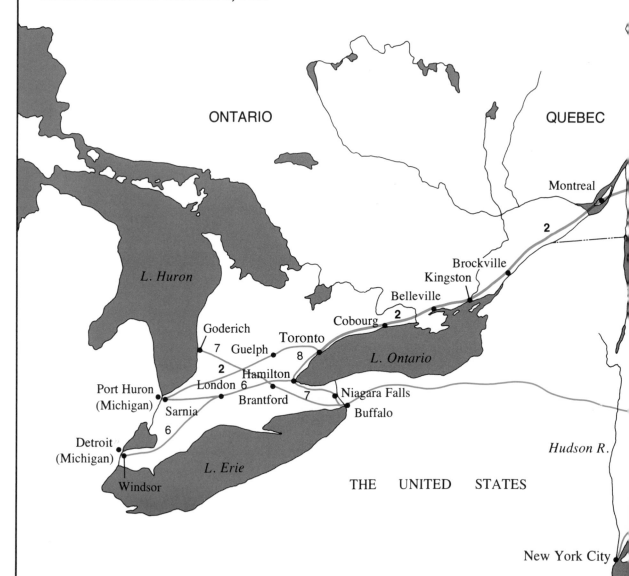

MAJOR CANADIAN RAILWAYS, 1867

1	Grand Trunk Railway of Canada East	6	Great Western Railway
2	Grand Trunk Railway	7	Buffalo & Lake Huron Railroad
3	St. Lawrence & Atlantic Railroad	8	Hamilton and Toronto Railroad
4	Quebec Richmond Railway	9	Nova Scotia Railway
5	Atlantic and St. Lawrence Railroad	10	European and North American Railroad
		11	New Brunswick & Canada Railway

N

ONTARIO

QUEBEC

Montreal

2

L. Huron

Brockville

Kingston

Belleville

Cobourg 2

Goderich

7   Guelph   Toronto

8

L. Ontario

2   Hamilton

London 6

Port Huron
(Michigan)   Brantford   7   Niagara Falls

Sarnia   Buffalo

6

Detroit
(Michigan)   Hudson R.

Windsor   L. Erie

THE   UNITED   STATES

New York City

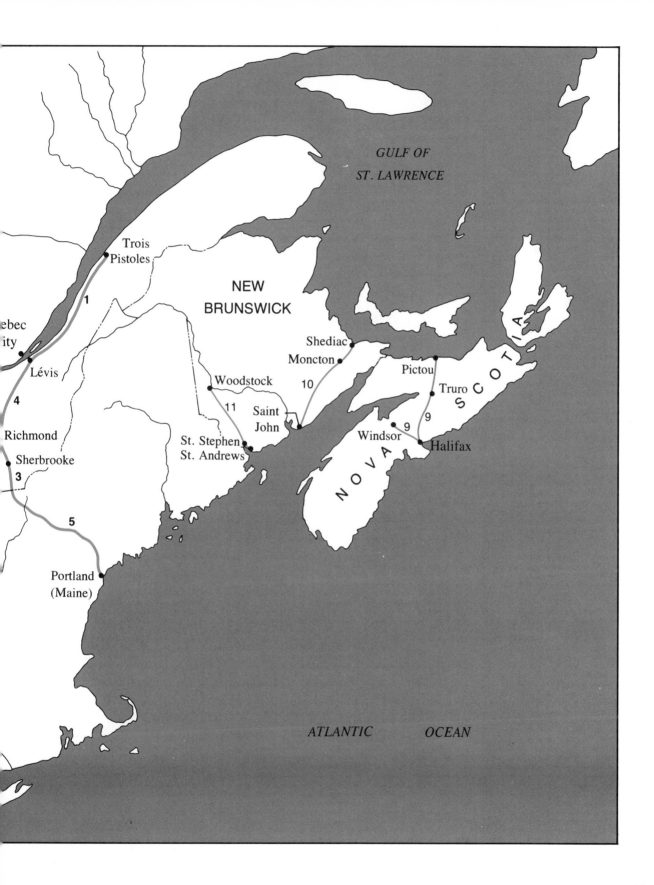

GULF OF
ST. LAWRENCE

NEW
BRUNSWICK

Trois
Pistoles

1

ebec
ity

Lévis

4

Richmond

Sherbrooke

3

5

Portland
(Maine)

Woodstock

11

Saint
John

St. Stephen
St. Andrews

10

Shediac
Moncton

Pictou

Truro

9

9

Windsor

Halifax

NOVA SCOTIA

ATLANTIC   OCEAN

Early on the morning of October 27, 1856, one train left Toronto and another left Montreal to launch the first through service between the two cities. The trains met at Kingston, Ontario, about two o'clock in the afternoon. After a thirty-minute stop, during which all the passengers were given a special lunch, the trains continued on their way along the single-line track. Late that night, one steamed into Bonaventure Station, the Montreal terminus of the Grand Trunk, the other into a small, brick station house at the foot of York Street, Toronto. Each had stopped at about sixty-four locations en route, yet the run had been made in the miraculous time of fifteen hours.

Peterboro', Haldimand, Colborne, Brighton, Trenton, Bellville, Shannonville, Napanee, Bath, Odessa, Prescott, Ottawa	Daily, (Saturdays excepted,) at 6 P. M.	9.30 P. M. Daily, (Sundays excepted,) at 9.30 P. M.

Letters, &c., Posted between the hours of 6 P. M. and 5.30 A. M., will be forwarded in charge of Mail Conductors on the trains. No Letters will be received for Registration after 5.30 P. M.

JOSEPH LESSLIE, P. M.

Post Office, Toronto, Oct. 25, 1856.

1032

GRAND TRUNK RAILWAY.

THE PUBLIC ARE RESPECTFULLY IN-
FORMED that the RAILWAY WILL BE OPENED THROUGH-OUT TO TORONTO,

On MONDAY, OCTOBER 27.

TRAINS WILL RUN AS FOLLOWS:

THROUGH TRAINS,

STOPPING AT ALL PRINCIPAL STATIONS,

Will leave MONTREAL every morning, (Sundays excepted,) at 7:30 A. M., arriving at TORONTO at 9:30 P. M.

Will leave TORONTO at 7:00 A. M., arriving at MONTREAL at 9:00 P. M.

LOCAL TRAINS,

STOPPING AT STATIONS,

Will leave BROCKVILLE, daily, for MONTREAL, at 8:30, A. M.; returning from MONTREAL at 3:30, P. M.

Will leave BELLEVILLE, daily, for BROCKVILLE, at 7:00, A. M. returning from BROCKVILLE at 3:15, P. M.

Will leave COBOURG, daily, for TORONTO, at 6:30, A. M.; returning from TORONTO at 4:45, P. M

The Trains will be run on Montreal Time, which is—
8½ Minutes faster than Brockville Time.

12	"	"	Kingston	"
14½	"	"	Belleville	"
23	"	"	Toronto	"

Freight Trains will not run between Brockville and Toronto during the first week.

Fares between Toronto and Montreal :

First Class....................................... $10 00

Second do.. 8 00

S. P. BIDDER,

General Manager.

Montreal, October 18, 1856.

1025

The Public Archives of Canada, C 5780

In 1860, the Grand Trunk's Victoria Bridge at Montreal was formally opened. Designed jointly by Robert Stephenson, son of the inventor of the steam locomotive, and Alexander M. Ross, the Grand Trunk's chief engineer, the bridge was a remarkable construction feat: a rectangular iron tube, 2009 metres long, which rested on two abutments and twenty-four piers.

from New York to Chicago, which would compete with the Grand Trunk line from Portland, Maine, to the American Midwest.

Despite its grand scheme, the Grand Trunk was not a financial success. (In fact, by the time of Confederation, governments had had to subsidize the Grand Trunk to the extent of $130 000 000.) The company needed more business and new markets for its services. In 1863, the financial backers of the Grand Trunk (bankers like the London, England, firm of Thomas Baring) formed the International Financial Society and bought the Hudson's Bay Company. Obviously, the Grand Trunk was aiming at some kind of extension into the Northwest to increase its profits.

THE INTERCOLONIAL

In the Confederation negotiations, the politics of union brought another railway matter back into focus. In the 1850s, politicians in British North America had discussed a railway to link the two Canadas with the Maritime colonies. Several delegations had even sailed to Great Britain to discuss financial arrangements. There was general agreement on the need for a railway; the delegates from Canada East and Canada West, however, would not accept the British terms for paying off the money that would have to be borrowed to build the railway. The whole proposal fell through. The Maritimers, of course, were angry and began to believe that the Canadians could not be trusted. The railway scheme was dropped for at least a decade.

By 1863, the situation had changed. Politicians in Canada West and Canada East wanted a new political arrangement and an opportunity to expand into the Northwest. Without the support of the Maritime Provinces, however, these aims of the Province of Canada were unacceptable to Great Britain. In the end, the men from Canada East and Canada West wanted Confederation enough to offer the Maritimers an intercolonial railway — and the offer was accepted. (Joseph Howe, in particular, saw the intercolonial railway as an opportunity to expand markets for Maritime goods in the Province of Canada.) In fact, Section 145 of the British North America Act summarized the agreement:

> Inasmuch as the Provinces of Canada, Nova Scotia, and New Brunswick have joined in a Declaration that the Construction of the Intercolonial Railway is essential to the Consolidation of the Union of British North America . . . and have consequently agreed that Provision should be made for its immediate Construction by the Government of Canada: Therefore, in order to give effect to that Agreement, it shall be the Duty of the Government and Parliament of Canada to provide for the Commencement within Six months after the Union, of a Railway connecting the River St. Lawrence with the City of Halifax in Nova Scotia, and for the Construction thereof without Intermission, and the Completion thereof with all practicable Speed.

Section 145 was repealed in 1893, when the Intercolonial was completed.

The terms are clear enough. The government of Canada, within six months after Union, was to start, build, and complete as quickly as possible a railway connecting the St. Lawrence with Halifax. But with railroads so closely linked to politics, there were complications.

First, there was the question of the Intercolonial route. Where would the line run between Halifax and Rivière-du-Loup? Any decision would mean good business for one region, and poor business for others. From the point of view of most settlement (and therefore the greatest opportunities for railway business), the best route appeared to be as follows: from Rivière-du-Loup south into northwestern New Brunswick, down the Saint John Valley to Saint John, and from there around the Bay of Fundy and on to Halifax. There was a strong lobby (pressure-group) working to make this the route. But Sir Georges Etienne Cartier had other ideas. He wanted the Intercolonial not only to join Halifax with the St. Lawrence, but also to help in colonizing the Gaspé region of eastern Quebec. According to Cartier's plan, the railway would push on from Rivière-du-Loup to Mont Joli, then turn south to Campbellton, New Brunswick, then on to Moncton, then Halifax. When the final decision was made, Cartier's plan won.

Another question had to be answered. Who was going to build the railway? (Not the actual construction — the foremen and construction workers might be the same whoever managed construction.) Who would take responsibility for organizing, completing, and paying for construction?

There were two possibilities. The first was the usual method, practised in the United States and in Europe. This was to give a privately-owned company a *charter*, the right to build a railway over a given route and under specified conditions. Although the company was usually assisted by government grants of money and/or land, the company itself would actually build, own, and operate the railroad. This method was used in the construction of the Grand Trunk, the Great Western, and many U.S. transcontinentals. In the case of the Intercolonial Railway, the Canadian government used another approach. Businessmen were not interested in the Intercolonial's prospects, so Canada itself would build and own the railway. To supervise construction and eventually run the railroad, the Canadian government appointed a Board of Railway Commissioners.

The building of the Intercolonial Railway and the policies of the Board of Railway Commissioners illustrate some peculiar features of nineteenth-century political life that may seem strange to us today. There were relatively few civil servants (government employees) to carry out policies, so planning, organizing, and operating a major construction project like the Intercolonial Railway was almost too much for the Canadian government to handle. The income of governments was tiny and was just about enough to cover the costs of day-to-day government. If you asked your parents about what taxes they have to pay to the federal government, they would probably give you a very long list — income tax, federal sales taxes, customs duties, excise taxes, and so on. But if you were able to ask your great-great-grandparents what taxes had to be paid in Canada when they were young, most of them would say they did not really know. Only a few — probably businessmen who imported goods from outside Canada — would be able to explain that the federal government got most of its money from customs duties on these goods. If, for any reason, the amount of goods imported into Canada declined, government revenues declined also.

Customs duties provided about 75 per cent of federal government revenues.

There is another political practice to keep in mind. This was called patronage. When an election came along, people were encouraged to work for and contribute to political parties. Some people worked or gave money because they believed sincerely that their political party was right. Others worked because they hoped that if their party won, they would be personally rewarded. In fact, in Canada's early days, there was actually something called the "spoils system," a term that came from the saying "to the victor, the spoils." The term meant that if control of the government passed from one political party to the other, all the civil servants (probably supporters of the old government) were fired, and a whole new civil service (probably supporters of the new government party) was appointed. There were jobs available in the post office department, in the customs service, and in railroads, to mention only a few.

These characteristics of nineteenth-century government became evident in the Intercolonial Railway project. The proposed route ran through fourteen federal constituencies, and, all along the line, the Board of Railway Commissioners tried to appoint government supporters to jobs such as station master or section boss. Also, the Board was limited by the revenues that the government received each year. It wanted to build the railway slowly — as money from customs duties became available — and, above all, as cheaply as possible. And the

The tariff has been a central issue in much of Canada's political history. So it might be a good idea to get a clear understanding of what tariffs are and why they are used. Tariffs are, simply, customs duties, and they have been around for hundreds of years. In the Middle Ages, for example, the rulers of countries put an extra charge on imports — goods entering their country — or on exports — goods leaving the country. These customs duties provided a means of raising money to run the country.

In addition to providing revenues for governments, tariffs also played a role in the development of trade and industry. Towards the end of the eighteenth century, Great Britain began its Industrial Revolution, and British manufacturers started to turn out better goods at lower prices than the rest of the world. The British knew that they could *manufacture* goods more cheaply than the countries to which they exported. If they did not have to pay customs duties in those countries, they could also *sell* their goods more cheaply than any local manufacturers, and thereby capture the markets — the customers — in those other countries. So, the British argued that all trade among countries should be free — that is, free of tariffs.

This British position came to be known as "free trade" or "laissez-faire": governments should leave trade and industry free to "do their own thing" and should not interfere by imposing customs duties, etc. This policy was adopted by Liberals in Great Britain, and was accepted almost as Holy Scripture by some nineteenth-century Liberals in Canada.

Tariff questions can become very complicated, but there are four basic points that need to be examined from the point of view of Canadian situations. The first of these is that the tariff can be used to provide "protection for infant industries." Canadian manufacturers argued that when a new industry was starting in Canada, the government should provide it with tariff protection. The costs of building a plant, setting up production, developing markets, and generally getting established meant that Canadian goods would be more expensive than goods imported from established foreign manufacturers. The tariff would raise prices for Canadian consumers, but it would also help industry to expand and provide jobs.

The second point relates to Canada's closest neighbor, the United States, whose economy has always been not only bigger but *ten times* as big as Canada's. What did this mean for Canadian manufacturers? To take an example, what happened if American factories produced 5 per cent more stoves than American consumers were prepared to buy? American stove manufacturers looked for markets for their extra stoves, and Canada, right next door, was a good possibility. But, that 5 per cent overproduction by the "elephantine" United States was equal to 50 per cent of the total

Canadian production. If Canadian stove manufacturers were already producing enough stoves for the Canadian market, the extra stoves exported to Canada would mean that there would be 150 stoves for every 100 Canadian buyers. The price of stoves in Canada would drop drastically. Canadian consumers would be happy, but Canadian manufacturers and their workers would be in trouble. The severe competition would cause Canadian stove factories to close, and Canadians would lose jobs. If the government wanted the Canadian economy to include stove manufacturing, it would have to provide Canadian factories with tariff protection against American manufacturers who "dumped" their excess production in Canada. Canadian manufacturers argued that Canada should not become a "slaughter market" where dumped foreign goods would kill Canadian industry.

The third point deals with a modern problem. Assume for a moment that all costs involved in making women's blouses are the same in Canada as in some foreign country. All costs, that is, except the price of labor. Let's say that in Canada, a person working in a blouse factory makes $3.00 an hour; in the foreign country, 65¢ an hour. Labor costs in the foreign country are lower; therefore, the final cost of the product is lower. Canadian blouse manufacturers cannot lower wages to 65¢ an hour — not only would they lose all their workers, it is illegal because of Canadian minimum wage laws. So blouse manufacturers will probably ask the government for tariff protection. What is the Canadian government to do? Should it permit Canadian consumers to buy the lower-priced foreign-made blouses? Or should it impose a tariff, to at least equalize the prices of Canadian and foreign-made blouses? With no tariffs, the Canadian consumer can buy cheaper foreign blouses; with tariffs, Canadian business and labor will be protected. What would you do? Remember, more than the price of the blouse is involved. A Canadian who is out of work has often earned the right to receive unemployment insurance payments, and the money for these has to come from other Canadians who are working.

The fourth point flips the tariff-protection coin to the other side. Canadian industries might just hide behind the tariff. Canadian manufacturers might insist that the government impose a high tariff, and then raise their prices until they are just slightly less than the price of foreign-produced goods, which have to pay import duties. That way, they could run their operation inefficiently, or produce goods of lower quality, but still be able to take advantage of the "captive" Canadian market. Their profits would come from the high prices paid by Canadian consumers. In this case, the tariff would protect the manufacturer, but certainly not the consumer.

These are just a few of the points in the tariff argument, which started before Confederation and is still with us today.

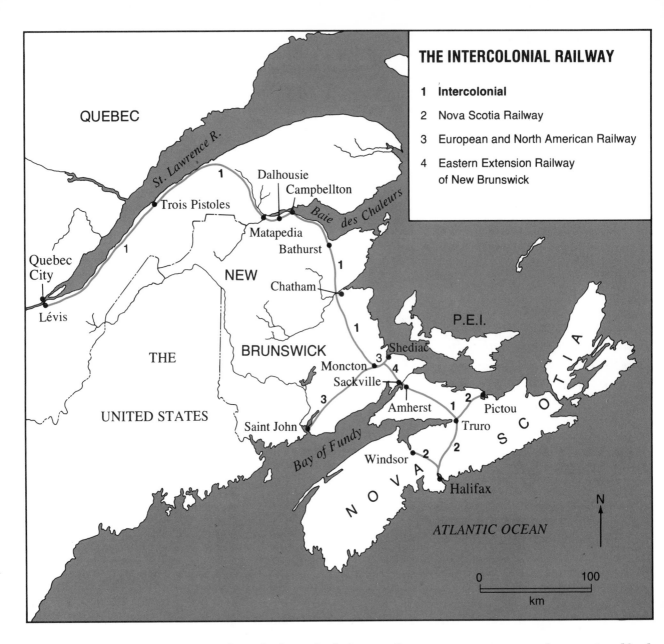

THE INTERCOLONIAL RAILWAY

1 **Intercolonial**

2 Nova Scotia Railway

3 European and North American Railway

4 Eastern Extension Railway
   of New Brunswick

Board might have had things all its own way, except that, in Sandford Fleming, they encountered a first-rate engineer-in-chief. His belief in careful planning and high-quality work and materials ensured that the Intercolonial was a much better railroad than the Board of Railway Commissioners ever intended it to be.

In 1845, at the age of eighteen, Sandford Fleming emigrated to Canada from Kirkcaldy, Scotland. Some incidents in his life are quite incredible. He camped out in the open on the shores of Lake Huron in a metre of snow and risked a balloon flight over Paris, France. He danced in a wolfskin cape with Indian friends and entertained the leading figures of the British Empire. He supervised and took a hand in the early survey work on a transcontinental rail route, and was the main force behind the laying of the telegraph cable from Britain to Canada and on to Australia. For Canada, one of Fleming's major contributions was his work on railways. He held top engineering positions on four of them: the Ontario, Simcoe and Huron; the Intercolonial; in the initial surveys for the Canadian Pacific; and the Newfoundland Railway. He was described, simply, as "the greatest man who ever concerned himself with engineering."

This was the person the Board of Railway Commissioners had to battle. They wanted wooden bridges and iron rails; Fleming insisted that the Intercolonial be built with iron bridges and steel rails. The Board was satisfied with a narrow-gauge line; Fleming decided to convert the railway to the more expensive standard gauge (used by most of the world's railways).

Fleming's work on the railway stopped when a new prime minister, Alexander Mackenzie, began to investigate the construction of the Intercolonial. Mackenzie was appalled by the waste and political patronage practised by the Board of Railway Commissioners (due to its Conservative Party connections) and decided to take over responsibility himself. Fleming, who was not in any way connected with the waste and corruption, was asked to give up his work on the Intercolonial and give his attention to the survey work on a transcontinental railway. Mackenzie, in addition to his duties as prime minister, took on the job of minister of public works, abolished the Board of Railway Commission-

In the 1870s, North American railroads were using 70-80 different local times. (On page 44, note the time differences between Montreal and Toronto.) It was Sanford Fleming who resolved this chaos. It was his idea to divide the globe into 24 time zones. In this scene in 1879, he is explaining standard time to a group of Toronto scientists and businessmen.

The Intercolonial Railway was one Confederation benefit for the Maritimes. Its construction and maintenance provided jobs for hundreds of workers. Settlements grew or expanded along its route. The value of farmland and forest in areas the railway served increased greatly. And the Intercolonial and the mining industry worked together to boost the economy. The mines produced coal, (which supplied the trains with fuel), and the trains carried the coal to markets in central Canada.

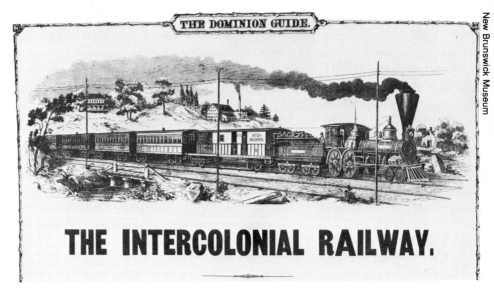

THE DOMINION GUIDE.

THE INTERCOLONIAL RAILWAY.

ers, and appointed C. J. Brydges (the former general manager of the Grand Trunk) as General Superintendent of Government Railways. Slowly, in spite of continuing financial difficulties (the result of falling government revenues), the Intercolonial crept toward completion. The last section, between Mont Joli and Campbellton, was finished in June 1876, and the first train from Halifax arrived at Lévis on July 6. The final cost to Canada, after the Intercolonial bought the Grand Trunk line from Rivière-du-Loup to Lévis in 1879, was to be almost $40 000 000. But as historian C. P. Stacey has pointed out, "the Intercolonial's value to Canada could not be measured in dollars. It was one of those great projects essential to an independent Canadian nationality, which have been forced upon this country by the proximity of the United States and which have been carried out by this country because private enterprise could not or would not do the job that was required."

A TRANSCONTINENTAL

Long before the Intercolonial Railway was completed, attention and interest had swung back to a Western rail line. The terms of the Confederation agreement with British Columbia in 1871 required that this railway be started within two years and completed within ten. Sir John A. Macdonald's government set itself to the task. Macdonald himself believed (along with many politicians of both parties) that the Canadian government could not undertake the job itself. Government financial resources were limited, there were not enough civil servants to oversee the work of construction, and the Intercolonial was showing how difficult it was for a government to do the job. A private company would have to undertake the project. The Grand Trunk might have been a possibility, but it was in deep financial trouble. Another private company would have to be found.

The first nibbles of interest came from a group of Canadians and Americans operating out of Chicago. They were represented by George McMullen, originally from Picton, Ontario, but now a Chicago businessman interested in any money-making deal; they were backed by Jay Cooke, the Philadelphia banker who controlled the finances of the Northern Pacific Railway in the United States. Cooke's aim was simple: if he could get control of the "Canadian" Pacific, and add it to his Northern Pacific, he would control the whole Northwest, and his railroad would reap the transportation and commercial benefits.

Macdonald had a meeting with McMullen and listened to his proposals, but nothing came of this. The prime minister, in historian W. L. Morton's words, wanted "to find a sound *Canadian* company to build a commercial railroad for political purposes." One obvious Canadian was Sir Hugh Allan, the Montreal shipping-line owner and millionaire. He had the money to back a private company, and he had a natural interest in linking his Atlantic shipping company with a transcontinental transportation system. And Allan was interested. Sir Francis Hincks had informed Allan of the interest of the Chicago group. Before long, Allan had entered into a secret agreement with the group to make the proposed Canadian Pacific a part of the Northern Pacific empire.

Sir Hugh encountered immediate opposition from Georges Etienne

Georges Etienne Cartier (1814-1873) fought to achieve and preserve Confederation. He believed that only in Confederation was there hope of preserving French language and culture. Time and time again, he told his fellow Francophones, "We French Canadians are British subjects like the others, but British subjects speaking French."

53

Cartier. The leader of the French-Canadian Conservatives wanted *Canadian* control of any transcontinental railway, added to which he still had an interest in the Grand Trunk building a line to the Pacific. But Allan was prepared to fight, and he carried the attack against Cartier right into his riding of Montreal East. Allan held the charter for an important section of railway planned for the north shores of the St. Lawrence and Ottawa rivers, from Quebec City to Ottawa. If this north shore railway were completed, there would be business and jobs in the riding of Montreal East. So Allan used this argument, and lots of money, to fight Cartier. He started spreading cash around — planting useful articles in newspapers, buying anti-Cartier votes in Montreal East for the upcoming election, even spreading money among Quebec Conservative MPs to weaken their support of their leader. In the end, Cartier had to stop opposing Sir Hugh Allan.

Cartier was defeated in Montreal East. He later ran and was elected in Proven-cher, Manitoba. See pp. 99-100.

But there were still others who crossed swords with Allan. Sir Hugh represented Montreal money; for political reasons, Toronto money should also participate in the railway to the Pacific. Madonald tried to persuade Senator David Macpherson, head of the Interoceanic Railway Company of Toronto and an old friend, to join with Allan to form the new company. But Macpherson and his colleagues in Toronto refused. They suspected that Allan was acting only as a front-man for the Americans.

For details of the Treaty of Washington, see pp. 33-37.

When Parliament met in April 1872, the first major item of business was the vote on acceptance of the Treaty of Washington. The British guarantee (attached to the Washington agreement) of loans of up to £2 500 000 for railways helped Macdonald keep his parliamentary support — and also fitted neatly into Ottawa's plans for a Pacific railway. Then, in spite of opposition from the Toronto *Globe* and some Ontario MPs, the Macdonald government went on to pass the Canadian Pacific Railway bill. The line from the Pacific Ocean to Lake Nipissing was to be completed by July 20, 1881; the company that built it would be named by the cabinet, not Parliament; the company would receive 20 234 300 hectares of land and $30 000 000. The railway appeared to be successfully launched.

In the summer of 1872, the government called a general election, as it was required to do by law. It was a typical, nineteenth-century election: money was the grease that lubricated the political machinery. In today's world, voters may be influenced by general promises of government programs, but in the 1800s, they were rarely satisfied with anything less than cash on the barrel-head. Promises of patronage, "treating" (buying a voter drinks), and outright bribery characterized the 1872 election. Once bribed, of course, the voter had to deliver on his promises; in the days before the secret ballot, he had to call out who he was voting for, in public (and probably under the nose of the man who had bribed him!). And because the election was a hard-fought affair, politicians needed a lot of money to get the votes they wanted.

Liquor outlets are still closed on election days in Canada, in reaction to this practice.

In the Canada of the 1870s, the wealthiest families lived in homes that were almost as large and ornate as palaces. Sir Hugh Allan built himself just such a palatial mansion, "Ravenscrag," on top of a hill overlooking Montreal. He is said to have enjoyed looking down on all other Montreal residents, rich or poor.

THE PACIFIC SCANDAL

When the election was over, the Conservative government was re-elected. Sir John A. could resume his task of getting a move on with the railway. By the end of 1872, a company was formed, with Sir Hugh Allan as president. When Parliament recessed, the work of nation-building was proceeding smoothly, and everything was under control. At least, that was the way things appeared on the surface. Beneath the surface, there was a bubbling, boiling pool of political lava, ready to blow Macdonald's government apart. The explanation is simple. Sir Hugh Allan had made his deal with the McMullen group from Chicago; and yet, Macdonald and Macpherson had insisted that American control of a Canadian railway was out of the question. (Cartier had been the most vocal opponent of American control, which helps to explain Sir Hugh Allan's efforts to weaken Cartier in Montreal East.)

During the election campaign in the summer of 1872, Macdonald had worked feverishly to bring together the Montreal money of Sir Hugh Allan and Macpherson's Toronto support. Publicly, Allan had agreed to break the American connection, but Macpherson had remained suspicious, and unwilling to join Allan. So Allan was even more important for the railway. As Allan's efforts in Montreal East were making Cartier's re-election unlikely, and as election campaign pressures generally mounted, Macdonald agreed to Allan's demand that he be president of the Pacific railway company. As a result, Allan made large sums of money available for Conservative election expenses, particularly for Cartier and Hector Langevin in Quebec. Macdonald also received money, which he distributed to Conservative candidates in Ontario.

After the return of the Conservative government, Macdonald worked through the fall of 1872 to get the Pacific railway company organized. In spite of Macpherson's refusal to join, the prime minister worked on. Writing to Cartier, he seemed optimistic: "We are making the best company we can . . . the thirteen directors are not all chosen yet, but they will all be settled by New Year's Day."

Then, on New Year's Eve, who should arrive from Chicago but George McMullen. His purpose was plain and simple: blackmail. He showed Macdonald proof that Sir Hugh Allan, in spite of his assurances and promises, had *not* broken off relations with his American associates. Then McMullen demanded that the Canadian government do one of two things: either keep Allan as president of the railway company *with American backing,* or get someone else. Macdonald was faced with a horrifying dilemma. He could not accept Allan with American support, and yet there appeared to be no one else to head the proposed company.

Macdonald managed to stall for time. He told McMullen that Allan's agreements with the Americans were Allan's business, not the government's. But through January and February of 1873, the prime minister must have felt like a man on top of a volcano. An eruption could come at any time.

The first rumblings came in early April. Lucius Huntington, an opposition MP, charged that the railway company was a front for American interests, and that Sir Hugh Allan had been offered the railway contract because he had contributed to the Conservative election campaign. With the support of a large majority in the House of Commons, Macdonald managed to stall further — a Select Committee of the House of Commons (with three government and two opposition members) would investigate the charges.

The volcano had been plugged, but only for the time being. In May, Parliament continued with important regular business: Macdonald introduced an act for the creation of a police force for the Northwest, and Prince Edward Island agreed to join Confederation. And then sadness; news arrived from London that Sir Georges Etienne Cartier had died, the victim of Bright's Disease, which had been sapping his strength for several years. The loss for Macdonald was devastating. The two men had worked together inseparably for almost a quarter of a century. They had understood and trusted each other fully, sharing the same vision of Canada and acting as if with one mind. Little wonder that Macdonald went to pieces when he learned of Cartier's death.

With Cartier gone, Macdonald watched the top blow off the volcano. On July 4, the Toronto *Globe* began to publish Allan's letters to his American associates; on July 18, three opposition newspapers published some telegrams that had been stolen from the office safe of John J. C. Abbott, Sir Hugh Allan's lawyer. All Canada could read the evidence:

August 24, 1872, Cartier to Abbott:
I shall be obliged by your supplying the Central Committee with a further sum of twenty thousand dollars . . . . P.S. Please also send

John J. C. Abbott became prime minister in 1891. See p. 138.

Sir John A. Macdonald ten thousand dollars more on the same terms.

August 26, 1872, Macdonald to Abbott:
I must have another ten thousand; will be the last time of calling; do not fail me; answer today.

Although no one suggested that Cartier or Macdonald had used any of these funds for personal purposes, the effects for the prime minister were disastrous. The idea that the government party had received money from Sir Hugh Allan, while at the same time negotiating with Allan over a major project like the Pacific railway, was an outrage to many Members of Parliament. Macdonald delivered a brilliant speech on November 3, which rallied his dwindling support. But the next day, even Donald Smith, who had been one of the prime minister's personal

Donald Alexander Smith is an outstanding example of the immigrant-Scot success story. His shrewd investments in bank bonds and railroad shares made him a millionaire several times over. In 1897, he also acquired great social prestige when Queen Victoria made him Baron Strathcona and Mount Royal.

Right: Alexander Mackenzie became Canada's second prime minister in 1872. A Canadian historian says Mackenzie "had none of Macdonald's charm, cynicism, or imagination. Mackenzie was a lesser but a more honest and . . . a far better man . . . intelligent in business, able enough for office in a work-a-day fashion."

Notman Photographic Archives, McCord Museum   The Public Archives of Canada, C 4953

envoys to the Red River in 1870, voted against Macdonald. (And Macdonald was not to forget it for a long time.) On November 5, Macdonald resigned as prime minister, and the Governor General, Lord Dufferin, invited the Liberal Party leader, Alexander Mackenzie, to form a government.

THE FIRST LIBERAL GOVERNMENT

Macdonald's resignation could be viewed as the end of an era in Canadian history. With Confederation, and with the Northwest, British Columbia, and Prince Edward Island brought into the union, the plan for Canada was almost complete. But the relative prosperity of the Confederation years appeared to be ending as a depression — a major slowdown of economic activity — began in Europe in 1873. The same depression affected the United States from about 1873 to 1878, and Canada a little later, from about 1874 to 1879. Business failures occurred both in Canada and the United States: for example, some Canadian banks went bankrupt; Jay Cooke's Northern Pacific Railway collapsed, dragging down other U.S. railroad companies and banks. As American businesses slowed down, trade between Canada and the United States fell off, and Canadian government revenues from import duties declined.

But the economic picture was not all bad. The completion of the Intercolonial Railway assisted manufacturers in Ontario and Quebec. During the depression of the 1870s, Ontario agricultural-machinery manufacturers (who sold at home, in domestic markets, and whose goods paid no duties) experienced almost steady growth. Along with the textile mills around Montreal, they began to take advantage of new markets in the Maritimes. Then, British agriculture experienced bad harvests and animal diseases in the late 1870s, and Canadian farmers began to increase their exports of grain and livestock to Great Britain. The outlines of a new Canadian economy were developing, even while the business depression was spreading gloom.

Alexander Mackenzie, 1822-1892

The man who inherited the depression was Alexander Mackenzie. Like so many men in Canadian public life at the time, he was a Scots immigrant. Although he had worked hard and become a successful Sarnia stonemason, many doubted his ability to be a good prime minister. The Governor General, Lord Dufferin, said about Mackenzie that, "he is honest, industrious and sensible, but he has very little talent." However, no one ever questioned Mackenzie's dedication to his responsibilities. John A. himself said that Mackenzie gave more time to Canada "than the country could claim or had a right to expect."

The country was prepared to support Mackenzie, as the Liberal victory in the 1874 general election demonstrated. But, in the eyes of many observers, the real power in the Liberal Party was George Brown, who used the editorials in his Toronto *Globe* like bolts of lightning to strike down his opponents. (Those opponents were usually the people

Left: Although George Brown was defeated in the 1867 election, he continued to influence the Liberal Party via the editorial columns of his Toronto newspaper.

Right: Like Macdonald, Wilfrid Laurier knew that English and French Canadians had to co-operate if Canada was to survive. His basic political belief was "a policy of true Canadianism, of moderation, of conciliation."

who did not see the Dominion of Canada the way Brown did — as an extension of Ontario.)

The party that Mackenzie led was unified only in its opposition to Macdonald's Conservatives. In addition to Brown, two other forces in the Liberal Party deserve mention. The first of these was represented by Edward Blake, a brilliant Ontario lawyer. In spite of his rather cool, perhaps shy personality, Blake was respected highly among Liberals. He was not happy with the Conservative position represented by Macdonald, but at the same time he had doubts about a traditional Grit or Reformer position. He was searching for a new Canadian view, and in the Canada First movement there were elements that might fit into his developing idea of Canadianism.

Edward Blake, 1833-1912

Canada First was never a very clear political movement, but its supporters were among the first to aim at a particular Canadian nationality — not necessarily anti-British, nor anti-American, but pro-Canadian. Blake, too, sensed this possibility for Canada, and his

59

thoughts were summed up in a speech he gave at Aurora, Ontario, on October 3, 1874:

> . . . the future of Canada . . . depends very largely upon the cultivation of a national spirit. We are engaged in a very difficult task — the task of welding together seven provinces which are accustomed to regard themselves as isolated from each other, which are full of petty jealousies, their provincial questions, their local interests. How are we to accomplish our work?

Blake was never able to work out totally satisfactory answers, but he did ask a fundamental Canadian question.

The close relationship between religion and politics in the Province of Quebec provided the background for the second development within the Liberal Party. Traditionally, the Roman Catholic Church had been a conservative force in Quebec, particularly in its efforts to preserve the French Canadian way of life. In politics, the Church generally supported the Conservative Party. Quebec Liberals, therefore, were in an awkward position. They recognized and accepted the Church's important religious and social role in the province, but they were opposed to Church involvement in politics. The confrontation between the Church and Quebec Liberals became more intense in the 1860s and 1870s. Within the Church itself, there was growing support for the Ultramontane movement, which condemned nearly all the political and social developments of the nineteenth century, including liberalism. One example of Ultramontane doctrine was provided by Louis-François Laflèche, who would one day become Bishop of Trois Rivières. Abbé Laflèche stated that all authority came from God. The rights of peoples to elect a government was passed on from God's powers, which were to be explained by the Church. (What effect would this argument have among Ontario Protestants?) Abbé Laflèche went on to state that priests not only had a right, but a duty, to tell their parishioners how to vote.

Wilfrid Laurier, 1841-1919

Opposition to this doctrine came from the French Canadian Rouges, particularly those who were members of the *Institut canadien*. The Institut provided its members with reading materials which Ultramontanes in the Church disapproved. When Joseph Guibord, a former member and vice-president of the Institut died, the Ultramontane Bishop Ignace Bourget of Montreal refused Guibord Catholic burial in a Church cemetery. The Guibord affair (1875) turned into a national and international controversy. Quebec society was split down the middle, with everyone taking one side or the other. The whole Ultramontane-Liberal confrontation dragged on for years, but in its midst there emerged an important new spokesman for the Liberals.

Wilfrid Laurier became MP for Drummond-Arthabaska in 1874. A distinguished young lawyer, he was an example of the moderate Liberals who wanted political freedom, but who wished to avoid conflict with the Church. His views on political liberalism were summarized in a speech at Quebec City in June 1877:

Our constitution invites all citizens to take part in the direction of the affairs of the State; it makes no exception of any person. Each has the right not only to express his opinion, but to influence, if he can, by the expression of his opinion, the opinion of his fellow citizens. This right exists for all, and there is no reason why the priest should be deprived of it. . . .

"This right, however, is not unlimited. We have no absolute rights. The rights of each man in our state of society end precisely at the point where they encroach upon the rights of others.

The right of interference in politics ends at the point where it encroaches upon the elector's independence.

The constitution of the country rests upon the freely expressed wish of each elector. It intends that each elector shall cast his vote freely and willingly as he deems best. . . .

It is therefore perfectly legitimate to alter the elector's opinion by argument and all other means of persuasion, but never by intimidation.

When Laurier delivered this speech, he was a relatively unimportant member of Mackenzie's government. When his speech was published, Laurier was on his way to becoming an important national political leader.

"THE GREAT LONE LAND"

While these movements were occurring within the Liberal Party, Alexander Mackenzie's government had to deal with problems in the rest of the country. One of these was "the Great Lone Land," the Northwest. W. F. Butler, an English soldier, explorer, and writer, did not exaggerate when he explained that "The Great Lone Land is no sensational name. . . . there is no other portion of the globe in which

Glenbow-Alberta Institute

A drawing of a settler's cabin near Winnipeg. In this typical living-room-cum-dining-room-cum-kitchen, two different types of stove provided heat, not only for cooking and baking but also for keeping the home warm during the long, cold, prairie winter. The family slept in the attic, which was reached by the ladder in the background.

travel is possible where loneliness can be said to dwell so thoroughly. One may wander five hundred miles in a direct line without seeing a human being, or an animal larger than a wolf."

Only in the postage-stamp Province of Manitoba was there major settlement. Here, some of the problems of land claims had been dealt with in the Manitoba Act of 1870. By its terms, Métis titles of land along the Red and Assiniboine rivers that had been established by Métis custom were confirmed. A further 566 560 hectares were granted to Métis children. By the time all the land claims were sorted out, this came to about ninety-seven hectares per person. In 1874, Métis heads of families were also given $160 in land scrip, but this scrip (a coupon or certificate that could be used only for the acquisition of land) often found its way into the hands of land speculators.

The Manitoba land claim settlement, however, was unsatisfactory for Métis who wanted to follow their traditional way of life, the buffalo hunt.

For details of these events, see pp. 97-107.

They left Manitoba and established settlements farther west. Some of these, like St. Laurent and Batoche near the South Saskatchewan River, became permanent, and were to play an important role in the events of 1885. Several other non-Métis settlements began to take shape along the North Saskatchewan in the 1870s. Some, like Fort Carlton and Fort Edmonton, were centred on Hudson's Bay Company posts. Telegraph Flats (later Battleford) was established when the survey for the Pacific railway was under way.

Dominion surveyors began the gigantic task of surveying the

The Public Archives of Canada, C 17566

In the nineteenth century, more and more buffalo were slaughtered by hide hunters. In the early 1880s, skulls and bones collected by the settlers were piled alongside the CPR line for shipment to fertilizer companies in eastern Canada.

Northwest in 1871, after the Manitoba situation had been settled. By 1873, about 2 000 000 hectares of prairie land had been surveyed, so it was possible for settlers to take up land according to the terms of the Dominion Lands Act of 1872. By the terms of this Act, immigrants to the Northwest over twenty-one years of age could apply for a quarter-section of land (sixty-five hectares). There was a $10 application fee, but this was the only charge. To gain complete title to the land, settlers had to occupy and "improve" (cultivate) the land for three years, after which they could have their title registered and also have the right to *buy* one more adjoining quarter-section.

Generally speaking, settlement in the West was slow in the 1870s, as world economic conditions discouraged heavy immigration. The settlers who did come were mostly English-speaking Canadians, and they favored not the bleak, open prairie, but the park-like areas fringing the valley of the North Saskatchewan River. Some immigrants who spoke neither English nor French as their mother language *did* arrive in the 1870s, as economic and other pressures drove them from their homelands. In 1876, after severe weather conditions and a volcanic eruption disrupted their life in their old home, Icelanders came to the Northwest and formed the Gimli settlement on the southwestern shore of Lake Winnipeg. By 1877, about 7000 German-speaking Mennonites (who had left their homes in the Russian Ukraine because of the threat of forced military service) had built up settlements in Manitoba which soon became thriving agricultural communities.

Standing in the way of all settlement, however, was another major problem. Who owned the land that was going to be taken up by homesteaders? To the extent that anyone actually "owned" the land, the "owners" were the Indian nations. But the Indians themselves did not think in terms of "ownership" of land; rather, they thought of "using" the land and its resources, just as their ancestors had done for centuries. Although there might be squabbles over hunting grounds with others — Europeans or Métis — they could "use" the land as did the Indians. For them, the arguments involved use, not ownership.

Settlers in the Northwest had no intention of just "using" the land, the way Indians did. They would "own" their quarter-section, plough the land and plant wheat — and they expected others to stay off "their" land. So there were two different concepts of what the land would mean to the people on it, and the possibility of conflict was recognized by Canadian government officials. In 1870, the undersecretary of state for the provinces asked the lieutenant-governor of Manitoba to

> ascertain and report . . . the course you think the most advisable to pursue, whether by Treaty or otherwise, for the removal of any obstructions that might be presented to the flow of population into the fertile lands that lie between Manitoba and the Rocky Mountains.

Only the even-numbered sections were available for homesteading. The odd-numbered lots were reserved for other purposes.

63

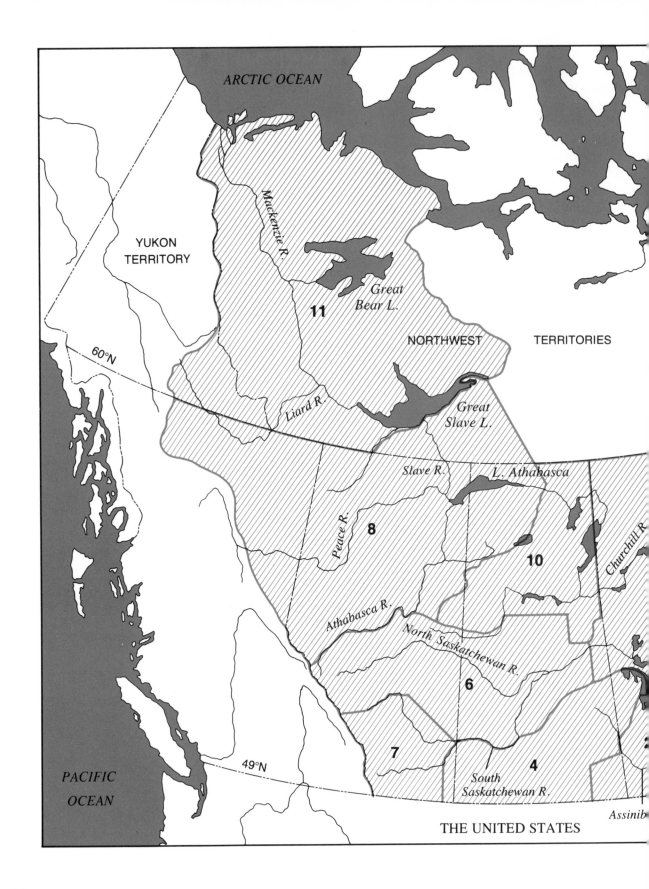

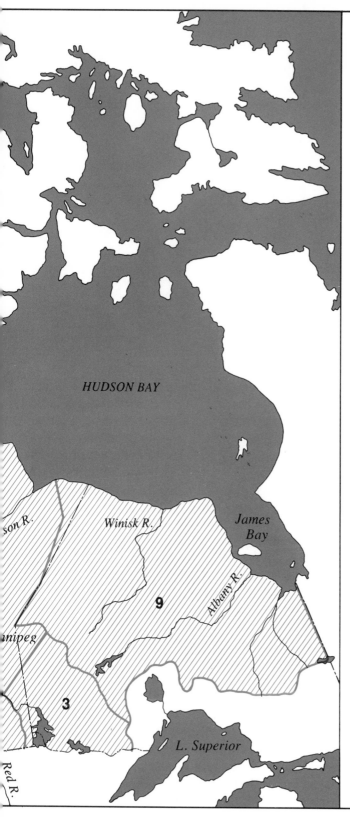

POST-CONFEDERATION TREATIES

Treaty No. 1, 1871:
Ojibwa and Swampy Cree in southern Manitoba

Treaty No. 2, 1871:
Ojibwa in southern and southwestern Manitoba, and in southeastern Saskatchewan

Treaty No. 3, 1873:
Ojibwa in northwestern Ontario and southeastern Manitoba

Treaty No. 4, 1874:
Cree and Ojibwa, mostly in southern Saskatchewan

Treaty No. 5, 1875:
Swampy Cree and Ojibwa, mainly in northern Manitoba

Treaty No. 6, 1876:
Plains Cree and Wood Cree in central Saskatchewan and central Alberta

Treaty No. 7, 1877:
Blackfeet, Blood, Piegan, Sarcee, and Stoney in southern Alberta

Treaty No. 8, 1899:
Cree, Beaver, and Chipewyan in northern Alberta, northeastern British Columbia, and south of Great Slave Lake

Treaty No. 9, 1905:
Ojibwa and Cree in that part of Ontario whose rivers drain down to Hudson Bay

Treaty No. 10, 1906:
Chipewyan and Cree, mostly in northeastern Saskatchewan

Treaty No. 11, 1921:
Slave, Dogrib, Loucheux, Hare, and Kutchin in lands drained by the Mackenzie River

In this painting of the making of Treaty Number 7 in October, 1877, Crowfoot is speaking to the treaty commissioners, Lieutenant-Governor Laird of the North-West Territories and Colonel James F. Macleod of the Mounted Police.

Included in the treaties was the provision for lands to be "reserved" for Indians (hence the term "reserves"). When Plains Indians began to feel the effects of the disappearance of the buffalo, they demanded in later treaties that the Canadian government guarantee food and medicine "in times of famine and disease."

The "obstructions" were the Indians, and in the eyes of the government, their "removal" would permit settlement to press forward.

To ensure that the Indians gave up all claim to the land, the Canadian government used a policy of treaty-making with the Indian nations. These treaties were never negotiated as agreements between equals. Ottawa offered gifts and annual payments of money to every Indian (to avoid outright conflict), and Indian spokesmen felt they had to accept the treaties in the hopes that they would somehow protect their people from the uncertain but threatening changes which appeared sure to come. But as the 1870s unfolded, the Indians were troubled by constant pressures on themselves and their hunting and fishing grounds. The arrival of large numbers of immigrants meant the coming of smallpox and the liquor trade, and it is hard to say which had worse effects. Gold-seekers, railway-builders, settlers — all threatened tribal lands and, directly or indirectly, the traditional Indian ways of life. As they negotiated for their people, the chiefs were all too aware of these pressures.

When a formal treaty-signing with the Indians took place, the Canadian government was represented by official negotiators, such as Lieutenant-Governor Morris of Manitoba and the North-West Territories. Their job required patience and skill, combining understanding of Indian wishes and respect for their spokesmen. The negotiators were often hampered by the views of short-sighted officials in Ottawa, who knew little of conditions in the West and begrudged every extra cent or gift that was included in a treaty. Fortunately, acting as interpreters and helping to smooth over negotiations were the Métis, who were described by Lord Dufferin as "the ambassadors between east and west."

In the treaty signings that took place after 1874, a new element was added to the Canadian group that participated in the negotiations. This was the North West Mounted Police, the force that represented the Canadian government's response to conditions in the Northwest.

Soon after Canada acquired Rupert's Land and the North-Western Territory, it became clear to Ottawa that if the government's authority was to be respected, there had to be law and order. Events in the Northwest proved this only too well. One Canadian observer, Colonel Robertson Ross, described what he had learned in 1872:

> At Fort Edmonton during the present summer whisky was openly sold to the Blackfoot and other Indians trading at the post by some smugglers from the United States who derive large profit thereby, and on these traders being remonstrated with by the gentleman in charge of the Hudson's Bay post, they coolly replied that they knew very well that what they were doing was contrary to the law of both countries, but as there was no force to prevent them, *they would do just as they pleased.*

Both Captain W. F. Butler and the Council of the North-Western Territory reported that lawlessness was general among all parts of the population, and recommended that a military force take over law enforcement. And no incident made the need for a police force clearer than the Cypress Hills massacre in May 1873, when a group of whisky traders from Fort Benton, Montana, slaughtered a large number of children, women, and men of an Assiniboine (Stoney) band.

On May 20, 1873, Parliament passed the act that brought the North West Mounted Police into existence. From the beginning, the NWMP combined police powers and military organization. As a police force, its authority of "Maintiens le Droit" extended to all the people in the Northwest — Indians, Métis, and new settlers. As for organization, its first commissioner, G. A. French, had been an officer in the British Army, and he insisted on strict military discipline within the force. Also, by a lucky choice, the uniform selected for the NWMP was military: white helmet for formal parades (a little round pillbox for regular duties), cavalry boots and spurs, dark blue cavalry breeches, and the most famous part of the force's uniform — the scarlet tunic. It is hard to overestimate the importance of that tunic. In the minds of the Indians, the old "medicine line" — the boundary between the United States and Canada — became a "color" line, with the blue of the U.S. Cavalry standing for treachery south of the 49th parallel, and the red of the Mounted Police for fair dealing in Canada.

The first job of the Mounted Police was to establish Ottawa's authority in the plains and foothills of what are now southern Saskatchewan and Alberta. After a winter of drill and organization at Fort Garry, Manitoba, Commissioner French assembled about 275 of his slightly more than 300

Maintiens le Droit = Uphold the Right, that is, maintain the law.

While still a boy, Jerry Potts, the son of a Scots trader and a Piegan woman, tracked his father's murderer to a Blackfoot encampment and there killed him. From that time on, Potts became one of the very few Métis who was allowed to enter a Blackfoot (Blackfeet, Blood, Piegan, or Sarcee) camp at any time and on any occasion. He was even accorded the honor of being allowed to attend some Blackfoot councils.

A scout of great ability, Potts was invaluable to the Mounted Police. He guided Colonel Macleod and his men to the place on the Oldman River where Fort Macleod, the first Police post in the West, was to be built. He helped the Police in their search for the Cypress Hill murderers. Perhaps most important of all, Potts persuaded many Indian groups to put their trust in the Police.

A Police patrol and Indian scout on the open plains. The men are wearing the original pillbox hats, which proved little use against prairie wind and weather and were replaced by the Stetson.

men at Fort Dufferin, near the American border. In July 1874, the force set out from the Red River on its Great March.

The westward march must have been quite an experience for the mounted policemen, many of whom had led a much tamer life in eastern Canada. First, there was the column of march itself. As well as the files of horses and men, there were wagons, Red River carts and their drivers, artillery pieces, and a couple of hundred head of cattle. On a normal day, this strange caravan was about eight kilometres long. Then there was the country — the big sky, the huge, near-flat prairies, the dangerous patches of alkali. And then there was the weather — dry in the summer with grasshoppers destroying the scanty pasture, water-holes covered with ice by mid-September, and then a snowstorm.

The force's objective was Fort Whoop-Up, the main "whisky fort" in a region that also boasted Fort Stand-Off and Fort Slide-Out. Fort Whoop-up had to be eliminated if the attack on the illegal whisky trade was to be successful. For about a month — from mid-September to early October — the Canadian police tried to find the fort, with no luck. Supplies began to run short. Commissioner French sent about one-third of his men to winter quarters in Fort Pelly, Manitoba, while he and the rest of his men turned south towards Fort Benton in Montana, the nearest available supply source. When the supply problem was taken care of, Commissioner French turned back to Fort Pelly, leaving Assistant Commissioner Macleod and a small detachment

The fort, built by American whisky traders, was located at the point where the St. Mary and Belly rivers meet to form the Oldman River.

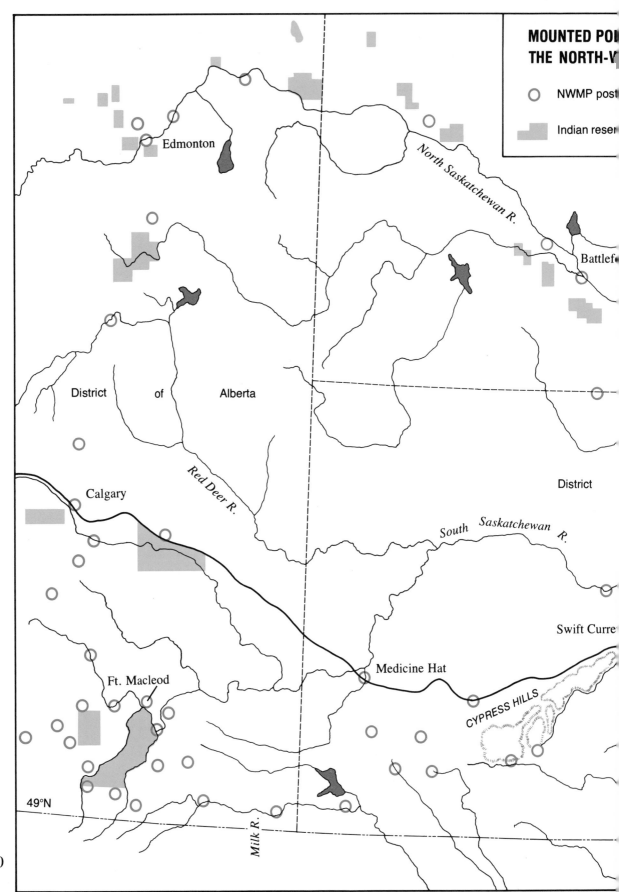

MOUNTED POI[ICE]
THE NORTH-W[EST]

○ NWMP post[s]

Indian reser[ves]

Edmonton

North Saskatchewan R.

Battlef[ord]

District   of   Alberta

District

Red Deer R.

Calgary

South   Saskatchewan   R.

Swift Curre[nt]

Medicine Hat

Ft. Macleod

CYPRESS HILLS

49°N

Milk R.

70

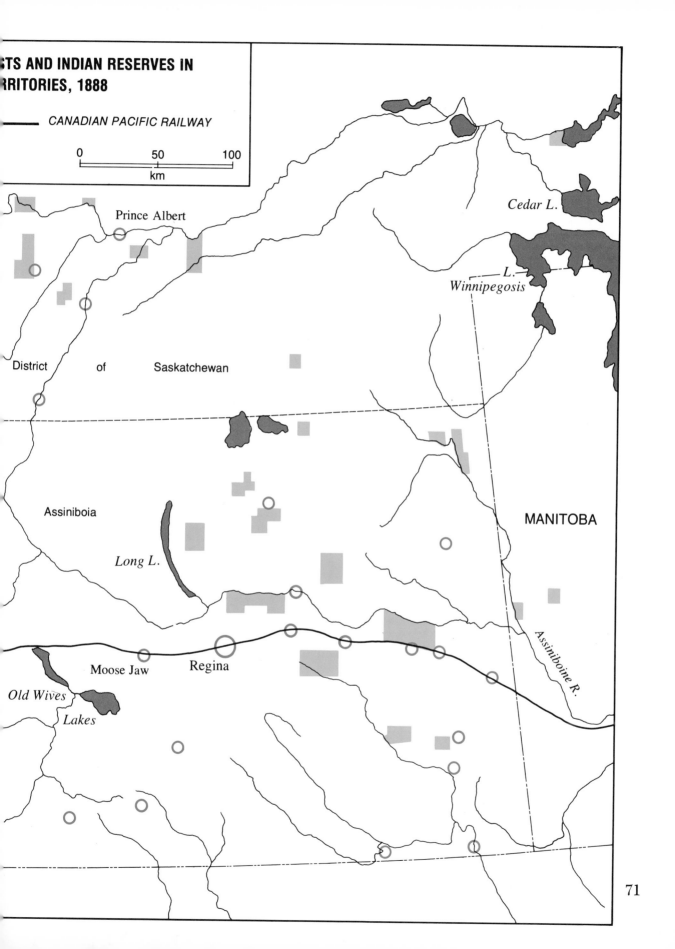

TS AND INDIAN RESERVES IN
RRITORIES, 1888

——— *CANADIAN PACIFIC RAILWAY*

0   50   100
km

Prince Albert

Cedar L.

L.
Winnipegosis

District   of   Saskatchewan

Assiniboia

MANITOBA

Long L.

Assiniboine R.

Moose Jaw   Regina

Old Wives

Lakes

Royal Canadian Mounted Police

to winter in southern Alberta. By mid-October, Macleod's men had found an empty Fort Whoop-Up and occupied it. Whisky traders elsewhere tried to keep up their dealings with Indians, but the force soon put them out of business. Barrels and jugs of whisky were emptied onto the ground, furs were confiscated, and fines were levied. In 1874 and 1875, the North West Mounted Police began to establish Canadian authority and a reputation for itself. In the Northwest, word quickly got around that the NWMP *could* maintain the law.

By 1876, the North West Mounted Police had settled into the West. With 309 men and 287 horses, they manned posts they had taken over or established — Fort Walsh on the south edge of the Cypress Hills, Fort Macleod, Fort Calgary (named by Commissioner Macleod after a castle on the Isle of Mull in Scotland), Fort Edmonton, Fort Saskatchewan, and Fort Pelly on the Swan River. A few hundred men managed to patrol tens of thousands of square kilometres.

The Mounted Police were fortunate — they did not have to deal with large numbers of people arriving in the West, at least not at the start. The confrontation between settlers and Indians that took place in the United States was mercifully avoided in Canada in the 1870s and 1880s. And the force was also lucky that it operated in territory that had been governed by the generally fair and responsible administration of the Hudson's Bay Company. But they themselves added to their good fortune by being fair and efficient policemen. In the words of Crowfoot, the leader of the Blackfeet tribe:

> If the Police had not come to the country, where would we all be now? Bad men and whisky were killing us so fast that very few, indeed, of us would have been left today. The Police have protected us as the feathers of the bird protect it from the frosts of winter.

72

THE TRANSCONTINENTAL — AGAIN

While the Police were bringing law and order to the Canadian West, Mackenzie was struggling along, trying to run Canada's government as prime minister and minister of public works. He was not blessed with good luck. Edward Blake joined the government as minister of justice in 1875, but his presence did not add strength to the government. Blake wanted to be prime minister himself, and there were enough Liberals prepared to support him to weaken Mackenzie's leadership.

The depression certainly did nothing to strengthen Mackenzie's government. It meant that fewer goods were imported; fewer imports meant lower revenues from tariffs; lower revenues in turn meant less money for government projects. One of these was the Pacific railway, which had to be completed by 1881. Mackenzie tried to find a private company to do the job, but in spite of the favorable terms he offered, there was not enough private money available for investment. So the government would have to build the railway itself. And it would have to do so with the badly reduced government revenues. These facts help to explain the very slow progress in building the rail link with the West while Mackenzie was prime minister.

The first challenge to Mackenzie's railway project, however, was political rather than financial. Should the British Columbia section of the railway follow a route from the prairies to Bute Inlet, across the Strait of Georgia to Vancouver Island, and then south to Esquimalt? Or should it take the Fraser Valley route, through Yale and New Westminster? The Vancouver Island route meant better business for Vancouver Island businessmen; the Fraser route meant greater prosperity for Fraser Valley merchants. Premier George Walkem of British Columbia supported the Island route, and he went to London to argue his case, over the head of the Canadian government. The British Colonial Secretary, Lord Carnarvon, worked out a compromise called the Carnarvon Terms: the Island route would be used (this would please the Island

Geological Survey of Canada, Ottawa

Coal was found on Vancouver Island near Nanaimo in 1849, the first mining in this area being done by the Hudson's Bay Company. Coal remained the chief basis of Nanaimo's economy for a century.

73

merchants), but the date of completion would be put off from 1881 to 1890 (this would ease the pressure on the Canadian government).

Then Edward Blake got into the act. He was opposed to the whole idea of the railway, even though it was clear that if the railway were not built, British Columbia would have good reason to leave Confederation. As prime minister, Mackenzie had to keep British Columbia satisfied, but he also needed the votes of Blake and his supporters. So Mackenzie was forced to accept Blake's changes in the Carnarvon Terms. Instead of an Island route, the railway would follow the Fraser Valley route (this was what Ottawa wanted, but Mackenzie had to keep in mind the views of the British Columbia MPs); but the government of Canada would pay British Columbia, as compensation for the change in route, $750 000. In the House of Commons, Blake's proposal carried the day; only the members from British Columbia voted against it.

In the Province of Manitoba, transportation promised to be a gold mine for those who gained control of steamboat services on the Red River. Operating out of St. Paul, Minnesota, an ex-Canadian named J. J. Hill used U.S. law to restrict his competitors and grab all the freight traffic on the Red River for his steamboat *Selkirk*. Then other groups got into the act to break the monopoly. Donald Smith, a Conservative MP and also chief commissioner of the Hudson's Bay Company, joined forces with a man called Norman Kittson and challenged Jim Hill's monopoly with a steamboat called the *International*. A group of Winnipeg and Minnesota merchants commissioned two steamers of their own to fight both Hill and the Smith-Kittson-HBC steamboat.

Then, to replace them all, construction was started on a rail line from Selkirk to Pembina. It was intended to link up with the St. Paul and Pacific Railway, which was supposed to be built from St. Paul to the Canadian border. This new Manitoba railway, lurching its way south from Winnipeg, was never very successful. But it did contribute to some noteworthy developments for the West and for Canada. It brought the first locomotive to western Canada, the *Countess of Dufferin*, which was shipped by steamer to Winnipeg in October 1877. But more important, it got Jim Hill and Donald Smith interested in the St. Paul and Pacific Railway, a fact that was significant for the future *Canadian* Pacific railway.

Mackenzie's policy for the Pacific railway was to go slow, paying expenses from revenues, and to concentrate on the section of the proposed route between Fort William, on Lake Superior, and Selkirk, Manitoba. Strictly speaking, it was not a railway at all, but rather a rail-water-rail route. The idea was to build about fifty-three kilometres of rail line from Fort William at the eastern end, and about one hundred and twenty kilometres at the western end, and use the system of lakes and rivers between these two sections to cut costs. The water system, unfortunately, had about seventy portages, and by 1878 even Mackenzie had dropped the idea of using water transportation and was planning a complete rail route.

The steamer Dakota, operated by Norman Kittson's Red River Transportation Company. (Kittson was the HBC's agent in St. Paul.) This steamship line was actually a joint venture by J. J. Hill, Kittson, and the HBC, which received a one-third discount on all river freight. The profits from freight traffic were glorious; a keg of nails cost ten times as much at Red River as in Ontario.

As minister of public works, Mackenzie was responsible for awarding contracts for railway construction. Here he found himself subject to the same pressures that Macdonald and the Conservatives had had. Railways were for transportation, yes, but in the minds of some businessmen their primary purpose seemed to be to provide easy opportunities to make money from government contracts. With Mackenzie in office, Liberal businessmen expected to make money. And they did. In fact, of eleven contracts awarded by Mackenzie's government, eight of them — for 95 per cent of all the money paid out — went to men who at some time or another were Liberal MPs. Even more questionable was Mackenzie's huge overpurchase of rails from a Montreal company in which the prime minister's brother, Charles, was a partner until at least May 1875.

Mackenzie also had to deal with the tariff question. Here, his own party was split. Some Liberals agreed with Mackenzie that the tariff should be raised, so as to increase government revenues. Other Liberals, however, thundered against the tariff, almost as if it were a sin.

"Protection [of industries]," said the Toronto *Globe*, "is . . . the devil's lie that nations are and ought to be each others' enemies." The leader of the opposition in the Commons took advantage of this split, which paved the way for the defeat of the Mackenzie government.

THE RETURN OF SIR JOHN

When he left office in 1873, Macdonald was tired and sick, and he wanted his party to choose a younger man as leader. For about two

John A. Macdonald is one of the most important figures in North American history. It was he, more than any other person, who shaped a nation out of a few scattered British colonies and a huge, near-empty West. As a result, the continent of North America was divided politically into two nations.

years, he took a much smaller part in politics, concentrating on his law practice in Toronto. But late in 1875, that long politician's nose of his smelled trouble in the Liberal Party, and his interest in public life revived. Macdonald zeroed in on the tariff issue. In the House of Commons in 1876, he called for a "readjustment to the tariff" (meaning a raise in tariff rates), which would "afford fitting encouragement and protection to the struggling manufacturers and industries, as well as to the agricultural products of the country." He was continuing the development of the tariff part of his National Policy, and this policy he took to the people.

His medium was the political picnic. This was not one of those cozy "fireside chats" offered by politicians today on television. Several thousand men, women, and children gathered to enjoy themselves — eating from the tables, meeting the politicians, and listening to the speeches. The speeches were really newsworthy; with no radio or television to pound out bits of news, every hour on the hour, the chance to listen to politicians and assess their policies was important to any citizen who took politics seriously. The first of these picnics was held at Uxbridge, Ontario, on July 1, 1876. Macdonald was at his best. He spoke, of course, without any public address system, but he did not need any. His friendly, easy style carried the message to his listeners. He wanted protection not just for manufactured goods, but also for farm products, to protect Canadian farmers against imports from the United States. And he attacked the prime minister most effectively. It was no use looking to Mr. Mackenzie, he said, to help the country out of the trade depression because "Mr. Mackenzie is a free trader." If the country were ever to come out of the depression and the National Policy be established, Mackenzie's government had to be defeated.

Two by-elections were held near Uxbridge on July 5, and the Conservatives won both. Macdonald's political picnics continued that summer and the next, and the Conservatives continued to win by-elections. The stage was set for the 1878 election.

Again, Mackenzie was dogged by bad luck and bad timing. Blake had resigned from the government in January, overworked and ill, and his supporters failed to give Mackenzie the backing he needed. The harvests in Ontario and Quebec were bad (a sure indication that the farmers' vote would go against the party in power). And then the prime minister set the election date for September instead of June, giving the Conservative Party another summer in which to hammer the government at political picnics. John A. continued to press for his National Policy: ". . . there has arisen in this country a *Canadian* party, which declares we must have Canada for the Canadians . . . ."

In the 1878 election, Canada's first election with the secret ballot, the Mackenzie government was crushed. The results of 1874 were reversed, and Macdonald, now sixty-three, took office as prime minister once again.

STUDY 2

1. On a map of the eastern half of Canada, trace the route of the Grand Trunk Railway, from Portland (Maine!) to Sarnia, Ontario (and, later, Chicago).
2. Why was the Intercolonial built by government, not by private enterprise?
3. Show the connection between railways and politics in the case of the Intercolonial — original purpose, route, method of construction, patronage, etc.
4. Imagine that you are a nineteenth-century railway promoter in Canada. Draw up a railway proposal, including all the reasons why the government should grant you the charter and why people should invest in your scheme.

    Then imagine that you are a rival promoter with your own plans for a railway. Present the case for *your* proposal. Explain the disadvantages of your competitor's plan and the dangers of investing in such a "hare-brained" scheme and point out the benefits of your own "sure-fire" scheme.
5. Why were some Canadian railways in the nineteenth century planned to encourage and aid colonization?
6. Describe, in your own words, what happened in the Pacific Scandal. If you were writing a melodrama based on these events, who would be The Villain? Why?
7. What do you think was Sir Georges Etienne Cartier's most important contribution to the development of Canada as a nation?
8. What problems did Sir Alexander Mackenzie face as prime minister and leader of the Liberal party? (Add to your answer as you go through the chapter.)
9. Summarize developments in the Northwest from 1871-1877. What additional sources of possible conflict would you add to your answer to Question 6, Study 1?
10. How did the North West Mounted Police earn their reputation?
11. On a sketch map, trace the two proposed routes for the transcontinental railway. How did politics affect the choice of route?
12. How did people vote before the secret ballot was introduced? What advantages, if any, were there in the old system?
13. Explain what "free trade" meant for the Canadian economy in the last half of the nineteenth century. What were the advantages and disadvantages of free trade for Canadians?

the Railway and Rebellion

The Old Chieftain was back. Sir John A. Macdonald had led the Conservatives back into power in the election of 1878 with his proposals for a National Policy. Now, with old political comrades like Sir Charles Tupper and Sir Samuel Tilley, it was up to him to put this policy into practice. The National Policy, it is true, was good politics for the Conservatives; it provided an excellent platform from which to attack the Liberals, who had struggled through the depression years of the 1870s. But it was not only political. Whatever the opposition might say, the National Policy was intended to support Macdonald's basic idea — the creation and strengthening of an independent nation in the northern half of North America.

THE NATIONAL POLICY

The National Policy was like a three-legged stool, which needed each of its legs if it was to stand. The three legs of the stool were these: the development and protection of Canadian industry, using the tariff to keep out competitive goods produced by foreign manufacturers; the construction of communication links to tie the country together; and finally, the filling up of Canada's empty spaces, particularly the West, through immigration. Each leg of the stool was dependent on the others. Without a railway, for example, there would be little immigration to the West. Without a populated West, there would be only limited markets for Canadian manufactured goods. Without a railway and healthy manufacturing industries, Canada as a free and independent nation would never gain the strength it needed to stand on its own.

In the winter of 1878-1879, Macdonald's new government turned its attention to a new system of tariffs. The minister of finance, Sir Samuel L. Tilley, listened to delegation after delegation of manufacturers, every one of whom wanted his product protected by the new tariff rates. When the new rates were finally passed through the House of Commons in the spring of 1879, the principle behind the tariff had changed. It still provided revenues for the government, but it was now clearly a "protective tariff," whose purpose was to protect Canadian markets for goods manufactured in Canada. Some of the new rates demonstrated this purpose: duties on agricultural implements, 25 per cent; duties on bricks, 20 per cent; duties on railway cars, 30 per cent. Moreover, the new system operated nationally, providing protection for a wide range of

According to Macdonald (the gent in the top hat), Canadian prosperity would result from the development of industry, which could grow only if a tariff wall was erected against cheaper imported goods, notably those from the United States. The National Policy would allow both industry and agriculture to enjoy the profits made in Canada.

products, including Nova Scotia coal, Ontario petroleum, and Montreal textiles.

There was another important aspect to the new tariff structure. It was intended to be permanent. Revenue tariffs could be adjusted from year to year, depending on government needs, but protective tariffs had to be permanent, to enable manufacturers to make long-range investment plans.

The tariff that protected manufacturers should also have helped workers in Canadian industry. However, in many cases, particularly in the factories in the larger cities, the position of labor was not improved. Workers continued to toil long hours for low wages, sometimes in appalling conditions. Not until the twentieth century did Canadian workers begin to benefit from the tariff policies that ensured their employers high profits.

For information on the labor movement in Canada, see Chapter 8.

The second part of the National Policy was the Pacific railway, the bonds of steel that would bind the country together. When Macdonald returned to office in 1878, he found that prospects for a successful railway were as bad for the Conservatives as they had been for the Liberals. Macdonald wanted a private Canadian company to build the line, but he still faced the old problem: where was he to find Canadian capitalists with enough money?

A solution to Macdonald's problem was forming, strangely enough, on the rolling plains of the *American* West. In Minnesota, a group of Canadian businessmen was turning "two streaks of rust on the prairie" into a successful railroad *and* into enormous personal fortunes for themselves. Their success was to provide the financial foundation for the Canadian Pacific Railway.

Here is how it happened. Back in 1876, Donald Smith had begun to take an interest in American railroads with lines into the Canadian Northwest. One railroad in particular, the St. Paul and Pacific, looked like an excellent prospect. Its iron rails were rusting on the prairie, and it was heavily loaded with debt — not much of a prospect, except to a shrewd businessman like Donald Smith. The St. Paul and Pacific had other lines, it had the promise of huge land grants from the Minnesota government if it completed a railroad to the Canadian border on time, and it would tie in very neatly with a line in Manitoba. So Smith organized a syndicate among several of his friends and business associates. It included J. J. Hill and Norman Kittson, of the Red River Transportation Company, and R. B. Angus, the general manager of the Bank of Montreal. Perhaps most important, it included George Stephen, Donald Smith's cousin and president of the Bank of Montreal. With the Bank of Montreal's financial support (which Stephen was able to obtain) and through the shrewd financial and political work of Hill, the syndicate gained control of the St. Paul and Pacific, settled its $28 million debt for only $6 million (paying with promises rather than solid cash), and then reorganized the road as the St. Paul, Minneapolis and

Donald Smith was involved deeply in the Canadian West, as MP for Selkirk, Manitoba, and Chief Commissioner of the HBC.

Manitoba Railway. The syndicate completed the line to the border on time (and so received the huge land grant). The first train left St. Boniface for St. Paul in December 1878. Settlers began to move in, and the railroad began to operate profitably. Given its original objective — to make money — the syndicate was successful. For a total initial investment from their own pockets of about $300 000, the syndicate members acquired assets of more than $300 000 000!

"Get their money before they have time to invest it somewhere else," was the advice that Macdonald received from his minister of agriculture, John Henry Pope. So it was with great interest in June, 1880, that the prime minister listened to a proposal by Duncan McIntyre to build a Pacific railway for the government. For behind McIntyre stood George Stephen and his associates. Stephen, yet another Scots immigrant, has been described by one Canadian historian as "perhaps the greatest creative genius in the whole history of Canadian finance." For Macdonald, Stephen was practically the perfect man to head a private company in the construction of the Pacific railway. He was a recognized leader in the Canadian business community, he was totally committed to Canada, and he had already proved his capability in the development of the St. Paul, Minneapolis and Manitoba Railway.

Other businessmen were interested in building a transcontinental railway, but no other Canadian group was prepared to undertake construction of a route through the forbidding stretch of rock and muskeg north of Lake Superior. Stephen's syndicate offered the only practical possibility. Throughout the summer of 1880, the government and the railway syndicate negotiated — Stephen holding out for better terms, Macdonald trying to reduce the syndicate's demands. By the fall, agreement was reached, and on October 21, the Canadian Pacific Railway (CPR) contract was signed.

The terms of the contract were not just princely, they were imperial. The government of Canada agreed to give the CPR $25 million and 10 million hectares of land, in a seventy-seven kilometre belt along the prairie right-of-way. In addition, the government agreed to turn over to the CPR several sections of government-built railway, including the St. Boniface-Pembina branch line in Manitoba, the uncompleted sections from Fort William to Winnipeg and, in British Columbia, from Port Moody to Savona Ferry. Altogether, the government signed over to the CPR about 1175 kilometres of track in these sections, worth at least $31.5 million. Among the tax concessions that the company received was permission to import building materials duty-free. Finally, Parliament was to authorize no other railroad south of the CPR main line. This gave the CPR a monopoly in what would become some of the most important wheat-growing areas of Canada's West. In return for all these terms, the CPR agreed to undertake the construction and operation of the railway, which was to be completed and running by May 1, 1891.

Macdonald faced a storm of opposition over these terms, from within

Duncan McIntyre controlled the Canada Central Railway, which ran from Ottawa to Callander on Lake Nipissing. It was to be an important link in the CPR.

This branch line had been leased by Smith and Stephen in 1878.

Glenbow-Alberta Institute

his own party and also from the Liberals. There was great argument, for example, over the monopoly clause, which gave all rail traffic in the Northwest to the CPR. Stephen had been firm in his demand that the railway have the monopoly; writing to Macdonald, he had asked "what do you think would be the position of the CPR or of the men bound to own and operate it, if it were tapped at Winnipeg or at any point west of that, by a line or lines running towards the United States boundary? What would, in such a case, be the value of the CPR line from Winnipeg to Ottawa? No sane man would give a dollar for the whole line east of Winnipeg. . . . *any and every line south* of the line of the CPR running towards the boundary line must be owned and controlled by the CPR, otherwise the CPR would be strangled." But the "monopoly clause" caused controversy in Parliament, and later it was to be a major reason for the West's resentment against the CPR in particular and the East in general.

The major thrust of the Liberal opposition was against the whole idea of an all-Canadian route. In its place, the Liberals argued for a policy of continental transport, which meant in effect going south of the Great Lakes (the old Grand Trunk scheme) to get to the Canadian West. Macdonald counterattacked fiercely. He called on the support of the House to "carry out an arrangement which will give us all we want, which will satisfy all the loyal, legitimate aspirations, which will give us a great, a united, a rich, an improving, a developing Canada, instead of making us tributary to American laws, to American railways, to American bondage, to American tolls, to American freights, to all the little tricks and big tricks that American railways are addicted to for the purpose of destroying our road."

It was a long, tiring debate, which finally drove Macdonald into a sick-bed. But by the end of February, the CPR contract had been passed in Parliament. George Stephen became president of the new company, with McIntyre, Angus, and Hill as directors. Knowing that Macdonald had neither forgotten nor forgiven the vote of 1873, Stephen and his colleagues persuaded Donald Smith, very much against his will, to stay in the background.

THE CPR

The building of the CPR was a massive undertaking — the biggest project in Canadian history until the twentieth century. It makes sense to describe its route in sections, just as it was built. The first part was to go from Callander on Lake Nipissing (where McIntyre's Central Canada stopped) to Port Arthur. From Port Arthur, the CPR would run to St. Boniface-Winnipeg, over a rail line that the government had brought almost to completion. The great prairie section was next; as originally planned, it was to run from Winnipeg through the Fertile Belt to Edmonton and the Yellowhead Pass. The Rocky Mountain route would run south from the Yellowhead Pass along the North Thompson River to Kamloops. Here, the railway would link up with the final section, from Kamloops down the Thompson and Fraser rivers to Burrard Inlet.

For political reasons, the contract for the British Columbia section of the line, from Yale to Kamloops, had actually been awarded in the spring of 1880. Andrew Onderdonk, a brilliant young American engineer, undertook the work, and on May 14, a ceremonial dynamite blast opened construction. Progress through the Fraser River canyon, however, was anything but a ceremony. Onderdonk had to build a railway in a canyon that has little room in it for anything but the Fraser River. He described the work on an eight-kilometre stretch near Lytton as "solid rock cuttings, rock slides of loose rock, large boulder cuttings and some heavy earthwork." What this meant was that Onderdonk's construction crews had to move almost 600 000 cubic metres of rock and earth in this stretch — 80 cubic metres for each metre of track. That is the same as a wall of earth and rock between the tracks 47 metres or 153

A Chinese work gang on the mountain section of the CPR. In British Columbia, several thousand Chinese were employed on the railway because they were willing to work for lower wages than Canadians or Americans. This was the chief cause among British Columbians of anti-Chinese discrimination. Macdonald regarded Orientals as "alien," but he would not exclude them from Canada. As he bluntly put it in Parliament, "It is simply a question of alternatives: either you must have this labour or you can't have the railway."

Notman Photographic Archives, McCord Museum

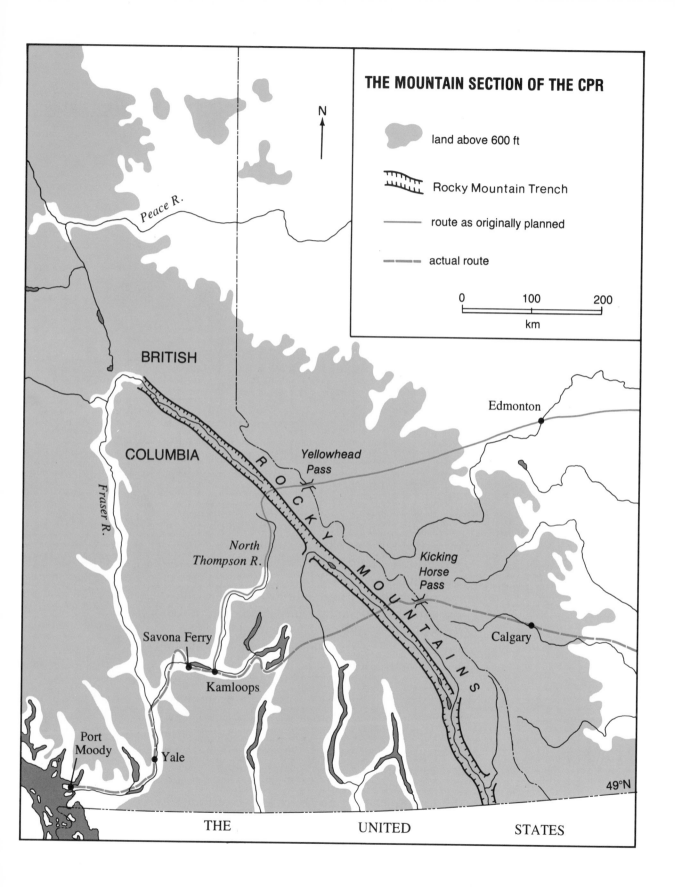

THE MOUNTAIN SECTION OF THE CPR

land above 600 ft

Rocky Mountain Trench

route as originally planned

actual route

0   100   200
km

Peace R.

BRITISH

COLUMBIA

Fraser R.

North
Thompson R.

ROCKY MOUNTAINS

Yellowhead
Pass

Kicking
Horse
Pass

Edmonton

Calgary

Savona Ferry

Kamloops

Port
Moody

Yale

49°N

THE   UNITED   STATES

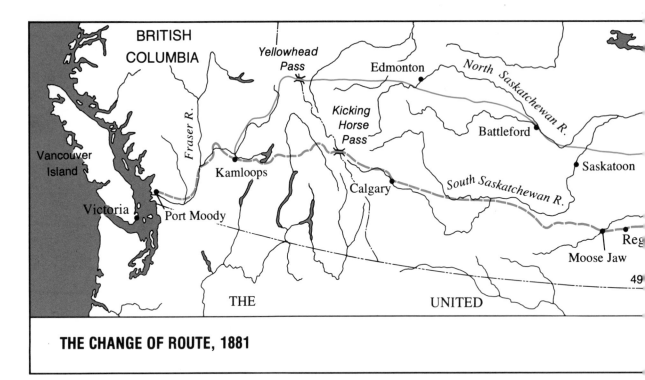

THE CHANGE OF ROUTE, 1881

feet high! And that did not include the many tunnels that had to be bored. Total costs ran to about $185 000 per kilometre.

The rock cuts ate up explosives. Onderdonk was forced to establish dynamite factories along the route. To avoid the high freight charges being levied on the old Cariboo Trail, he had a special steamship built — the *Skuzzy* — to get supplies in. With the aid of its own engines, extra winches, and 150 men pulling on ropes, the *Skuzzy* was able to make it through the Hell's Gate Rapids of the Fraser River.

Onderdonk's section of the CPR needed a small army of laborers, between 8000 and 9000 men. Of these, the majority were Chinese immigrants. At one time, about 6500 Chinese worked in Onderdonk's gangs, and the reaction of many British Columbians to them was openly racist. As long as there was work on the railway, the Chinese were only segregated — living in their own camps, staying among themselves. Later, when the railway construction boom was over and jobs were hard to get, British Columbians became actively hostile to the Chinese. In March 1885, the British Columbia government refused to allow Chinese immigrants to land in Canada. At this point, Sir John A. had to step in. (Immigration came under the powers of the federal government.) Macdonald's response was a head tax of $50 for every Chinese immigrant, except students, officials, or merchants.

For his part, Onderdonk had no problem with the Chinese. Railway building required heavy labor; and the Chinese were prepared to work long hard hours. As far as Onderdonk was concerned, the Chinese were right for the job. What mattered above all was building the line, which

This head tax was raised to $100 per person in 1901 and to $500 in 1904.

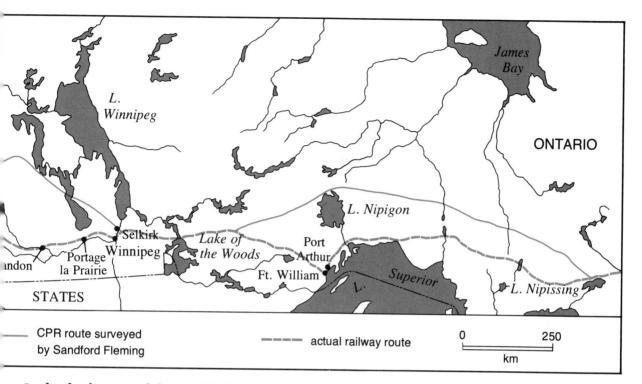

L. Winnipeg

James Bay

ONTARIO

L. Nipigon

Selkirk

Lake of the Woods

Port Arthur

Portage la Prairie

Winnipeg

Ft. William

Superior

L.

andon

STATES

L. Nipissing

_____ CPR route surveyed
by Sandford Fleming

- - - - - actual railway route

0   250
km

Onderdonk proved he could do. In 1882, the young engineer was awarded the construction contract for the Yale-Port Moody section, and in 1884, he received another contract, this time for the section from Savona Ferry to Eagle Pass.

Eagle Pass? Why would Onderdonk build towards Eagle Pass when the route as originally surveyed was to go through the Yellowhead Pass, 224 kilometres farther north? The answer lies in a decision made by the CPR management almost as soon as construction began. The route of the main line was changed to run from Winnipeg west into what is now southern Alberta, instead of northwesterly to Edmonton and the Yellowhead Pass. The CPR management knew that the Kicking Horse Pass was quite a lot higher than the Yellowhead Pass (which would probably mean greater construction costs); it also knew that no practical pass had yet been found through the Selkirk Range, the next mountain barrier west of the Rockies. But the change of route was a huge gamble the CPR management felt it had to take. There was useful coal in southern Alberta, and a southern route to a Pacific terminus would be a lot shorter than going through the Yellowhead Pass. Most important, south of the 49th parallel, the Northern Pacific Railroad had recovered from its financial difficulties and was building a main line from Fargo, North Dakota, to Portland, Oregon. The line threatened to take future business away from the CPR, and this CPR management had to prevent.

Before anyone was at all sure that the Rockies could be crossed south of the Yellowhead Pass, construction had begun on the prairie section. In 1881, about 440 kilometres of railway were built. But J. J. Hill was

The Kicking Horse Pass had not yet been surveyed to see if a rail line could be built through it. The CPR was gambling that the pass would take the railway through the Rockies.

The CPR advanced across the prairies with amazing speed. Migrating animals, such as antelope, found their return blocked by lines of rails "and terrified by the sight . . . gathered in hundreds on the north side, afraid to cross. . . ." Here, a rail-laying gang uses a winch to lift the steel off a flatcar and lower it onto the ties.

unsatisfied with this progress. The general superintendent of construction was fired, and an American who had begun his railroad career as a telegraph operator took over: William Cornelius Van Horne.

How does something as big as a railway or a hydro-electric project or a pipeline actually get built? Businessmen or politicians set the objectives; surveyors and engineers draw up the plans of the project and provide on-the-job expertise; skilled and unskilled workers turn the plans into their final physical form. But who ensures that objectives and skills are brought together to successfully complete the project? That is the job of the organizer, and the CPR could not have found a better one than Van Horne.

He was not an engineer; his job was to organize skills and materials so that objectives would be reached. And for Van Horne (who set himself a personal goal in 1882 to complete 805 kilometres of track), it was a huge job. Out in front were the surveyors, measuring and marking where the line would be laid. Then came the bridge-building gangs, working in shifts all day and night to erect bridges and trestles. The grading gangs were next — small armies of men preparing the right-of-way for track-laying. Think of the organizing skills required in managing all these workers. Another problem for the organizer: Where would the men eat and sleep? (One solution was special two-storey rail cars, with bunks above and kitchen and dining halls below.) With no bulldozers or power shovels, horses provided a lot of muscle. (More problems for the organizer: Who would look after feed for the horses? Who would take care of harness and horseshoes?) Then came the track-laying: trolleys with ties and rails were brought to the "end of steel"; ties were laid and rails were spiked; the empty trolleys were pushed off to the side, to be picked up later; then, new loaded trolleys were brought up to the end of steel, and the sequence started all over again.

Supporting the efforts of the construction gangs were the supply trains, carrying steel rails from Britain and Germany and wooden ties from the forests of eastern Canada. Van Horne had men checking on these all along the supply route, noting when each train passed and telegraphing the news to Van Horne in his private headquarters car.

With Van Horne driving the line forward, three to five kilometres of first-class railway were laid every day during the summer of 1882. Another successful construction season followed in 1883, and by the end of the year, the CPR was approaching the Kicking Horse Pass. Behind the railway stretched a line of new towns, like beads on a necklace. Brandon, Manitoba; "Pile o' Bones," the site of an old buffalo hunters' camp, re-christened Regina; Moose Jaw, where an early traveller was said to have repaired his Red River cart with the jaw of a moose; Swift Current; Medicine Hat, its name taken from Indian legend; and Calgary, NWMP post and cow-town.

INDIAN GRIEVANCES

Throughout 1882 and 1883, everything was well organized and proceeding according to plan — except for one important consideration. In the rush to complete the railway, no one had bothered to explain to the Indians what was going on.

A minor incident developed in 1883, when Chiefs Piapot and Long Man of the Cree staged a sit-down demonstration in the middle of the CPR right-of-way west of Moose Jaw. The Mounted Police (three of them) were called in. After giving the Indians half an hour to move on, they knocked down the teepees that were blocking the right-of-way, and the Indians stepped aside. Later that same year, a much more serious event occurred. When CPR construction crews crossed onto the lands of a Blackfoot reserve, Chief Crowfoot warned that there were 700 Blackfoot warriors ready to halt them. Recognizing how dangerous the situation was, Father Albert Lacombe, who had worked among the Indians for more than thirty years, quickly telegraphed news of the situation to Van Horne. In reply, he asked Father Lacombe to explain to Crowfoot that the Indians would receive compensation. When the old chief understood that the Blackfoot would receive a further land settlement, he was able to calm down his angry young men, and the danger passed.

The Hands Studio, Ottawa   Glenbow-Alberta Institute

Left: In an effort to bring back the great herds, Indians perform the Buffalo Dance in front of their friends, the Mounted Police, at Fort Qu'Appelle, District of Saskatchewan.

Right: This photograph of the Blackfoot chiefs, Crowfoot and Three Bulls, and Father Albert Lacombe was taken during their 1886 tour of eastern Canada. It was the sincerity of men like Lacombe, his Protestant counterpart, the Reverend John McDougall, and Colonel Macleod that induced many chiefs to accept Ottawa's authority over the prairies.

The Indians were being faced with an enormously difficult change in their lifestyle — from a free, almost nomadic, hunting life in which they were highly skilled, to a static (or, as they saw it, stagnant) farming life, which demanded new and different skills. As Indians adjusted painfully to this change, the years from 1879 to 1882 were marked by starvation and death among the tribes, and they began to suspect the good faith of the Canadian government. When supplies ran short and Indians demanded the food that had been promised them in the treaties, the government agents told them that no supplies could be given out. When an Indian walked across a homesteader's land (which only a few years before was as free as a prairie antelope), he might be shot at. Even the Mounted Police, enforcing what the Indians saw as white men's law, began to lose the respect of the tribes. The Canadian Empire being formed in the Northwest tended to forget the legal rights of Indians, and to ignore their sensitivities. Without the concern of men like Father Lacombe, and without the statesman-like qualities of chiefs like Crowfoot, Canada might have experienced the bloodshed that characterized the settlement of the American West.

THE CPR RUNS OUT OF MONEY

The railway was pushing on. Beyond Calgary and approaching the Kicking Horse Pass, it now had to make its way through what Edward Blake had called a "sea of mountains." Wave after wave of them lay between the prairies and the Pacific coast. But, to justify the gamble of the southern route, a way had to be found through the mountains. And, with a lot of exploring and a bit of luck, a way was found.

Back in 1865, a survey crew led by Walter Moberly, at the time assistant surveyor-general for Canada, had discovered a break in the Gold Range: Eagle Pass. In 1881 and 1882, the CPR sent another surveyor to find a practical rail route through another mountain barrier, the Selkirk Range. The man was Major A. B. Rogers, "a snappy little chappy" whose language was colorful and whose expertise with chewing tobacco was a sight to behold. He started his surveys on the west side of the Selkirks; then, by following the Beaver River Valley, he was able to find the eastern approaches to the pass that would later bear his name. He overcame many hardships and difficulties because he had a tremendous motivation: "Find a pass," J. J. Hill had told Rogers, "and I'll name it for you." In spite of attacks by black flies and mosquitos (Rogers said he was bitten so badly that his ears shook like raw liver when he walked!), the tough little surveyor made his way back to the Kicking Horse Pass to the end of steel. Here, the news of his important find was telegraphed to Montreal. Rogers eventually got a cheque for $5000 from the CPR for his work — cheap for the 240 kilometres of line that the Rogers Pass saved the railway!

The mountain section of the line could now advance. Temporary trestles took the place of bridges; grades almost two and a half times greater than acceptable standards had to be used in the passes; snow sheds had to be built to prevent the line being blocked. But the CPR gradually crept forward, toward Onderdonk's section in British Columbia.

The most difficult part of the CPR route was the section north of Superior, from Callander to Port Arthur. Van Horne described it as "two hundred miles of engineering impossibilities." Again, the planned route was changed, brought closer to Lake Superior to make the transportation of supplies easier. Materials were brought in by twelve steamers — three of them specially built (in Scotland) so that they could be cut in half, taken through Canada's canal system, and reassembled on the Great Lakes. A dynamite factory was built on Superior's north shore to provide the blasting gangs with the powder they needed. Sometimes nitroglycerine was used, and this extremely dangerous explosive killed many men and boys.

The route ran over the world's oldest rock, the granites of the Canadian Shield. But even this oldest of rock had not been worn flat by time. The Shield in northern Ontario has high bluffs, rolling hills of rock, and swampy, water-logged depressions called muskeg, sometimes so deep

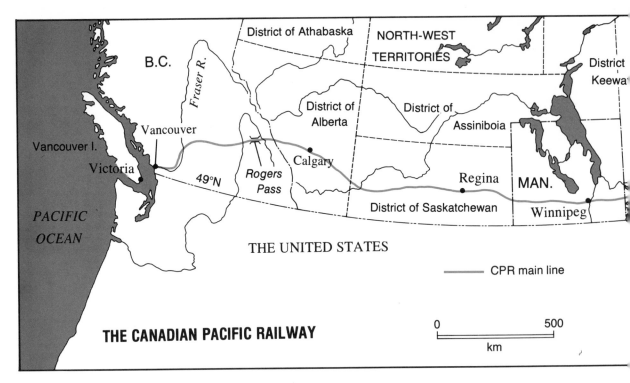

THE CANADIAN PACIFIC RAILWAY

as to seem bottomless. Imagine the anger and exasperation of the builders on a stretch of muskeg — a thick matting of tree roots and dead or dying vegetation supporting a few trees — their work accompanied by the high whine of mosquitos and bloody black-fly bites. The line is cleared, the track is laid, and then, with an enormous gurgle, it sinks into the swamp. And this happened not once, but seven times! And not one, but *three* locomotives sank into the same swamp. Contractors lost their shirts hauling in gravel and rock, only to see the materials swallowed by the muskeg. One particularly bad kilometre of the Superior section cost $435 000; many others ran as high as $186 000 each to build. In fact, construction costs along the whole Superior route were astronomical.

Costs and debts: these were the rocks on which the CPR threatened to founder. However generous the terms of the CPR appeared on paper, the money and land grants were earned only after completion of stipulated lengths of line. Every forty kilometres of completed track brought a cash payment to the company. The payment was earned easily on the prairies, where forty kilometres took little more than a week to build. But in the Rockies and north of Superior, forty kilometres sometimes took months to build. The terms for the land grants were similar. Every thirty-two kilometres of track brought a transfer to the CPR of a number of hectares of land, which the CPR could then sell to settlers and thereby get its hands on cash. But in practice, the process did not work out so smoothly. For example, of the four million prairie hectares that the CPR had earned by 1882, only a little over one million were close to the main

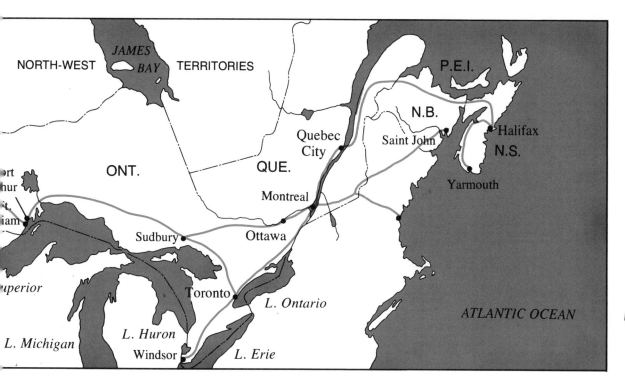

line. Some of this land was so dry that it was difficult to sell as farmland. The remainder of the land, situated farther to the north, was away from the main line and therefore unlikely to command a high price.

Even though the income of the CPR developed more slowly than expected, George Stephen was prepared to spend money to develop rail links for his company in eastern Canada. Duncan McIntyre's Canada Central was bought outright by the CPR in 1881; the Montreal-Ottawa section of the Quebec, Montreal, Ottawa, and Occidental Railroad was bought from the Quebec government in 1882. In 1884 came the lease of the Ontario and Quebec Railroad, projected to run from Toronto through Peterborough, Ontario, to Montreal. This lease was very important for the CPR, for it brought with it control of two other railroads — the Credit Valley Railway (Toronto-London-St. Thomas) and the Toronto, Grey, and Bruce Railway (Toronto to Owen Sound). All of these Ontario lines provided the CPR with important new business — and a rail network in Grand Trunk home territory. For the Grand Trunk, the CPR was serious competition; the old, Ontario-based company determined to use all its financial and political weapons to drive its upstart competitor out of business.

The CPR was certainly vulnerable. By the end of 1883, it had received $21 million from the government and from land sales. But at the same time, it had been required to pay out about $59 million. Much of the $38 million difference came from the sale of CPR shares. But, as Van Horne's construction costs continued to pour in, the CPR found itself in serious financial difficulty. Further sales of shares became impossible, as the offered purchase price fell below what Stephen could afford to accept. The CPR would have to borrow money. Yet even the Bank of Montreal, with which Stephen was so closely associated, was reluctant to lend any. Only an official letter from Sir Charles Tupper, the minister of railways and canals, finally induced the Bank to agree to a relatively small loan. But Stephen needed big money — $22 500 000 — and the only possible source was the government of Canada itself. Sir John A. was against it. He told Stephen he might as well ask for the planet Jupiter. But then the prime minister reconsidered. The CPR *had* to be supported, for if it failed, the government would fail, the Conservative Party would fail, and, in Sir John A.'s view, the whole idea of Canada based on the National Policy would fail.

The Conservatives introduced a bill to lend the CPR the necessary money on February 1, 1884. It immediately came under attack from the Liberal opposition, which the Grand Trunk supported in every way it could. Even some Conservative members from Quebec and the Maritimes used the opportunity of the bill to lever money from the government for railways in their provinces. In the end, after a long tough fight by Macdonald, the CPR got its loan. However, this still did not solve all the financial difficulties. Stephen and Smith borrowed money personally — pledging their own personal assets — to prevent the CPR from going under. But there simply was never enough money to pay all the bills. Pay cars failed to arrive at construction sites, and workers went on strike. After another year of financial struggle had gone by, Sir John A. refused to lend the CPR any more public money. It was all over. The CPR had hit bottom. On March 26, 1885, the railway company was headed for the graveyard of bankrupt North American transcontinentals.

Almost everyone, including the CPR president, George Stephen, had argued that the Superior section of the railway should not be built because it would — and did — cost millions of dollars in materials and wages. By 1884, there were 15 000 men laboring between Lake Nipissing and Port Arthur, and their pay alone amounted to $1 100 000 a month.

THE ORIGINS OF THE NORTHWEST REBELLION

On March 27, a telegram arrived in Ottawa. Métis riflemen had killed twelve Mounted Police and volunteers, at a place called Duck Lake, a few kilometres north of Saskatoon. Eleven men were wounded. Apparently some kind of rebellion had broken out. What was happening in the Northwest?

The origins of the Northwest Rebellion are not hard to find. Each of the population groups in the Northwest — Indians, Métis, and recent settlers — had a long list of grievances. For the Plains Indians, the late 1870s and early 1880s were disastrous. In 1879, the last of the great buffalo herds began to disappear, as "civilization" came to the Great Plains. Railroads obstructed the herds' migration paths; "sportsmen" with rifles slaughtered thousands of the animals, taking only the tongues and hides and leaving the carcasses to rot. Since the Plains Indians depended so heavily on the bison, the disappearance of the herds meant that the whole Indian way of life began to fall apart. (This helps explain why the chiefs who signed treaties wanted guarantees of rations if disease or "general famine" threatened their people.) Government officials encouraged the Indians to take up farming, but this was asking a lot of nomads. Farming was hardly as interesting as following the buffalo. In any case, agriculture required Indians to learn a completely new set of cultural skills and attitudes. How do hunters suddenly learn to domesticate animals instead of killing them? How does a people — any people — suddenly learn how to plough, plant seed, harvest the grain, and save some grain so that they can use it as seed after the winter? For the Plains Indians, the change from hunting to agriculture was probably more difficult than a change from urban living to hunting would be for a Canadian city dweller today.

Little consideration was given to the Indians' special problems. For example, in 1883 and 1884, falling government revenues in Ottawa led to budget cuts in all government departments, including the Department of Indian Affairs. Supplies promised in treaties were cut off; for the Indians, this could mean starvation and death. The department was run on a day-to-day basis by a penny-pinching civil servant called Lawrence Vankoughnet (the deputy superintendent-general), but the politician responsible for the department, the superintendent-general of Indian Affairs, was Sir John A. Macdonald himself. Was the prime minister not affected by the words of Father Doucet? "It is hard to recognize in the victims of famine, thin and emaciated, without vigour in their voices, the magnificent savages that I had formerly seen. They are no longer men but walking skeletons."

Pressured by insecurity and a shortage of food, the Indians confronted government officials. In 1879, some broke into Fort Qu'Appelle to get provisions; in the same year, a Mounted Policeman was killed by an Indian. In 1883, Cree and Blackfoot challenged the railway. In

Left: According to some Police reports, the Cree chief Big Bear was the most troublesome Indian on the prairies. But much of this reputation stemmed from his caution when being pressured to sign a treaty or move onto a reserve.

Right: Chief Poundmaker was also labelled "troublesome," because he objected to Ottawa's invasion of tribal lands. He earned his name from the patience and skill with which he lured buffalo into a pound. An adopted son of Crowfoot, Poundmaker maintained tribal discipline and held many impatient Cree in check.

1884, Indians at Crooked Lake demanded food from their farm instructor; he refused, as the government had ordered. His pupils stormed the storehouse and barricaded themselves against the Mounted Police. Another similar incident occurred the same year. Again, a demand for food; again, refusal. This time, however, the Indians became a furious, rioting mob. Only after the Mounted Police gave the Indians food and after Chief Big Bear convinced his people to calm down was a major uprising avoided.

Government officials in the East knew about these events from the regular reports they received, but they took no action to help the Indians. So it became the policy of chiefs like Big Bear and Poundmaker to organize united resistance so that Ottawa would *have* to grant better treaty terms.

The situation of the new settlers reflected other problems in the Northwest. The third part of Macdonald's National Policy — immigration and settlement of the West — had achieved only limited success. There were only a few settlements worth noting. In 1874, at the junction of the Battle and North Saskatchewan rivers, Telegraph Flats was established. In 1877, it became the new capital of the North-West Territories, and was renamed Battleford. In 1878, a small group of

Poundmaker got his name as a maker of buffalo pounds. These were enclosures into which buffalo were driven for killing.

Ontario farmers established a community in the Carrot River Valley. There was also a sprinkling of farm settlement in the North Saskatchewan River Valley, along the route that Sandford Fleming had originally proposed for the transcontinental railway. However, when the CPR line was shifted closer to the U.S. border, settlers and settlement were affected in two ways. First, the focus of settlement moved south, as new towns sprang up in the wake of the railway. Secondly, new settlers went south rather than north. Several co-operative or company settlements were started: in 1882, for example, a Major Bell from Ontario organized the Qu'Appelle Valley Farming Company near Indian Head. Lady Gordon Cathcart sent a group of tenants from her Scottish estates to found farmsteads near Moosomin. In 1884, twenty families of laborers from London, England, came to what is now southern Saskatchewan to try their inexperienced hands at prairie farming.

The change in the CPR route also affected the northern settlers. They had taken up land in the expectation that the railway would provide close transportation and increase the value of their farms. Now, they were stuck at the end of long, bumpy wagon roads. Moreover, they were uncertain about their land claims. The Land Board officials in Winnipeg administered the complicated laws badly, confusing settlers who were already on the land and discouraging others from even trying to settle.

The third group in the Northwest was the Métis. Some of these people had been born and raised in the North-West Territories, and their chief settlement was at St. Albert, near Edmonton. Many others had come from Manitoba to the District of Saskatchewan, where they established several centres, including, on the South Saskatchewan River, St. Laurent, St. Antoine de Padoue (better known as Batoche), and St. Louis de Langevin.

The disappearance of the buffalo affected the Métis in the same way that it had affected the Indians. Their preferred way of life became impossible, and they had to concentrate on farming. Farming meant land, and land meant land claims, surveys and titles — all the factors which had contributed to the Red River troubles in 1869-1870. The Manitoba Act of 1870 had provided a land settlement of 566 560 hectares for Red River Métis. The administration of this settlement, however, was unbelievably slow: it began only in 1873, and then took several years to complete. A good number of Manitoba Métis, unhappy with the changes in the Red River settlement and fed up with delays over their land claims, left the province and drifted west, where they founded the St. Laurent and Batoche settlements.

In the early 1880s, the Saskatchewan Métis began to be concerned about their claims to the long, narrow river lots that they had taken up along the rivers. Their position was complicated by several factors. Some Métis had rights to the land. Some, however, had already received land in Manitoba and were entitled to no more. Others had received scrip — a land certificate — and had sold it to speculators for extremely low prices, perhaps $50 or $60 for a scrip for ninety-seven

The York Colonization Company from Ontario settled eight townships near Yorkton, Saskatchewan.

Some settlers who came were totally out of their element. The English gentlemen who arrived at Cannington Manor, for example, brought with them dinner jackets, cricket bats, and tennis rackets; the ladies, evening gowns. While hired laborers looked after the farming, the "very good class of people" danced or went fox-hunting.

For details of the Manitoba Act, see pp. 27-28.

Gabriel Dumont had entered his application in 1883.

For lot-survey details, see p. 20.

This photograph of a group of Métis on the open prairie was taken sometime in the period 1872-1875. In all probability, they were emigrating from Manitoba to the valley of the North or South Saskatchewan rivers. There, in St. Laurent, Batoche, and other centres, they built houses of logs plastered with clay and dug large, semi-underground ice houses for keeping meat and fish during the winter. They grew potatoes, barley, and hay and raised a few cattle.

hectares. Legally, it was argued, their claims had been settled. (A commission established by Ottawa to investigate Métis land claims in 1885 reported the following: of 779 Métis who had signed petitions demanding settlement of land claims, only 193 qualified. The rest had either received land under the terms of the Manitoba Act, or were from the United States, or were squatters who were not really Métis at all.) Moreover, in the eyes of some government officials, the Dominion Lands Act (1872) gave Métis the opportunity to apply for homestead land just like anyone else. Why couldn't the Métis follow the rules? The Métis responded that these rules should not apply to them. Some of them argued that they, like the Indians, had a right to inherit the land from their Indian mothers.

However, the most important factors in the Métis land claims question really had little or nothing to do with land at all. They had to do with matters of trust and pride. When government surveyors began to lay out the lots near St. Laurent, they used the square survey system. They could just as well have laid out long, narrow lots (as Métis had had in Manitoba) as square ones. When the land agent in Prince Albert suggested the long-narrow-lot-survey in 1882, his suggestion got a "no" from Ottawa. The French-speaking Métis wanted the government to send out French-speaking surveyors, land agents, and magistrates to deal with Métis problems. Instead, the land agent sent to Prince Albert was an Anglophone who ignored the Métis situation entirely. When Bishop Grandin of St. Albert wrote to a cabinet minister in 1884, he summed up the Métis fears and frustrations:

> They, as well as the Indians, have their national pride. They like to have attention paid to them and could not be more irritated by the contempt of which they feel themselves rightly or wrongly the victims.

By 1883, various settlers in the West had begun to demand action on their grievances. The Manitoba and Northwest Farmers Union was formed and sent delegation after delegation to Ottawa to get the government going. In 1883 and 1884, one of Canada's early poets, Charles Mair, travelled all the way to Ottawa several times to explain the

The Public Archives of Canada, C 4164

Royal Canadian Mounted Police

situation and try to convince the government that change had to come quickly. Nothing succeeded. According to one government official, Westerners were making trouble for the government because they were Liberals. Sir John A. Macdonald viewed the farmers' protests as unimportant. "No amount of concession," he said, "will prevent people from grumbling and agitating." The grumbling and agitating, as Macdonald termed it, played an unimportant role in the events of the Northwest Rebellion, but within a few years it would be the basis of a farmers' movement that would change the politics of Manitoba.

The people in Saskatchewan, particularly the Métis, decided on a more immediate course of action. Four of them, led by Gabriel Dumont, rode south to Sun River, Montana. There, on June 4, 1884, they met Louis Riel, showed him a letter from Prince Albert settlers requesting his help, and asked the one-time Red River leader to return with them to the District of Saskatchewan. Riel agreed.

THE REAPPEARANCE OF RIEL

What had Louis Riel been doing since the troubles in Red River? In 1871, in spite of the hostility of Ontario newcomers in Manitoba, Riel and Ambroise Lépine had organized the Métis into companies for defence against American Fenian invaders. In the 1872 election, Riel stood as candidate for Parliament for the Manitoba riding of Provencher — and won. To provide a seat for Sir Georges Etienne

This photograph of Louis Riel was probably taken about 1879, while staying with friends in the eastern United States. It was about this time that he began moving west, first to northern Minnesota, and then farther west still to the Territory of Montana. Here, he travelled with Métis buffalo hunters, sometimes acting as their purchasing agent, sometimes himself engaging in the trade in robes and hides. He also acted as interpreter and negotiator for Indians and Métis in their dealings with the U.S. Army and the Montana government.

In 1883, now a married man with a family to support, Riel became a school teacher at the mission of St. Peter's on the Sun River.

Cartier (who had been defeated in Montreal East), and also to remove Riel from the political scene, Macdonald's government offered Riel $1000 if he would withdraw in favor of Cartier and go to the United States. Riel agreed, and Cartier was elected for Provencher. In 1873, after Cartier's death, and again in the general election of 1874, Riel was elected MP for Provencher. In the meantime, however, the Ontario government had posted a $5000 reward for Riel's capture and arrest, because of the alleged "murder" of Thomas Scott. Riel had to go secretly to Ottawa, where, unrecognized by the Clerk of the House, he was sworn in as a Member of Parliament and signed the roll. Only when Riel was going out the door did the Clerk glance at the roll and see, to his astonishment, the name "Louis Riel."

Riel never served as a Member of Parliament. The House of Commons, in a vote split along language lines, voted to expel Riel. Then, in 1875, the House voted to give amnesty "to all persons concerned in the North-West troubles. . . . that a like amnesty should be granted to L. Riel and A. D. Lépine conditional on five years' banishment from Her Majesty's Dominions." Riel became an outlaw, wandering restlessly in the United States and occasionally slipping over the border into Canada. Burdened with feelings of persecution and convinced that he had a divine mission to save his people, Riel became mentally unbalanced. He spent the period between 1875 and 1878 in and out of mental hospitals in Quebec, sheltered and protected by friends. After his release from

Beauport Asylum in 1878, Riel visited a French Canadian community in New York State. The local parish priest, Father Fabien Barnabé, arranged for Riel to go to the American West, where he would work with the Jesuits in the Catholic frontier colonies in Minnesota or in North Dakota.

By 1884, he was teaching school at Sun River, Montana, where Dumont and his companions found him. After hearing their plea that he return and lead them, Riel, now forty, accepted the challenge. In Prince Albert, in July, he delivered a carefully prepared speech that contained his proposals for a non-violent solution to the problems of the Northwest. Riel called for free title for Métis lands, more lands for homesteading, and representation for the Northwest in Parliament. Immigrant settlers and French and English Métis supported him with enthusiasm. Once again, he had become the spokesman for people who believed they had legitimate grievances.

In late 1884 and early 1885, some efforts were made to organize negotiations that would lead to a settlement. Riel discussed matters with a Territorial Council official; a petition in French and English was sent to Ottawa. But nothing came of these efforts. Macdonald refused to make any concessions.

Failing to get a positive response from Ottawa, Riel's attitude began to harden. He believed that his people were being persecuted, and felt himself called to be their prophet. Inspired by religious visions, Riel called for a new Church among the Métis, for he believed that the old Church had failed his people. Bishop Grandin of St. Albert, he said, would be the Pope of his new Church. Stirred by Riel's religious and mystical ideas, many Métis were prepared to follow him. However, several priests among the Métis considered Riel's ideas to be heretical. As events developed, the Church (which had never given him much support to begin with) became a strong opponent of Riel.

Riel was also losing other supporters. English Métis and settlers moved away from him, as the possibility of physical violence — even armed rebellion — appeared to become an increasingly important factor in Riel's plans. And the Indians, the most numerous group in the Northwest, were at best lukewarm in their responses to Riel's proposal that they unite with the Métis. The Indians had learned that if Métis had to choose between their Indian and their European heritage, they generally chose the latter.

In March 1885, Riel was developing a strategy similar to the one used in the Red River developments of 1869-1870. He would seize Fort Carlton, as he had seized Fort Garry; he would declare a provisional government, as he had in 1869; from this position of strength he would negotiate with the Dominion government in Ottawa. But conditions had changed. Canada now held legal title to the Northwest; the establishment of a provisional government would be interpreted as an act of treason. More important, the North West Mounted Police were on hand to enforce Canadian law. As reports about the uneasy situation around Prince Albert filtered south, Lieutenant-Governor Dewdney of the North-West Territories ordered Commissioner Irvine to go to Prince Albert with Mounted Police reinforcements.

THE FIGHTING BEGINS

Riel reacted swiftly and angrily to the news of Dewdney's action. The Métis leader seized the local Indian agent and other government officials as prisoner-hostages. On March 19, the feast day of St. Joseph (the patron saint of the Métis), Riel proclaimed his provisional government. On March 21, he demanded that Fort Carlton with its garrison of NWMP and militia volunteers surrender. The Mounted Police officer in charge, Superintendent Crozier, refused. As the fort was running short of supplies, Crozier sent some men to get provisions from a store near Duck Lake. They were turned back by the Métis. Crozier then gathered most of his men together and set out for Duck Lake in force.

A short distance from the store, Crozier and his men encountered a large body of Métis and a few Indians. Crozier went forward to talk; an argument developed; soon Crozier's interpreter was struggling with an Indian to get his rifle back. Someone fired a shot, and Crozier's men opened fire. By now, the Métis had crept around to three sides of the police force, and they too opened fire. Boxed in by Métis fire, Crozier had little choice but to retreat to Fort Carlton. His losses were the twelve killed and eleven wounded referred to in the March 27 telegram. But whether either side wanted to solve its problems through bloodshed is a good question. Riel was appalled by the fighting, and towards the end of the fire-fight, he ran out between the two sides and shouted that they should stop. "For the love of God, don't kill any more. There's too much blood spilled already."

Riel's cry summed up the tragedy of both the Red River troubles and the Northwest Rebellion. Riel was a political person, aiming at a political solution of political problems, although his most effective political asset was the military strength of the Métis. Unfortunately, political confrontation turned into military conflict. When this happened, political rules were dropped, and military rules came into play. Riel's use of military means to achieve political aims provoked a military response, with tragic consequences for both sides in the rebellion.

The news of Duck Lake encouraged some of the more embittered Indians to take similar action to work off their frustrations. Several Hudson's Bay Company stores were pillaged. On April 2, a group of Big Bear's Cree invaded the post at Frog Lake, where a small HBC trading post and Roman Catholic mission formed the centre of a settlement. Big Bear himself was away hunting, otherwise he might have been able to prevent the outbreak of shooting at Frog Lake, during which members of his band killed nine people, including two priests. Two weeks later,

When Commissioner Irvine arrived at Fort Carlton a few hours later, he decided to abandon it and return to Prince Albert.

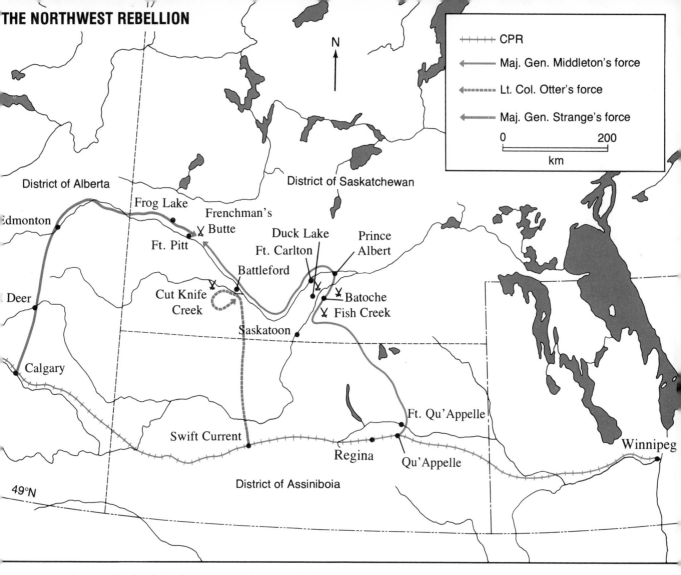

THE NORTHWEST REBELLION

Legend:
- CPR
- Maj. Gen. Middleton's force
- Lt. Col. Otter's force
- Maj. Gen. Strange's force

0 — 200 km

District of Alberta

District of Saskatchewan

Edmonton · Frog Lake · Frenchman's Butte · Ft. Pitt · Duck Lake · Ft. Carlton · Prince Albert · Battleford · Cut Knife Creek · Batoche · Fish Creek · Deer · Saskatoon

Calgary · Swift Current · Ft. Qu'Appelle · Regina · Qu'Appelle · Winnipeg

District of Assiniboia

49°N

some settlers who had fled to Fort Pitt decided to abandon the fort and take refuge downriver at Battleford. This gave the Indians possession of another fort. When news of all these events reached Ottawa, there was only one interpretation: rebellion.

This time, Sir John A. Macdonald was not just at the end of a telegraph line as he had been in 1869-1870. Now he was also at the end of a railway, which meant that troops could be moved swiftly to the West. William Van Horne guaranteed he could move militia and army units to the West in eleven days — if he had forty-eight hours notice. He was as good as his word. The regular troops moved first, then came the militia, the citizen-soldiers. They came from all across the Dominion, including the Halifax Provisional Battalion from the Maritimes, the 9th Voltigeurs from Quebec City, the Queen's Own Rifles from Toronto, the Winnipeg Light Infantry from Manitoba, and the Rocky Mountain Rangers from Calgary. They formed a force of about five thousand men, to deal with a rebellion that never fielded more than about four hundred fighting men.

Left: When the Police at Fort Pitt paraded for this photograph, they had no idea that they would be forced to abandon the fort to Big Bear's band of Cree. Short of ammunition and pressured to retreat downriver by local settlers who had crowded into the fort for protection, the officer in charge reluctantly agreed to withdraw to Battleford.

Right: Someone once said that 99 per cent of a soldier's time is spent waiting for something to happen. Here, a group of bored infantrymen at Batoche have fallen asleep in the hot spring sunshine.

In command of the Canadian forces was Major-General Frederick Middleton, an experienced British regular officer. He decided to use the CPR main line as his base and move his men northward in three main columns. He himself would lead the main force from Qu'Appelle towards Riel's headquarters at Batoche. From Swift Current, Lieutenant-Colonel William Otter would lead a column of six hundred and fifty men north in the direction of Battleford. From Calgary, Major-General T. B. Strange would march north to the North Saskatchewan River and move downstream on the Métis concentration around Batoche.

Every column had to cope with problems. As winter turned to spring, the thawing ground made transportation difficult, and wagons and guns bogged down. Strange's column ploughed through mud up to their knees, as they struggled to get their artillery across swampy ground. When Middleton's column reached the South Saskatchewan River at Clark's Crossing, transportation services were so poorly organized that it took four days to get half his men across the river.

The first confrontation between Métis and Canadian militia took place at Fish Creek, just south of Batoche. When news came that Middleton was at Clark's Crossing, Riel and Gabriel Dumont hurried south with about two hundred men and took up positions in a thickly-wooded ravine. The Métis plan was to ambush the Canadians as they crossed Fish Creek, but General Middleton's scouts spotted the trap. A general fire-fight resulted, with the Métis successfully holding off the militia as the relatively inexperienced militiamen from the East stormed over the ravine skyline and into the Métis rifle-fire. The battle turned into a draw. General Middleton counted his losses and decided to withdraw. Gabriel Dumont saw many of his men slip away to the north and many of his horses shot. If either side had the advantage, it was the Métis.

Meanwhile, from his base at Swift Current, Colonel Otter moved north to Battleford. General Middleton thought there was no real danger in the Battleford area; Otter's job was simply to keep an eye on things while Middleton took care of the real problem, Louis Riel and the Métis at Batoche. Many of the settlers in the Northwest, however, feared that there was a much greater danger than that posed by the relatively few Métis. Events at Frog Lake and Fort Pitt had aroused fears of a general Indian revolt.

Riel had sent out messengers to the Indian bands to get their support, but the Indians' reaction was mixed. In their hearts, they feared the consequences of war because they knew well the power of Ottawa. Crowfoot decided to stay out of the trouble, in the hope that his people's loyalty would be rewarded by better treaty terms from the Department of the Interior. "We will be loyal to the Crown," said Crowfoot's message to Sir John A., "whatever happens." Other Indian leaders decided to wait and see. A few hotheads pressed for war, but most of their leaders managed to restrain them.

When Colonel Otter reached Battleford, he found a broken-down fort, about five hundred or so settlers, a few Mounted Policemen, and two rusty old cannon. After the settlers had sought safety in the fort, the Indians slowly burnt down the settlement, setting fire to a few dwellings every night. Otter decided that he would take part of his force to "punish Poundmaker," as he put it in a telegram to Governor Dewdney. Otter's superior officer, General Middleton, told him that he had better remain

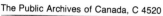
The Public Archives of Canada, C 4520

After every battle, there was always the grisly task of sewing up the dead in their blankets for burial as soon as possible.

105

at Battleford, but Otter decided to go after Poundmaker. With about three hundred and twenty-five men, the militia leader left Battleford and headed for Cut Knife Creek, where Poundmaker's camp was supposed to be. But the camp was gone, moved a little farther west. Otter's men took up a position on Cut Knife Hill. Cree and Stoney warriors crept into the ravines surrounding the base of the hill. Again, as at Fish Creek, the militia on top of the hill, silhouetted against the sky, were easy targets for the Indians. Otter had to pull out. For his part, Poundmaker chose not to "punish Otter." He ordered his men not to attack the retreating militia. Slaughter was not the answer to the Indians' problems.

Back at Fish Creek near the South Saskatchewan River, General Middleton had become extremely cautious and most reluctant to attack the Métis again. He waited for two weeks at Fish Creek, trying to solve his transportation problems, and arranging for support from the Hudson's Bay Company steamboat *Northcote*. The plan was that the *Northcote* would steam down the river with a few soldiers to take the Indians and Métis by surprise from the river side of Batoche, while the main body of his troops attacked from the southeast side of the town. By May 9, Middleton was ready to move towards the chief Métis centre at Batoche.

The battle for Batoche turned into a strange encounter. To begin with, the *Northcote* arrived on the scene well ahead of Middleton's land force, but even so, Gabriel Dumont's men were ready for it. The Métis plan was to stretch a strong ferry cable across the river to stop the steamboat. While the militiamen on the *Northcote* and the Métis and Indians on the river bank exchanged rifle fire, the steamboat drifted towards the cable. Although the Métis had not lowered the cable enough for serious damage, it did tear off the funnels, steam whistle, and mast. Temporarily disabled, the *Northcote* drifted downriver, out of action.

Ironically, the ferry concession had been granted to Gabriel Dumont.

To prepare for the impending militia attack, the defenders of Batoche had dug deep, well-sited rifle pits. When Middleton's troops finally went into action, therefore, they again made excellent targets for the entrenched riflemen. For three days the militia infantry advanced on the Métis positions, but the Métis held them off. On the fourth day, some of the Canadian troops were pulled out of the line and sent back to camp to eat dinner, leaving the rest to hold the line. Unknown to Middleton, Riel's men were in a serious position, being practically out of ammunition. On the fourth day, May 12, as the commanding general sat down to dinner back in camp, the militiamen who had been left in the line started to advance against the Métis. The advance turned into a charge, and soon the militia had overrun the rifle pits. Middleton extended the attack, and by nightfall, Batoche had fallen. The only job left was to capture the Métis leaders. Gabriel Dumont, after searching unsuccessfully for Riel in the post-battle confusion, had slipped away to

J. Ross Robertson Collection, Metropolitan Toronto Central Library

The Cree chiefs Big Bear (2) and Poundmaker (5), each sentenced to a three-year prison term, pose for the press on the front steps of Stoney Mountain Penitentiary, Manitoba. Neither survived for long the shock of imprisonment. Released after a few months, Poundmaker went almost immediately to visit his foster father, Crowfoot, on the Blackfoot Reserve, and died there, apparently of a heart attack. Big Bear was not freed until almost two years later, and he, too, died within a few months.

the United States. Riel himself surrendered to Middleton on May 15.

The backbone of the rebellion was broken. There remained only the completion of Major-General Strange's operation north from Calgary. Composed largely of French-speaking militia, his force reached Edmonton on May 1, and by the 14th was ready to move down the North Saskatchewan. Strange's objective was to pursue and capture Big Bear, whose Cree band controlled the area around Fort Pitt. When the Indians learned of Strange's approach, they took up positions on a hill called Frenchman's Butte. The Cree position was well fortified, and Strange's force was down to not much more than two hundred. A frontal attack failed, and the troops retreated. But the Indians, short of ammunition and frightened by the unfamiliar artillery fire, also pulled back. On May 29th, the day after the encounter, Inspector Sam Steele of the Mounted Police set out in pursuit of Big Bear and his band, but his efforts to capture the Indian leader were unsuccessful.

When Middleton heard about Frenchman's Butte, he hurried to Fort Pitt to take over the pursuit of Big Bear. The Cree chief led Middleton a merry chase. Four columns, over a thousand men, chased Big Bear for nearly a month. The chase ended only when the chief surrendered himself at Fort Carlton on July 2.

The Northwest Rebellion was over. Riel had surrendered; Poundmaker had led his band to Battleford and captivity on May 26; now Big Bear had come in. It remained only to count the cost. In money, the rebellion cost the Canadian government about $5 000 000, most of it spent on pay for soldiers, food and supplies, and transportation charges. If a fraction of this amount had been spent before the uprising, the rebellion might have been prevented. On the other side of the ledger, there were some positive results. Foreign newspapers had confidently predicted that the Dominion would fall apart; it did not. The participation of both French- and English-speaking militia created a sense that the country was united. And to settlers in the West, the government's quick action demonstrated that Ottawa at least cared about their affairs.

For the Métis, however, the Northwest Rebellion and its consequences meant the disappearance of their hope for a Métis nation as a distinct ethnic group. Some drifted away farther north, while others accepted the life of the reserves. Ironically, some did finally receive scrip or land title — a clear indication that at least some of the Métis had a right to the land that the government had been so reluctant to grant.

The military conflict was over, but the political climax of the Northwest Rebellion was still to come — the trial of Louis Riel. Since these proceedings have become a focal point in our history, they deserve careful consideration. Three topics merit study — the trial itself, the question of Riel's mental state, and the verdict imposed on Riel.

The Métis leader was brought to Regina, where proceedings against him began on July 20, 1885. The charge was high treason. There seems to be little doubt that Riel was guilty as charged. The six-man jury — all English-speaking residents of the North-West Territories — took only about one hour to reach their verdict: guilty, with a recommendation for mercy. The major issue in Riel's trial, however, was not whether he had committed treason, but whether he was sane or insane. Riel's lawyers argued from the beginning that he was insane and therefore not responsible for his actions. Two doctors from Ontario who had examined Riel (for very short periods only) stated that they believed that Riel was sane. On the other hand, Dr. François Roy of the Beauport Asylum near Montreal (where Riel had been a patient in 1877) said that he did not believe that Riel "was in a condition to be master of his acts." Dr. Roy had not seen Riel since 1877, but he was prepared to stand by this opinion.

The jury was in a difficult position. In 1885, the legal definition of insanity was that a person was insane if he did not know right from wrong. There was no provision for an absence of self-control, or for "temporary insanity." All that mattered legally was: did the person know right from wrong? If he did, he was sane. And Riel did not help his own defence very much — he was desperate to clear his life, and the family name, of "the stain of insanity." When asked if he had any-

When the militiamen returned home, they were greeted with civic receptions to honor their service in the West.

thing to say after the verdict had been delivered, Riel replied: "Should I be executed — at least if I were to be executed — I would not be executed as an insane man. It would be a great consolation for my mother, for my wife, for my children . . . for my countrymen."

On August 1, Judge Hugh Richardson of Regina sentenced Riel to death by hanging. Three appeals were made on Riel's behalf, and all of them failed. Three reprieves were granted, but time ran out. On November 16, 1885, Louis Riel was hanged in Regina.

In a telegram to Lieutenant-Governor Dewdney, Macdonald had expressed his satisfaction with the conviction of Riel and then went on

A view of Regina, the capital of the North-West Territories, at the time of Riel's trial and execution. In the summer and fall of 1885, the city was an armed camp, because of persistent rumors that Gabriel Dumont would rescue Riel from his cell in the Mounted Police barracks. As one member of the Police recorded it: "When the sun had risen, we could see the polished arms of the sentries — a perfect ring — around the barracks. Scouts were out in every direction, trotting off in the distance. Bugle-calls rang out in the clear air. An inner cordon of fifty men was posted around the guard-room. . . ."

Saskatchewan Archives Photograph

to say: "There is an attempt in Quebec to pump up a patriotic feeling about him — but I don't think it will amount to much." How wrong he was!

The controversy over Riel's execution began well before the death sentence was carried out. By September, French-Canadian Conservative newspapers were arguing that the government could never permit Riel to hang. In a by-election in the Ontario riding of East Durham, the Liberals used the same argument — the Conservatives would let Riel off. The Conservative candidate in the by-election assured the voters that the government *would* hang Riel. The Conservatives squeaked through after a hard fight, but Sir John A. Macdonald's political fate in Ontario was summed up by a Conservative supporter: "God help him next time if he doesn't hang Riel." Ontario's mind was made up. Riel had started a rebellion back in 1869-1870, and he had murdered Thomas Scott and then got off without being punished. Now he had been convicted of high treason for starting another rebellion, and this time, justice would be done.

In Quebec, sympathy for Riel grew among French Canadians. His lawyers' arguments that Riel was insane convinced many. Since both judge and jury had been English-speaking, the verdict could only be explained as anti-French prejudice. But even an English jury had recommended mercy. Moreover, Riel had been the spokesman for a French-speaking minority, whose rights had to be protected. It was the government's duty to protect these rights, even in the face of the will of the majority.

As Macdonald listened to the shouts for death and the shouts for pardon, he was faced with a particularly thorny political problem. To intervene and have Riel's sentence changed meant the sure loss of votes in Ontario. On the other hand, to do nothing and let Riel hang meant the loss of support in Quebec. The prime minister was sure that, in the long run, Catholic Quebec would not take the part of a man who had tried to set up his own church and who had lost the support of the bishops and many priests. He decided not to intervene. From Macdonald's point of view, the issue was a political one. And he had never based his policies on "racial" differences.

But, the use of these differences as a powerful political rallying cry never seems to be far below the surface of politics in Canada. Responsible politicians have recognized both its possibilities and its perils. The leading French-Canadian Liberal, Wilfrid Laurier, emphasized the dangers in the House of Commons debate on Riel's fate:

It would be simply suicidal for the French Canadians to form a party by themselves. Why, so soon as the French Canadians, who are in a minority . . . in the country, were to organize as a political party, they would compel the majority to organize as a political party, and the result must be disastrous to themselves. We have only one way of organizing parties. This country must be governed

110

and can be governed only on questions of policy and administration.

Another French-Canadian leader, however, *was* prepared to use Riel for political profit. This was Honoré Mercier, a lawyer who had become leader of the Quebec Liberal Party in 1883. He was a brilliant orator, and he took advantage of the agitation over Riel's execution to address a huge public gathering in Montreal on November 22, 1885:

> . . . Riel, our brother is dead . . . a victim of fanaticism and betrayal; of the fanaticism of Sir John and his friends; of the betrayal of three of our own people who, to maintain their cabinet posts, have sold their brother. . . . Riel died on the scaffold, as the patriots of 1837 died . . . as Christ he forgave his murderers. . . . In the face of this crime, in the presence of these failings, what is our duty? We have three things to do: unite to punish the guilty, break the alliance which our deputies made with Orangeism and seek in an alliance more natural and less dangerous, protection of our national interests.

Mercier was calling for the establishment of a "national" party — one based on the French-speaking "nation." In less than sixteen months, his Parti National became the government of Quebec.

*   *   *

The year 1885 was an important time mark for Canada. The Northwest Rebellion and the execution of Louis Riel revived bitter feelings. For almost half a century, Canadians had found ways of joining together to solve political problems, starting with Louis Hippolyte Lafontaine and Robert Baldwin in the 1840s, and continuing through the Macdonald-Cartier partnership. In 1885, French-English conflict had again become

On a misty November morning in 1885, William Van Horne (1) and Sandford Fleming (2) watch as Donald Smith (3) hammers in the "last spike" of the CPR, in Eagle Pass, British Columbia. It was most appropriate that Smith, a former HBC commissioner, should drive home that spike. The ceremony recalled those other fur-trading Highlanders — Mackenzie, Fraser, McLeod, McLoughlin, Simpson, Douglas — who had penetrated the western mountains and established a transcontinental pattern of communications, which the CPR would continue.

Glenbow-Alberta Institute

Early in 1887, the CPR extended its main line a few miles from Port Moody to a new town that Van Horne had christened Vancouver. On May 23rd of that year, the first Canadian transcontinental passenger train steamed into Vancouver bearing the proud motto "Ocean to Ocean."

an important issue in Canadian politics, and threatened to pull the country apart. In that same year, 1885, the CPR was completed. (In May, Van Horne completed the eastern section north of Lake Superior; the section from Port Moody to Kamloops was finished in July.) On November 7, barely a week before Riel's execution, the official last spike of the CPR was hammered in by Donald Smith at Craigellachie, in Eagle Pass. In completing the railway, Canada had created the bonds of steel which, more than any other single factor, guaranteed our nation's continued independence.

And so, on the one hand, the revived tension over linguistic and religious differences threatened to pull the country apart, while on the other hand, the railway pulled the country together. Both of these factors, in the years after 1885, would present Canadians with new and complicated challenges that would lead ultimately to a complete reorientation of Canadian politics.

1. What were the three main features of the National Policy? Explain why each "leg" was necessary to support the "stool."
2. Explain in your own words the difference between a "revenue" tariff and a "protective" tariff.
3. Prepare notes for short biographies of Donald Smith and George Stephen, emphasizing similarities and differences between the careers and characters of the two men.
4. Imagine that you are an opposition Member of Parliament during the CPR debate in 1881. What arguments would you use to attack the terms of the CPR contract? What arguments would you present in support of a "continental" instead of a "national" transport policy? Keep in mind any points that the government is likely to use to counter your arguments.
5. Choose any section in the building of the CPR and describe a day in the life of a construction laborer.
6. Make a sketch map of the route of the CPR showing the towns that grew up along the route.
7. One of the CPR's continuing problems was raising money. The CPR's rivals, particularly the Grand Trunk, tried to make it difficult and even impossible for the CPR to borrow money in London and New York. What do you think were some arguments that Grand Trunk officials used?
8. Prepare a time-chart, beginning in 1871 and ending in 1891, of events in western Canada as seen through the eyes of a Blackfoot Indian. Remember to choose events and issues that are important from the Indian point of view — weather conditions, food supply, land use, buffalo herds, etc.
9. Summarize briefly the grievances of Métis and settlers of the North-West Territories before the 1885 Rebellion. Use your answers to Question 6, Study 1, and Question 9, Study 2, to write a summary paragraph on this topic.
10. What do you think was the most important factor in Riel's decision to return to the South Saskatchewan in 1884?
11. Make a list of the military engagements of the Northwest Rebellion. Include dates, the forces on each side, and the outcome. What adjectives would you choose to describe the conflict?
12. The jury in Louis Riel's trial reached a verdict of guilty, but added a recommendation for mercy. Why, in your opinion, was this recommendation disregarded?
13. The railway joined the country together; the controversy over Riel pulled it apart. Which, in your opinion, has had a greater effect on the political history of Canada?

CHAPTER 4

Confederation: unity or diversity?

In 1883, a Toronto man called Archibald Hodge took the Canadian government to court over a game of billiards. Does this sound ridiculous? Perhaps it does, but then the court case really involved much more than a game of billiards.

It all started on Saturday, May 7, 1881. Hodge's St. James Hotel had closed at 7:00 p.m., the legal closing time. In one of the rooms, however, a game of billiards went on. For this, Hodge was fined twenty dollars, because one of the rules of the Toronto Liquor Licence Commissioners said that no games could be played in taverns after closing hours. In going to court, Archibald Hodge was not really disputing the amount of the fine. He was testing the right of the Toronto Liquor Licence Commissioners to fine him at all. The issue was a constitutional one, because it involved the powers of government and the way these powers were divided in Canada between the Dominion and the provincial governments. To realize the importance of Hodge's court case, it is necessary to understand the division of powers in the British North America Act (BNA Act), how any argument over the division of powers is decided, and what all this means for Canadians.

WHICH GOVERNMENTS HAVE WHICH POWERS?

The basic document of the Canadian constitution is the British North America Act, passed by the British Parliament in Westminster in 1867. Section 91 of this Act lists the powers of the Parliament of Canada; Section 92 sets out the "Classes of Subjects" to be handled exclusively by the provincial legislatures. The control of education, another provincial right, is dealt with in Section 93.

The BNA Act, of course, could not provide a perfect separation of powers for Canada. For example, with education assigned to the provinces and minority rights to Parliament, which level of government, federal or provincial, would be responsible for minority rights in education? Furthermore, no constitution can foresee all future developments. What happens if new "Classes of Subjects" are invented? How does a constitution written in the nineteenth century take care of a development like educational television, when one level of government has control over communications and the other level has control over education? Obviously, there has to be some statement in a constitution that can be used to answer such questions. There has to be a general statement of principle that defines the higher, or overriding, power.

NFB Photothèque, Photo by Crombie McNeill

Parliament is composed of three parts: the Monarch, represented in Canada by the Governor General; the Senate; and the House of Commons. Bills are debated and passed (or rejected) first by the Commons and then by the Senate. However, even after a bill has been passed by both Commons and Senate, it does not become law until it has been signed by the Governor General.

In this modern photograph, taken from behind the Governor General's chair, the Senate and the judges (centre foreground) of the Supreme Court of Canada attend the opening ceremonies of a new session of Parliament.

VI. DISTRIBUTION OF LEGISLATIVE POWERS

Powers of Parliament

91. It shall be lawful for the Queen by and with the Advice and Consent of the Senate and House of Commons, to make Laws for the Peace, Order and good Government of Canada, in relation to all Matters not coming within the Classes of Subjects by this Act assigned exclusively to the Legislatures of the Provinces; and for greater Certainty, but not so as to restrict the Generality of the foregoing Terms of this Section, it is hereby declared that (notwithstanding anything in this Act) the exclusive Legislative Authority of the Parliament of Canada extends to all Matters coming within the Classes of Subjects next hereinafter enumerated; that is to say —

Legislative Authority of Parliament of Canada

1. The Public Debt and Property.
2. The Regulation of Trade and Commerce.
3. The raising of Money by any Mode or System of Taxation.
4. The borrowing of Money on the Public Credit.
5. Postal Service.
6. The Census and Statistics.
7. Militia, Military and Naval Service, and Defence.
8. The fixing of and providing for the Salaries and Allowances of Civil and other Officers of the Government of Canada.
9. Beacons, Buoys, Lighthouses, and Sable Island.
10. Navigation and Shipping.
11. Quarantine and the Establishment and Maintenance of Marine Hospitals.
12. Sea Coast and Inland Fisheries.
13. Ferries between a Province and any British or Foreign Country or between Two Provinces.
14. Currency and Coinage.
15. Banking, Incorporation of Banks, and the Issue of Paper Money.
16. Savings Banks.
17. Weights and Measures.
18. Bills of Exchange and Promissory Notes.
19. Interest.
20. Legal Tender.
21. Bankruptcy and Insolvency.
22. Patents of Invention and Discovery.
23. Copyrights.
24. Indians, and Lands reserved for the Indians.
25. Naturalization and Aliens.
26. Marriage and Divorce.
27. The Criminal Law, except the Constitution of Courts of Criminal Jurisdiction, but including the Procedure in Criminal Matters.
28. The Establishment, Maintenance, and Management of Penitentiaries.
29. Such Classes of Subjects as are expressly excepted in the Enumeration of the Classes of Subjects by this Act assigned exclusively to the Legislatures of the Provinces.

And any Matter coming within any of the Classes of Subjects enumerated in this Section shall not be deemed to come within the Class of Matters of a local or private Nature comprised in the Enumeration of the Classes of Subjects by this Act assigned exclusively to the Legislatures of the Provinces.

Exclusive Powers of Provincial Legislatures

92. In each Province the Legislature may exclusively make Laws in relation to Matters coming within the Classes of Subjects next hereinafter enumerated, that is to say, —

1. The Amendment from Time to Time, notwithstanding anything in this Act, of the Constitution of the Province, except as regards the Office of Lieutenant-Governor.
2. Direct Taxation within the Province in order to the Raising of a Revenue for Provincial Purposes.
3. The borrowing of Money on the sole Credit of the Province.

4. The Establishment and Tenure of Provincial Offices and the Appointment and Payment of Provincial Officers.
5. The Management and Sale of the Public Lands belonging to the Province and of the Timber and Wood thereon.
6. The Establishment, Maintenance and Management of Public and Reformatory Prisons in and for the Province.
7. The Establishment, Maintenance, and Management of Hospitals, Asylums, Charities, and Eleemosynary Institutions in and for the Province, other than Marine Hospitals.
8. Municipal Institutions in the Province.
9. Shop, Saloon, Tavern, Auctioneer, and other Licenses in order to the raising of a Revenue for Provincial, Local, or Municipal Purposes.
10. Local Works and Undertakings other than such as are of the following classes: —
    (a) Lines of Steam or other Ships, Railways, Canals, Telegraphs, and other Works and Undertakings connecting the Province with any other or others of the Provinces, or extending beyond the Limits of the Province:

(b) Lines of Steam Ships between the Province and any British or Foreign Country:
(c) Such Works as, although wholly situate within the Province, are before or after their Execution declared by the Parliament of Canada to be for the general Advantage of Canada or for the Advantage of Two or more of the Provinces.
11. The Incorporation of Companies with Provincial Objects.
12. The Solemnization of Marriage in the Province.
13. Property and Civil Rights in the Province.
14. The Administration of Justice in the Province, including the Constitution, Maintenance, and Organization of Provincial Courts, both of Civil and of Criminal Jurisdiction, and including Procedure in Civil Matters in those Courts.
15. The Imposition of Punishment by Fine, Penalty, or Imprisonment for enforcing any Law of the Province made in relation to any matter coming within any of the Classes of Subject enumerated in this section.
16. Generally all Matters of a merely local or private Nature in the Province.

Education

93. In and for each Province the Legislature may exclusively make Laws in relation to Education, subject and according to the following Provisions: —
(1) Nothing in any such law shall prejudicially affect any Right or Privilege with respect to Denominational Schools which any Class of Persons have by Law in the Province at the Union:
(2) All the Powers, Privileges, and Duties at the Union by Law conferred and imposed in Upper Canada on the Separate Schools and School Trustees of the Queen's Roman Catholic Subjects shall be and the same are hereby extended to the Dissentient Schools of the Queen's Protestant and Roman Catholic Subjects in Quebec:
(3) Where in any Province a System of Separate or Dissentient Schools exists by Law at the Union or is thereafter established by the Legislature of the Province, an Appeal shall lie to the Governor General in Council from any Act or Decision of any Provincial Authority affecting any Right or Privilege of the Protestant or Roman Catholic Minority of the Queen's Subjects in relation to Education:
(4) In case any such Provincial Law as from Time to Time seems to the Governor General in Council requisite for the due Execution of the Provisions of this Section is not made, or in case any Decision of the Governor General in Council on any Appeal under this Section is not duly executed by the proper Provincial Authority in that Behalf, then and in every such Case, and as far only as the Circumstances of each Case require, the Parliament of Canada may make remedial Laws for the due Execution of the Provisions of this Section and of any Decision of the Governor General in Council under this Section.

Legislation respecting Education

The basic principle in the BNA Act was this: in the event of any doubt or conflict, the Parliament of Canada would have the overriding authority and power. Under Section 91, the Parliament of Canada has the right "to make Laws for the Peace, Order and good Government of Canada, in relation to all Matters not coming within the Classes of Subjects by this Act assigned exclusively to the Legislatures of the Provinces . . . ." In other words, any powers that were unstated in the BNA Act or left over — *residual powers* — were assigned to the Parliament of Canada. And even in some matters assigned to the provinces, the Parliament of Canada was still to have the final say. For instance, under Section 95, the provinces could legislate on agriculture and immigration, but only if their laws were "not repugnant to any Act of the Parliament of Canada." Under Section 93, which deals with the provincial responsibility for education, Parliament could pass "remedial Laws" to enforce certain guaranteed minority rights. So it is clear from the BNA Act that in Canada's federal system, the central or national authority — Parliament — was *intended* to be a much more powerful partner than the provincial legislatures.

But what was going to happen if Parliament and the provinces disagreed in the interpretation of their powers? According to the BNA Act, the disagreement would be taken to the courts, where judges would decide how the law was to be interpreted. Since the BNA Act was passed by the British Parliament, the final or highest court of appeal was also a British institution, the Judicial Committee of the Privy Council. Composed of high-ranking judges and law officers, its responsibility was to interpret British law. In constitutional matters relating to the BNA Act, therefore, it was the Judicial Committee of the Privy Council that decided whether laws passed by the Dominion Parliament or the provincial legislatures were legally within their respective powers.

The powerful position given to the federal government by the BNA Act was more the work of Sir John A. Macdonald than that of any other Canadian. He viewed the new Dominion of Canada not as a collection of provinces, but as one single nation. In Macdonald's opinion, the Parliament of Canada would be as all-powerful in Canada after 1867 as the British Parliament had been before 1867. When the BNA Act was being written, Macdonald tried to make sure that Parliament would be more powerful than the provinces in several ways. First, the really important powers were given to the Dominion government, not to the provinces. Second, the lieutenant-governors of the provinces, appointed by the federal government, were to be "officers of the Dominion," not representatives of the Queen. And every provincial bill had to be signed by a lieutenant-governor before it could become law. If he refused to sign it, the bill had to be examined by the Dominion government, which decided whether or not the provincial legislation would be allowed to become law or disallowed (cancelled). In addition, Macdonald aimed at bringing under the control of the Dominion one important power —

In 1892, the Judicial Committee of the Privy Council decided that lieutenant-governors, although appointed by the Dominion government, were also representatives of the monarch.

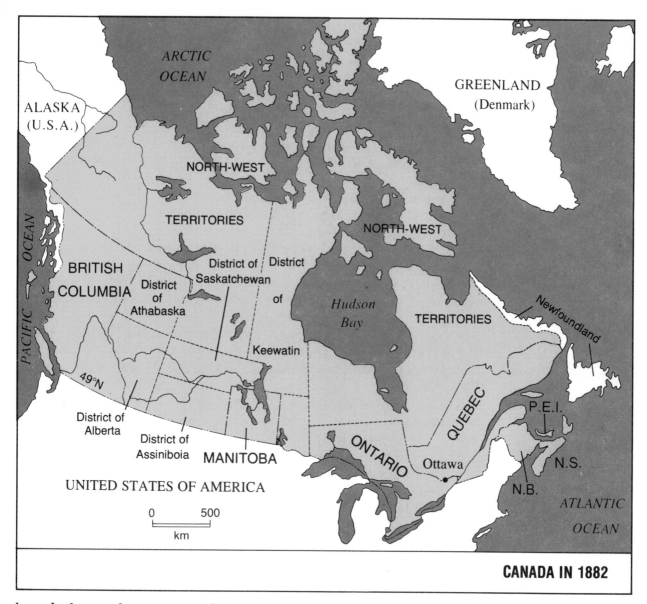

ARCTIC OCEAN

GREENLAND (Denmark)

ALASKA (U.S.A.)

NORTH-WEST

TERRITORIES

NORTH-WEST

PACIFIC OCEAN

BRITISH COLUMBIA

District of Athabaska

District of Saskatchewan

District of

Keewatin

Hudson Bay

TERRITORIES

Newfoundland

49°N

District of Alberta

District of Assiniboia

MANITOBA

ONTARIO

QUEBEC

P.E.I.

Ottawa

N.S.

N.B.

UNITED STATES OF AMERICA

0   500

km

ATLANTIC OCEAN

CANADA IN 1882

laws dealing with property and civil rights — that had been given to the provinces in the BNA Act. Provision for this was made in Section 94: "Notwithstanding anything in this Act, the Parliament of Canada may make Provision for the Uniformity of all or any of the Laws relative to Property and Civil Rights. . . ." In Macdonald's scheme of things, the Dominion government was to have *sovereignty* — the overriding legal power — in Canada.

ONTARIO VS. OTTAWA

During Macdonald's terms of office as prime minister, there were many challenges to the authority of the Dominion government. Some of these originated in Ontario, where a Liberal premier, Oliver Mowat, pressed hard for what he considered to be Ontario's rights.

Beneath the legal surface of constitutional confrontation, there were personal feelings that probably contributed to Macdonald's and Mowat's attitudes. Both were brought up in Scottish families living in Kingston, Ontario; together, they served in the ranks of the Kingston "Loyal Scottish Volunteer Independent Light Infantry Company." Mowat went away to Toronto — a short, round Grit; Macdonald stayed in Kingston — a tall, lean Conservative. But their political paths continued to cross.

A face-to-face confrontation came in 1861, in the legislature of the Province of Canada. Macdonald had just delivered an excellent speech, arguing that, in any future union, Canadians had to avoid the errors that had led to the outbreak of fighting in the United States only a week earlier (the beginning of the Civil War). Canadians had to strive to establish a powerful, sovereign, central government. In the same speech, Macdonald had made some jokes about Mowat's position on "representation by population," which upset Mowat greatly. In his reply to Macdonald, he suggested that John A. had purposely twisted the facts. Macdonald started to burn. By the time the session was finished, he was boiling. He marched over to Mowat, ready to fight. "You damned pup," shouted the forty-six-year-old Macdonald at the forty-one-year-old Mowat, "I'll slap your chops!" Macdonald went on to lead the Dominion government. Mowat succeeded Edward Blake as premier of Ontario in 1872.

The confrontation between the Canadian and Ontario governments centred on three major issues: control over the sale of alcoholic beverages; control over particular waterways in Ontario; and definition of the boundary line between Ontario and Manitoba.

In 1877, Mowat's government passed the (Ontario) Liquor Licence Act. This gave Ontario the power to grant licences to innkeepers and to tavern keepers. It was intended to show that the government of Ontario had the right to control the sale of alcohol within the province. (At the same time, it meant that some of Mowat's Liberal supporters received inn and tavern licences.) When Macdonald's government returned to office in 1878, it passed the Canada Temperance Act, which gave the Dominion control of the consumption of alcohol. Now here was constitutional conflict. Which government, according to the BNA Act, had the right to control alcohol?

The issue seemed to be decided in 1882. A man called Russell from Fredericton, New Brunswick, took the Dominion government to court, arguing that the Canada Temperance Act was *ultra vires* — Latin for "beyond the powers" — of Parliament, since it interfered with property and civil rights, a provincial responsibility. The Judicial Committee of the Privy Council heard the case and decided that the Canada Temperance Act fell "within the general authority of Parliament to make laws for the order and good government of Canada." So the issue seemed to be decided in favor of the Dominion government. To consolidate the government's position, Macdonald introduced the Dominion Licence Act, which would also give Ottawa control over the granting of liquor licences.

This only served to reopen the issue. In 1883, the Judicial Committee of the Privy Council heard the case of Mr. Hodge and his billiard table. Hodge's lawyers argued that the twenty-dollar fine levied by the Toronto Liquor Licence Commissioners was illegal, because it was imposed under the Ontario Liquor Licence Act. The Judicial Committee of the Privy Council disagreed. There were two "aspects," it said, to the case. Canada had the general power of prohibition through the Canada Temperance Act, but the provinces had the power to licence inns and taverns through Section 92. And, the judgment went on to say, within the limits of their power, provinces had sovereignty!

Now it was Mowat's turn to attack. The Ontario legislature passed a new law: anyone who took out a licence from the Dominion authorities had to pay further heavy fees to the Ontario government. (This was the same thing as imposing fines on those who obeyed the Dominion law.) Macdonald used the federal power of disallowance to cancel the new provincial law. Mowat, however, took the case before the Judicial Committee in 1884 and won. The Province of Ontario had triumphed over the Dominion government, and provincial sovereignty in this matter was established.

While the liquor licensing tug-of-war was still going on, another constitutional controversy had developed. Peter McLaren, a Conservative lumberman from Perth, Ontario, made some improvements on the Mississippi River west of Ottawa, so that his company's logs could be floated downriver to Arnprior. Boyd Caldwell, a Liberal lumberman from Lanark, Ontario, made arrangements with McLaren to use the

In the late nineteenth century, the timber trade formed a large part of Ontario's economy. Gigantic rafts of squared timber, complete with several small shanties (bunkhouses) and a cookhouse, were guided down the Ottawa and St. Lawrence rivers by gangs of shantymen.

121

river and its improvements for a fee. McLaren claimed that Caldwell failed to pay as agreed and refused to let him continue using his river improvements. So Caldwell took McLaren to court to force him to open the river. Mowat's government then entered the squabble. In 1881, the Ontario legislature passed an "Act for protecting the public interest in rivers, streams and creeks." This law proposed to make available to the public all dams, timber slides, and other improvements that private businessmen had provided at their own expense. Macdonald was furious. "The credit and fair name of Canada" were put in jeopardy by what he called a "law of confiscation." Moreover, the Act had been passed by a (Liberal) government — one of whose members was a relative of Caldwell — while the Caldwell-McLaren dispute was still before the courts. The Act was disallowed by the Dominion government. In fact, Ontario passed the Act four times, and the Dominion disallowed it three times. Finally, in 1884, it was declared *intra vires* — within the powers — of the provincial government by the Judicial Committee of the Privy Council. This was another important decision in the sovereignty struggle between Ontario and Ottawa.

According to the BNA Act, navigable waters came under the authority of the Dominion government.

A totally different matter, the question of Ontario's boundaries, was not really new. Prior to 1867, the Province of Canada had, from time to time, disputed the Hudson's Bay Company's claim to Rupert's Land. When the Dominion of Canada took over the Hudson's Bay possession in 1870, the dispute continued. The Ontario government adopted the old claim and demanded some sort of compensation. In August 1878 (not long before the election won by the Conservatives), Liberal commissioners appointed by the Liberal government of Alexander Mackenzie awarded about 373 000 square kilometres north and west of Port Arthur, as far as the Lake of the Woods, to Ontario (with its Liberal government). Manitoba (with a Conservative government) was thus cut off from direct access to Lake Superior. When the Conservatives were returned to office, however, Macdonald was determined to cut Ontario down to size. Acting on a report by a select committee of the House of Commons, he reduced Ontario's expansion and moved the boundary of Manitoba eastward, being careful not to fix it precisely. Macdonald thus ensured that the two provinces would squabble over the exact position of their common boundary.

Port Arthur and Fort William have been joined to form the city of Thunder Bay.

The problem was more than a dry legal argument. Manitoba declared Rat Portage (the modern Kenora) a Manitoba town; Ontario protested that it was inside the boundary as determined in 1878. Both provinces granted timber-cutting licences in the disputed area; both even held elections in the same area. The situation was becoming almost comic. Finally, in 1884, Oliver Mowat took his province's case before the Judicial Committee of the Privy Council and won a judgment in favor of Ontario. Therefore, in all these issues — in liquor licensing, control over provincial rivers and streams, and now, in the matter of boundaries — the Province of Ontario had triumphed over Canada.

DISCONTENTED PROVINCES

Ontario's was not the only challenge to the Dominion government. Other provinces were also discontented with Ottawa's conduct of Canadian affairs. Honoré Mercier — Quebec's first "nationalist" premier and a strong believer in provincial autonomy — invited the premiers of all the provinces to a conference in Quebec City, to be held in October, 1887. From the beginning, this conference was a curious event, regarded by some as simply a provincial attempt to embarrass the federal government. However, the items discussed and the decisions reached indicated a possible new direction for Confederation in Canada, a direction that proved important for the future.

The premiers of all the provinces were invited, but Sullivan of Prince Edward Island and Davie of British Columbia declined. The provincial leaders who did attend — Mercier of Quebec, Mowat of Ontario, A. G. Blair of New Brunswick, W. S. Fielding of Nova Scotia, and John Norquay of Manitoba — were all opposed to various Dominion govern-

In an 1889 issue of the humorous weekly publication Grip, *Toronto cartoonist John Wilson Bengough pokes fun at Honoré Mercier's dream of the future map of the Dominion.*

123

In Montreal harbor in the 1880s, the old and the new could be seen side by side. The sailing ship was slowly but surely being superseded by steam vessels. And, with the exception of bulk shipments of wheat, mineral ores, and coal, the railway was taking a great deal of freight business away from ships, sail or steam, travelling inland between Montreal and Lake Superior.

ment actions. All but Norquay were Liberals (or, in Mercier's case, opposed to the Conservatives); it was not difficult for the Conservatives in Ottawa to suggest that the whole conference was just Liberal politics. But although the premiers were united in their opposition to the Canadian government, they did not necessarily share the same grievances or the same aims.

Oliver Mowat, who was named chairman of the conference, wanted support in his constitutional battle with the Dominion government. At the same time, however, he knew that what most of the other provinces wanted from Ottawa was more money. As far as Mowat was concerned, this could be dangerous. Ottawa raised much of its revenue in Ontario; if Ottawa were to give more money to the other provinces, Ontario would end up paying most of the bill.

Mercier in Quebec was concerned with practical financial problems and with political nationalism. His government needed more money for interest payments on the provincial debt and for its ministry of agriculture and colonization — a very important ministry, planned to encourage French-Canadian colonization within Quebec. Mercier therefore aimed at obtaining larger federal payments for his province. At the same time, he had built his Parti National and his government on the idea of "nationality" (defined by the language, religion, and other aspects of French-Canadian culture) for the Province of Quebec. To protect this "nationality," according to his point of view, he needed to achieve provincial control over developments within the province, that is, provincial sovereignty. Here might be a basis for agreement between Mercier and Mowat.

The premiers of Nova Scotia and New Brunswick had different objectives. Both provinces were experiencing serious economic changes as the old, wooden, square-rigged sailing ships built in the Maritime Provinces were being replaced all over the world by iron steamships — built outside Canada. Both provinces watched with alarm as many of their young people emigrated to the New England states, where economic prospects appeared brighter. The Maritime fishing industry was also suffering. In 1885, the American government dropped the fishery sections of the Treaty of Washington (1871), with the result that Maritime fishermen could no longer sell their catches duty-free in American markets. And the Intercolonial Railway had not helped the Maritime economy. Joseph Howe had seen the Intercolonial as a means of transporting Maritime goods to central Canada; however, with the exception of Nova Scotia coal going west, all the traffic was coming the other way. Sheltered behind the protective tariffs of the National Policy, manufacturers in Ontario and Quebec were rapidly taking over Maritime markets. This generally bleak economic outlook, plus a widespread unhappiness about financial arrangements with Ottawa, spurred Maritime interest in Mercier's conference.

In 1886, Premier Fielding of Nova Scotia had introduced a motion in his province's Legislative Assembly that "the financial and commercial interests of the people of Nova Scotia, New Brunswick, and Prince Edward Island would be advanced by these provinces withdrawing from the Canadian Federation and uniting under one Government. . . ." The motion was carried, and Fielding had an election issue. He won the provincial election, with an increased majority. In the following year, however, the Conservatives won a convincing majority of the Nova Scotia seats in the Dominion general election. So the people were prepared to support Fielding, but not to the point of separation. At the premiers' conference, therefore, Fielding could voice Nova Scotia's discontent, but he could not threaten that it was prepared to separate from Canada.

Premier John Norquay of Manitoba was in an awkward position. As a general rule, his government supported the Conservatives in Ottawa. However, the CPR monopoly on the prairies had raised major opposition in Manitoba, and Norquay felt compelled to present his province's concerns at Quebec. Clause 16 of the CPR contract forbade the construction of any other railways south of the CPR main line. The monopoly granted in this clause was intended to help the CPR fight competition from American railroads such as the Northern Pacific. As it happened, however, the monopoly clause meant that the CPR controlled *all* railway matters south of the main line (most of agricultural Manitoba at the time), including freight rates and the building of new branch lines. In 1880, the Manitoba legislature had chartered a railway, the Manitoba and South Eastern, which was to be built in the forbidden territory. The Dominion government, therefore, disallowed the Manitoba charter; the railway was rechartered by Manitoba and again disallowed by Ottawa. Whereupon, the farmers of Manitoba

The CPR did much to make Canadians tourists. For instance, the return fare from Toronto to Halifax was only $40. And, thanks to the CPR's fleet of "Empress" liners, a Torontonian could go to China and back for $447.50, or around the world for $610.

became angry with the Dominion government. They would have to continue to pay CPR rates to move their grain to Lake Superior, and these rates they considered too high. In 1883, they formed the Farmers' Protective Union of Manitoba and drafted a "Bill of Rights." Their list of demands included an end to the CPR monopoly and power for the Manitoba legislature to charter branch rail lines. The branch line issue was very important for farmers, who needed to be able to deliver their bulky grain without travelling great distances. However, even though Premier Norquay had managed to improve the Dominion's money grants to Manitoba, discontent over freight rates and concern for provincial control over provincial affairs remained strong. And so Norquay had agreed to attend the conference.

Other demands in the Bill of Rights were "provincial rights" for Manitoba, including control over Crown lands, and a return to revenue tariffs.

These issues and events, then, were the background of the Quebec Conference in 1887. The provincial premiers produced a number of resolutions in their discussions, most of which were accepted by their legislatures. Although these had very little immediate impact on Canadian politics, the conference itself was to mean a great deal for the future, and for this reason the resolutions are worth noting. For example, it was resolved that the Dominion government should no longer be able to disallow provincial legislation; the northern boundaries of Ontario and Quebec should be determined once and for all; new financial arrangements between the federal government and the provinces should be worked out. This was an approach to Confederation far different from that of Macdonald's.

THE QUESTION OF SOVEREIGNTY

The "provincial rights view" was summarized in a statement in the Toronto *Globe* on March 9, 1888. Some of the major points in the article were as follows:

> The Confederation had its origin in a bargain between certain provinces, in which bargain the Provinces agreed to unite. . . . The Dominion was the creation of these Provinces; or, in other words, was created by the British Parliament, at the request of the Provinces. The Dominion being non-existent at the time the bargain was made, it was plainly not a party to the bargain. The power to revise the created body must lie in the hands of those who created that body. The overwhelming majority of those who created the Dominion being in favour of the revision of the Confederation compact, the British Parliament is not entitled to look any further or to consult the wishes of the Dominion Government in the matter. The resolutions of the Quebec Conference . . . will therefore furnish the British Parliament . . . the reasons and the authority for a revision of the Confederation pact. . . .

This is a strong statement of the *compact theory* of Confederation: that

"CENTRALIZATION;"

OR, "PROVINCIAL AUTONOMY ABOLISHED."

IS THIS WHAT SIR JOHN IS AIMING AT?

J. W. Bengough's cartoon ridicules Macdonald's view of sovereignty. Seven provincial premiers humbly beg concessions from King John.

the provinces made a compact (agreement) to form a federal union. And this viewpoint raises many problems. If the Dominion is a creation of the provinces, can it be abolished by the provinces? If it can, must the decision to abolish Canada be unanimous, or can it be done by a majority of the provinces? Only the provinces of Canada, Nova Scotia, and New Brunswick wanted the creation of a Dominion. Does this mean then that only the four original provinces — Nova Scotia, New Brunswick, Quebec, and Ontario — have the right to change the compact? Have "new" provinces like Manitoba (and Saskatchewan and Alberta), which are creations of the Dominion government, the same right? And what is the position of the provinces that later joined Confederation — British Columbia and Prince Edward Island (and, in 1949, Newfoundland)?

The compact theory might have become nothing more than an interesting footnote to history, except for another decision of the Judicial Committee of the Privy Council in 1896. Again, it was legislation (the Ontario Local Options Act) that involved control of the alcohol trade. The Act's details do not matter; the important thing is the decision of the Privy Council:

> The exercise of legislative power by the Parliament of Canada in regard to all matters not enumerated in Section 91, ought to be strictly confined to such as are unquestionably of Canadian interest and importance, and ought not to trench upon [infringe upon] provincial legislation with respect to any of the classes enumerated in Section 92. . . . If . . . the Parliament of Canada has authority to make laws applicable to the whole Dominion, in relation to matters which in each province are substantially of local or private interest, upon the assumption that these matters also concern the peace, order, and good government of the Dominion, there is hardly a subject enumerated in Section 92 upon which it [Parliament] might not legislate, to the exclusion of the provincial legislatures.

The Civil War in the United States had been fought over the issue of sovereignty.

This strong statement in support of provincial rights was, in a way, a revolutionary interpretation of the constitution, as important for the definition of sovereignty, in Canada, as the Civil War had been, in the United States. In its 1896 judgment, the Judicial Committee of the Privy Council was saying that the provinces, in matters over which they had control, were every bit as sovereign as the Parliament of Canada. The residual powers of the government in Ottawa stopped where the rights of the provinces began. Sir John A. Macdonald's idea of a union in which the provinces were to be subordinate to the federal government had been rejected.

Again, a number of questions arise from this revolutionary interpretation. What if Canadians wish to change their constitution? Do they need the agreement of a majority of the Members of Parliament? Or of a majority of the provinces? Or do they need the agreement of both the federal and the provincial governments? What happens if one government — federal *or* provincial — does not wish the change? And taking the compact theory and the 1896 decision one step further, what happens if one or several provinces wish to "leave" Canada? Does any province have a constitutional "right to secede"? If one province, or several, should choose to become totally sovereign and independent, could the other provinces or the federal government do anything about it?

These questions suggest that the comparison to the American Civil War is not an idle one. In 1861, several American states decided that they were sovereign and had the right to secede from the American Union; the government in Washington thought otherwise. As a result, Americans fought a long and bloody civil war in order to settle that issue.

MAJORITY RULE AND MINORITY RIGHTS

Against the background of the Northwest Rebellion and of the constitutional conflict over provincial rights, a whole new series of questions about Canada arose in the late 1880s. They were more personally pressing than physical problems like boundaries or railways, more real than abstract constitutional questions about sovereignty. They touched on things that Canadians felt deeply about — their religion, their identity, and their role or position within the nation's structure.

Open controversy began in 1888, when Premier Mercier of Quebec tried to settle a problem that had been simmering in the province for years. The Society of Jesus — the Jesuit Order — was suppressed by Pope Clement in 1773. By 1800, the last Jesuit in Canada had died, and the estates of the Order, which amounted to about 360 000 hectares, became the property of the British Crown. In 1831, the British government turned over the estates to the government of Lower Canada, and at the time of Confederation the estates became the responsibility of the Province of Quebec. The revenues from the estates continued to be used to support education. Soon after 1840, members of the Order were invited to return to Canada by the bishop of Montreal. The Order grew rapidly in importance and influence and announced that it wanted compensation for the estates that had been lost at the turn of the century. In 1888, Premier Mercier's government negotiated a settlement, which became the basis of the Jesuit Estates Act. To settle the Jesuit claims, the government of Quebec would make a final payment of $400 000, to be divided between the Jesuits and other Roman Catholic institutions. Mercier's difficulty was not the money, but finding an acceptable way of dividing the $400 000. Which Catholic groups in Quebec were to receive funds? And which group got how much? Mercier knew very well that if his government made these decisions, it would only make enemies. So the Jesuit Estates Act included a provision that the money was to be distributed among Catholic institutions "as the Pope might decide," in other words, by the head of the Roman Catholic Church in Rome, Italy. The Act was passed in the provincial legislature, and Macdonald's government had no intention of disallowing it. It appeared that a thorny Quebec problem had finally been settled.

Not so. By the end of 1888, reaction against the Jesuits Estates Act had begun to develop among Ontario Protestants. The Orange Lodge in particular found it infuriating that any legislation by a Canadian province would allow a foreigner to make a decision in a Canadian matter. Extremists among the Protestants began to agitate against the Act — and against all Jesuits, Roman Catholics, and French Canadians. By January of 1889, a grass-roots movement to disallow the Jesuit Estates Act had begun. A motion was introduced in the House of Commons for disallowance; it was defeated, overwhelmingly, 188-13. The major arguments for disallowance were presented by D'Alton McCarthy. In

Revenues from the estates had been used for the Order's educational and charitable work.

The Jesuit Order had been re-established in 1814.

D'Alton McCarthy, 1836-1898

McCarthy's view, Canadian nationality should be based on the principle of majority rule. The majority must rule if a true Canadian nationality was ever to come into existence. (And given the nature of the Canadian majority, Canadian nationality would have to be Anglophone.) In the March 1889 debate on the Jesuit Estates Act, he argued that "where there is no community of language, there is no common nationality in the highest sense." For McCarthy, the argument was clear: common nationality required a common language, the common language should be that of the majority, the majority of Canadians were English-speaking — therefore, English should be established as the language of Canada.

Among McCarthy's first moves to achieve this goal was the formation of the Equal Rights Association in Toronto in June, 1889. Despite what its name implied, this group really aimed at establishing the supremacy of the English language in Canada. The Conservative MP for Barrie, Ontario, carried forward his campaign on two other fronts: in the House of Commons, and in a speaking tour in the West. In Parliament, in January 1890, he introduced a bill to abolish Section 110 of the North-West Territories Act, which allowed the use of either English or French in the courts, in the Territorial Assembly, and in government publications in the Territories.

The resulting debate was an embarrassment for many members. Macdonald's government was in a particularly awkward position. Anglophone Conservatives believed in the rule of the majority; Francophone Conservatives supported minority rights — in this case, the rights of the French-speaking minority in the North-West Territories. Macdonald himself entered the debate, stating that he had

> no accord with the desire . . . that there should be an attempt to oppress the one language or render it inferior to the other; I believe it would be impossible if it were tried, and it would be foolish and wicked if it were possible.

The House of Commons voted against McCarthy's bill, but the question remained. Which principle would win out — majority rule or minority rights? Or would it be possible, in some typical Canadian way, to find an acceptable compromise between the two?

In the House of Commons, the pressures of practical politics averted an English-French division on the question of majority rule versus minority rights. In the West, and particularly in Manitoba, the confrontation was sharper. In a speech at Portage la Prairie, Manitoba, on August 5, 1889, D'Alton McCarthy attacked the use of French in Canada and called for English domination of the Dominion. His speech came at a time when Manitobans were prepared to listen to him, and it led directly to the Manitoba Schools Question.

Some of the factors in the background of the Manitoba school and language laws should be noted. First, denominational schools had been guaranteed in the Manitoba Act of 1870. Most Catholics in Manitoba

Denominational schools are those organized and conducted by religious groups.

were French-speaking, so Catholic schools meant, in practice, Francophone schools. Second, Manitoba in 1890 was quite different from Manitoba in 1870. The overwhelming majority of new settlers were English-speaking and Protestant, and of this group by far the largest percentage came from Ontario. They brought with them their belief in secular (non-denominational) public schools, not tied to particular religious teachings. And many brought Ontario-style politics with them — politics based on a uniform society where the majority ruled.

There were three possible choices for the organization of Manitoba schools. The first was to continue the existing arrangement, under which the government of Manitoba would provide grants to Protestant *and* Catholic schools throughout the province. Its opposite was the creation of a *single*, non-denominational, public school system. This would use English as the language of instruction (because it was the language of the majority) and have only limited general religious exercises instead of particular denominational prayers or teaching. The third possibility was a system modelled on that of Ontario, in which the province provided a general public school system, but members of a religious minority, under defined conditions, could direct that some of their taxes be used for the support of separate schools.

When the Manitoba language and school legislation was introduced in February 1890, it was clear that the government's policy was aimed at creating an Anglophone society. One bill abolished the official use of French in the Legislative Assembly, government publications, the civil service, and the provincial courts. Another bill changed the schools to a single provincial system with no separate school option, which meant the end of government support for minority (Catholic) schools. Catholic parents could organize (and pay for) their own separate schools, but, like all other citizens, they would still have to pay taxes to support the provincial system of education. Outside the legislature, opposition to these laws was led by Archbishop Taché, who saw his people threatened as they had been in 1869-1870. Inside the legislature, opposition came

A one-roomed school in Manitoba in the 1890s. The stout, bearded gentleman at the left end of the group is very likely the chairman of the local school board. (He must be very curious as to which boy or girl broke the window.)

131

The argument over educational rights in Manitoba was extremely emotional. The Ottawa Free Press expressed one side of the argument in this cartoon, entitled "Ye Good Knyghte and Ye Wicked Giant." (The "Good Knyghte" is the Conservative government in the person of Sir Charles Tupper.)

For details, see pp. 139-140.

from both French- and English-speaking Catholic members. Despite all opposition, in March the Manitoba schools legislation became law. Majority rule had prevailed over minority rights.

But Section 22 of the Manitoba Act of 1870 stated that Catholics had a right to such schools as "by law or practice" they had enjoyed at the time of union. So the passage of the Manitoba Schools Act was really only a beginning. There were to be seven more years of political and legal controversy, which involved politicians in Ottawa, before a solution was finally found.

CANADIAN-AMERICAN RELATIONS

While the controversy over education and religion was developing in Manitoba, another question about Canada and Canadian nationality had arisen. It was an old question, with new elements. It focussed on the east coast fisheries and the rights of American fishermen in Canadian waters and ports. The fisheries question in turn raised the larger question of Canada's general trade relations with the United States, and this introduced the problem of Canada's independence from the United States.

By the Treaty of Washington of 1871, Americans were permitted to fish in Canadian waters and use Canadian ports to buy bait and supplies. By the same treaty, Canadians were permitted to fish in American waters and sell their catches duty-free in American markets. The United States decided to drop the fishery agreements in the Washington Treaty; on July 1, 1885, privileges for both sides stopped (hence the discontent of fishermen in the Maritime Provinces). American fishermen, however, continued to fish in Canadian waters, and so Canadian officials boarded American fishing vessels to enforce Canadian law — 700 vessels in 1886, 1362 in 1887. While the Canadian action was legal, it was also very dangerous. American fishermen were angry; American politicians listened to them; and the United States was still ten times as strong as Canada. Furthermore, there were American politicians who had built their political careers on anti-British (and therefore anti-Canadian) sentiment, and they were not prepared to make any concessions to their northern neighbor. So Maritime fishermen and other Canadians sought some means to improve commercial relations with the United States.

One proposal supported by a few Maritime MPs and by Sir Richard Cartwright of the Liberal Party was commercial union with the United States. This meant that the two nations would enter into a complete tariff union, with a common set of tariffs against the rest of the nations in the world (including Britain) and free trade between Canada and the United States. It was really an impossible "pie-in-the-sky" proposal that went against Canada's National Policy. It would leave Canadian industries with no protection whatever against their most important competition: factories in the United States. Moreover, it was also unacceptable to the Americans, who were not prepared to give Canadians anything like an equal say in determining tariff policy. Most dangerous of all for Canada was the possibility that commercial union might lead to political union — to the annexation of Canada by the United States. No Canadian who believed in an independent nation in the northern half of North America could ever accept such a scheme.

The idea of commercial union grew out of both the fisheries problem with the United States and the Liberal Party's search for a popular, vote-getting policy. Soon after he became Liberal leader in 1887, Wilfrid Laurier asked for suggestions for a Liberal policy on commercial relations with the United States. Commercial union had been one proposal. While that idea was rejected, another similar policy seemed a vote-getting possibility.

In 1888, Sir Richard Cartwright proposed that Canada adopt a policy of "full and unrestricted reciprocity" (free trade) with the United States. Both Liberals and Conservatives had supported reciprocity with the United States in natural products — coal, wheat, barley, fish, lumber. However, this new Liberal proposal meant that, while each country would maintain its own system of customs duties, *all* tariffs between the two countries would be abolished. This scheme appealed to Liberal policymakers, because it did not involve the same danger of U.S. annexation of Canada as did commercial union. Most Canadian politicians, however, knew very well that the Americans were not the least bit interested in unrestricted reciprocity. When the House of Commons debated Cartwright's motion, it was soundly defeated.

In 1889 and 1890, Canadian politics were diverted from the tariff issue by the Manitoba Schools Question and by alleged scandals within the

Reciprocity in trade between two countries means that both have agreed to a common set of conditions for the flow of goods from one country to the other. Full and unrestricted reciprocity between two countries means that both have agreed to a free flow of all goods without any conditions.

133

Conservative Party. By the fall of 1890, however, Sir John A. Macdonald was grappling with the tariff question once again. The Americans had introduced a new, high-tariff policy, which threatened to eliminate Canadian markets in the United States. The Conservative government would have to negotiate some kind of agreement to minimize the damage to Canadian trade. Moreover, the American secretary of state, James G. Blaine — one of the American politicians well-known for his anti-British sentiments — was working on a fisheries agreement with Newfoundland. This, Macdonald believed, was really an attempt to draw the colony away from Britain and Canada.

The prime minister asked for a full discussion of Canadian-American problems. Blaine said he was willing to talk privately — provided there was no public announcement of the discussions. Early in 1891, the Canadian government asked if it could announce that the two nations had been discussing trade relations, because Macdonald wanted to show Canadians that his government had been active on the question. Blaine not only refused, he authorized this statement: "There are no negotiations whatever on foot for a reciprocity treaty with Canada. . . ." Macdonald accepted the setback and tried to continue negotiating, but he was told that Blaine had no time to see Canadian representatives until later that year. When the American attitude became clear, Macdonald knew that there was no use waiting for anything positive to come from trade negotiations with the Americans. He asked the Governor General to dissolve Parliament and call a general election.

JOHN A.'S LAST ELECTION

For details of the National Policy, see pp. 79-81.

Macdonald organized his election campaign very carefully. He reminded the voters of the National Policy, emphasizing the importance of the CPR and protection for Canadian industry. He also attacked the Liberals, taking advantage of a powerful political weapon that Liberal supporters themselves had forged. In January 1891, the Conservatives had received parts of a remarkable political pamphlet, prepared for possible use in the United States Senate. In addition to suggesting ways in which the United States might damage the Canadian economy, its writer said he believed "political union with the United States was the manifest destiny of Canada." Such a statement might have been expected from an American annexationist, but the author of the pamphlet was none other than Edward Farrer, the chief editorial writer of the Toronto *Globe*, Canada's leading Liberal newspaper. This was the same Edward Farrer who had had a highly publicized interview with Secretary of State Blaine, during the very period when Blaine said he had no time to speak with official Canadian representatives.

John A. pulled all this together in his main election speeches:

> . . .As for myself, my course is clear. A British subject I was born — a British subject I will die. . . . During my long public service of nearly half a century, I have been true to my country and

THE OLD FLAG,
THE OLD POLICY,
THE OLD LEADER.

Elections are won and lost for all kinds of reasons, but there seems little doubt that the "British connection" and the "loyalty" cry carried the Conservatives back into power in 1891. The party lost seats in both Ontario and Quebec, but it gained enough in the Maritimes and in the West to win.

This photograph of Sir John A. Macdonald was taken shortly before his death. Even as a young man, his face was prematurely lined, probably the result of long evenings spent at the bedside of his invalid first wife. And his closest friends knew that, to his dying day, he never got over the loss of his first son, who died at thirteen months of age.

its best interests, and I appeal with equal confidence to the men who have trusted me in the past, and to the young hope of the country with whom rests its destinies for the future, to give me their united and strenuous aid in this, my last effort, for the unity of the Empire and the preservation of our commercial and political freedom.

Macdonald's response to the Liberal policy of full and unrestricted reciprocity, therefore, was "loyalty" — with the emphasis not so much on British roots and institutions as on loyalty to Canada "and its best interests." He made this point in his first campaign speech in Toronto: "This election . . . will show to the Americans that we prize our country as much as they do, that we would fight for our existence."

So "loyalty" became the central issue in that winter election campaign. The February snowstorms made campaigning particularly difficult for Macdonald, who tried to follow his usual hectic schedule in spite of his seventy-six years and a severe chest cold. By February 24, he had collapsed. Only shortly before election day on March 5 was he able to leave his sick bed and return to Ottawa. Here he received the election results; once again he had led the Conservatives to victory.

John A. had only a few weeks to live. He was present when Parliament opened in late April, but he suffered a stroke on May 12 and then two more at the end of May. While Ottawa and much of Canada waited and hoped for his recovery, the old man slowly sank. On Saturday, June 6, he died.

The years have left us political cartoons and nicknames like "Old Tomorrow" and a number of sharply witty anecdotes about Sir John A. Macdonald. But history has also handed down to us the record of Macdonald's achievement: his consistent and persistent efforts to create and maintain an independent nation in the northern half of North America, and his clear understanding of the need for constructive compromise among Canadians if Canada was to continue as a nation. In the twentieth century, as Canadians concern themselves over the relations between English- and French-speaking Canadians, some historians remember the execution of Louis Riel and Macdonald's part in it. But they might also remember the Macdonald-Cartier alliance. And they might note that when eulogies were delivered in the House of Commons after Macdonald's death, the spokesman for the Liberals was Wilfrid Laurier, a French Canadian, and for the Conservatives, another French Canadian, Sir Hector Langevin. The conclusion of Langevin's eulogy in the House speaks for itself:

> Mr. Speaker, I would have wished to continue to speak of our dear departed friend, and spoken to you about the goodness of his heart, the witness of which I have been so often, but I feel that I must stop; my heart is full of tears. I cannot proceed further.

THE CONSERVATIVES WITHOUT MACDONALD

Macdonald's death left the ruling Conservative Party in a terrible position. The Old Chieftain had held the party together; now it was going to fall apart if an effective new leader could not be found. The obvious choice as Macdonald's successor might have been Sir Hector Langevin. He had attended the Charlottetown Conference as a delegate from Canada; he had succeeded Cartier as leader of the Conservatives in Quebec; he had served with and supported Macdonald for the better part of thirty years. But Langevin had become involved in political scandal. Thomas McGreevy, Conservative MP for Quebec West, had been arranging department of public works contracts for business associates for years. He had also received contributions from these business associates for political expenses. Some of these funds helped pay for Langevin's campaigns, and Langevin was minister of public works. When formal charges were laid in the House of Commons in May 1891, it became impossible for the Conservatives to accept Langevin as

A Jumble of John A.s
"Any election is like a horse-race, in that you can tell more about it the next day."
"One strong point I admire about Sir Oliver Mowat is his handwriting."
"I know enough about the feeling of this meeting to know that you would rather have John A. drunk than George Brown sober."
"He [Riel] shall hang though every dog in Quebec bark in his favor."
"Let us be English or let us be French, but above all let us be Canadians."

The charges were made by Israel Tarte, who had been Langevin's campaign manager in 1878. He was later Laurier's campaign manager. (See p. 142.)

Charles Tupper,
1821-1915

John J. C. Abbott,
1821-1893

John Thompson,
1844-1894

leader. Macdonald himself might have chosen D'Alton McCarthy had not McCarthy's arguments for an Anglophone Canada made him totally unacceptable to French-speaking Conservatives. And Sir Charles Tupper, whom Macdonald had named as his successor back in 1877 ("when I do retire, he is a man who will well fill my place"), preferred to stay on in his position of Canadian High Commissioner in London.

No one was totally acceptable to all sections of the party, so a makeshift government was arranged under dual leadership. Senator Sir John J. C. Abbott, a loyal, long-time Conservative, became prime minister. Sir John Thompson became leader for the Conservatives in the House of Commons, where he acted as deputy prime minister. Although Thompson was perhaps the most able minister in the government, he had several political weaknesses. He was a Protestant who had renounced his religion to become a Roman Catholic, and this did him no good at all in the eyes of Protestant Conservatives. Worse

Left: John J. C. Abbott accepted the prime ministership most reluctantly. As he put it: "I hate politics . . . . I hate notoriety, public meetings, public speeches, caucuses, and everything that . . . is apparently the necessary incident of politics — except doing public work to the best of my ability."

Right: When Abbott resigned in 1892, the blunt-spoken Sir John Thompson became Conservative leader. He was, if anything, too honest. As one Conservative said of him: "He won't even consider whether a thing is good for the party until he is quite sure it is good for the country."

still, Thompson had been minister of justice in Macdonald's government and had defended the decision not to intervene in the execution of Louis Riel. This made Thompson unpopular among French-Canadian MPs.

The government's first problem was the Langevin-McGreevy affair. Thompson decided that the only hope for the government was to have a full, complete, and open inquiry. It proved disastrous for the two Quebec Conservatives: Langevin was forced to resign, and McGreevy went to jail. Other problems beset the Conservatives, but they were overshadowed by an enormous scandal in the Province of Quebec. Honoré Mercier's government had subsidized the construction of the Baie des Chaleurs Railway on the south side of the Gaspé Peninsula. Money from the contractor had found its way back to Quebec cabinet ministers. So yet again there was a railway scandal, this time a disaster for Mercier's Parti National and for the federal Liberals. Honoré Mercier was forced from office, and, in a series of federal by-elections, the Conservatives took a net total of sixteen seats from the Liberals in Quebec, increasing their majority to almost sixty in the House of Commons. The first major crisis for the Conservatives after Macdonald's death, therefore, seemed to have been weathered.

Mercier's party was composed mostly of Liberals who supported federal Liberals in federal elections.

Two years later, Sir John Thompson died suddenly, and the Conservative Party started to come apart at the seams. The main reason was the Manitoba Schools Question. As the final act in the drama of the Manitoba Schools Question was played, there were profound changes in Ottawa, and Canada moved into a new political era.

Manitoba Schools Question.
See pp. 130-132.

Differences have always characterized Canada – differences in language, religion, ethnic origin, political views. This has made it extremely difficult to describe a "typical" Canadian. Sometimes, the differences have created an exciting and stimulating variety of points of view and opportunities; sometimes, they have been exaggerated for political purposes. For example, Anglophones or Francophones have found that if they wished, they could make mountains out of their differences. Protestants and Roman Catholics have found it all too easy at times to disagree with one another. Wise politicians have always tried to avoid exploiting such fundamental differences as a basis for politics. How could the country be governed if political parties were based on religion? Or if there were a French party and an English party?

Sir John A. Macdonald had understood that emphasizing differences only led to political trouble. So when Sir John Thompson urged Macdonald to let the legality of the Manitoba Education Act be decided in the courts and not by Parliament, Macdonald had agreed. A series of four court decisions ended with that of the Judicial Committee of the Privy Council, whose 1892 decision declared the Act valid. The Roman Catholics of Manitoba then began to talk of "remedial legislation" by Parliament, which would enforce the Manitoba Act of 1870. The controversy was thus thrown back into the lap of the federal government. The Conservatives, under Sir John Thompson, had had two options.

They could have disallowed the Manitoba legislation, and then endured Liberal criticism that they were interfering with "provincial rights." Or they could have introduced and passed a remedial act to enforce Catholic educational rights as set out in the Manitoba Act. But the second option was also a dangerous one for the Conservatives. The Catholic bishops, particularly those in Quebec, wanted remedial legislation; if the Dominion government passed the necessary law, Protestants in Ontario would doubtless complain that the Conservatives had given in to the Catholics and, therefore, to Quebec.

Once more, the Conservatives moved the matter out of the public spotlight. They requested a decision from the courts as to whether the federal government had the right to pass remedial legislation. By the time of Sir John Thompson's death, the question had been referred as far as the Judicial Committee of the Privy Council. On January 29, 1895, this highest of all courts decided that the government of Canada *did* have the right to pass remedial laws. Once again, the Conservatives had to face the issue.

Mackenzie Bowell, 1823-1917

After Thompson's death, they could not have been worse prepared to deal with such a difficult issue. The new prime minister, Sir Mackenzie Bowell, was without any notable qualities of leadership. Moreover, he owed his rise within the Conservative Party to the fact that he had been Grand Master of the Orange Lodge and a leader of extremist Conservatives who had little use for anything French or Roman Catholic.

Although Bowell lacked the wisdom and the sensitivity to solve the Manitoba problem, he at least showed, in the words of one historian, "a snarling courage." On March 21, 1895, his government pushed a remedial order through Parliament, requiring the Manitoba government "to restore to the Roman Catholic minority the said rights and privileges of which said minority has been so deprived." The Manitoba government danced around the remedial order. In Winnipeg, Liberal Premier Greenway replied that the Dominion government did not really have enough information, and that his government would "cheerfully assist in affording the most complete information available." But his government would not change the school law. So, if the federal government wanted to force Manitoba to carry out the order, it would have to pass remedial legislation, which, by law, Manitoba would have to obey. Bowell lost control of his cabinet, some ministers threatening to resign if the remedial legislation were delayed, others insisting that it be put off. Ultimately, there was a cabinet rebellion, and seven members resigned. It became obvious that Bowell had to go.

The "Cumberland War Horse," old Sir Charles Tupper, took over as Conservative leader. Under his direction, the government brought before the House of Commons a remedial bill for Manitoba. After weeks of frustrating debate, marked by unbelievably long filibusters (the House of Commons once sat for 130 hours straight), Tupper withdrew the proposed legislation. There was nothing left to do now but

Left: Sir Mackenzie Bowell was Canada's fifth prime minister. The owner-editor of a Belleville, Ontario, newspaper, he hated all Liberals and Roman Catholics and was the parliamentary leader of a group of right-wing Conservatives sometimes referred to as "the lunatic fringe."

Right: Sir Charles Tupper became the sixth prime minister. The party owed him its leadership. He had brought Nova Scotia into Confederation and then set about winning over his fellow Nova Scotian and long-time political foe, Joseph Howe. And Tupper's bulldog determination and fiery speeches had rallied the Conservatives in many House of Commons debates.

to obtain the opinion of the voters in the course of a general election. When the ballots were counted, the results of the 1896 election were as follows:

	Liberals	Conservatives
Nova Scotia	10	10
New Brunswick	5	9
P.E.I.	2	3
Manitoba	2	4
British Columbia	4	2
N.W. Territories	2	1
Ontario	43	44
	68	73

With totals so close in all these provinces, Quebec's decision would settle the outcome.

Wilfrid Laurier campaigning. He once explained his politics in the following words: "I am a Liberal. I am one of those who think that everywhere in human things there are abuses to be reformed . . . there is always room for . . . the attainment by a larger number of an easier way of life."

For one group in the Province of Quebec, the issue had been clear. At least six of the Catholic bishops insisted that remedial legislation should be enacted, and that voters should support candidates who wanted the law passed. This meant in effect that the electors should vote Conservative. For the Liberal leader, Wilfrid Laurier, the issue was more complicated. On the one hand, he was a French Canadian and a Catholic; on the other hand, if he were elected he would be a *national* leader. He finally took a stand; he was against forcing Manitoba to accept change. The election became a direct confrontation between the authority of the bishops and the popularity of Laurier. And to Laurier's personal appeal were added the outstanding organizational and political skills of Israel Tarte, a one-time Conservative and now the manager of Laurier's Quebec campaign. Tarte knew that what happened in Quebec would decide the fate of the Liberal Party. So he told Liberal candidates in the rest of the country to be as anti-Catholic as their voters expected them to be, play up Laurier's stand on provincial rights, and "leave Quebec to Laurier and me." He knew where the votes in Quebec were.

On election day, Quebec voters went against the bishops and for Laurier, their favorite son. The results astonished nearly everyone: Conservatives 16, Liberals 49. With this massive Quebec support, Wilfrid Laurier brought to an end almost a quarter century of Conservative rule in Canada.

Tarte edited the Conservative newspaper *Le Canadien.*

STUDY 4

1. Explain or define the following expressions and terms: British North America Act; Parliament; legislature; distribution of powers; residual powers; lieutenant-governor; Judicial Committee of the Privy Council; and sovereignty.
2. Write a brief report on the three major challenges that Ontario presented to the authority of the Dominion government.
3. Summarize the history of the boundary between Ontario and Manitoba from the point of view of Manitoba.
4. What were the main grievances of the Maritime Provinces in the 1880s? How many of these problems, in your opinion, were due to policies of the Dominion government?
5. Manitoba farmers focused their discontent on the CPR monopoly clause. Were they justified in doing this? Explain.
6. State in your own words the compact theory of Confederation. Do you support the compact theory generally? Would you make exceptions for particular provinces? Which, and why?
7. Why did the Jesuit Estates Act cause such a controversy?
8. Write a brief résumé of the main events of the Manitoba Schools Question. In your summary, try to separate the political and legal aspects of the question.
9. Explain the difference between the traditional (Conservative and Liberal) policy of reciprocity with the United States and Sir Richard Cartwright's proposal for "full and unrestricted reciprocity." What is the difference between "commercial union" and "full and unrestricted reciprocity"?
10. Find in this chapter material that should be added to your file on Canada-U.S. relations, which you started in Study 1.
11. If you had to choose Sir John A. Macdonald's most important contribution to Canada, what would it be? Why?
12. Investigate further the career of Sir John Thompson. What, in your opinion, might have been the results in the election of 1896 if Thompson had continued to lead the Conservatives?
13. Joseph Israel Tarte, Wilfrid Laurier's campaign manager in the 1896 election, was a Conservative. How can you explain his support for the Liberal leader?
14. Account for Laurier's victory in the 1896 election. Your explanation should take into account the national picture as well as the relationship between religion and politics in Quebec, going back to the Guibord affair (pages 60-61).

techniques and technology

The election of Wilfrid Laurier's first government is a good place to stop and examine Canada's progress. For 1896 was a milestone in the development of the nation. It was the year in which Canada had its first French-speaking prime minister and it was the starting point of the Liberals' domination of federal politics. The year 1896 was also the start of a period of immigration that would establish the basis of our multicultural society.

The focus on political leaders in the previous chapters is one way of looking at Canada's past. There is also social history, on the everyday level of ordinary people — farm and fisher folk in their homes in the Maritimes; settlers in their sod houses on the prairies. Another way is to investigate how people lived in the closing years of the nineteenth century. What tools did they work with? What techniques did they use? In short, what technology did they have? What technology did they develop in response to the challenge of their environment? And what part did technology play in producing the Canadian nation?

*   *   *

Technology is one of those big-sounding words that seem difficult to define. But it really is not all that complicated. A good working definition can be developed by combining three elements. The first is our understanding of the things we perceive in the world around us. The second is our use of this understanding to make tools and develop techniques to solve the problems we face in everyday life. The third is the result (or results) of this use, for us and for our environment. If we think of the automobile as an example, we can illustrate these three elements. We understand that rapidly burning gases expand. We use this understanding to build a tool — an internal-combustion engine. We place this tool in an automobile, and its effect on all of us and our environment can be seen everywhere.

One of the reasons that technology sounds mysterious is that many people associate it with complicated machinery or powerful engines or electronic computers. But technology did not begin in the twentieth century or even with the Industrial Revolution. It started with people, from the very beginning, for it is people who make technology. When people first used a bone as a weapon, they did not know the "scientific facts" about bones that we know today, but they knew all they needed to

Confederation Life Collection

know for their purpose: they could use a bone to hit an enemy over the head. That was technology. A sharp, pointed stick used to dig up earth to plant seeds and grow food is just as much technology as was, later, the horse-drawn plough or, today, the tractor-pulled plough. (What will the "earth digger-upper" of tomorrow be?) In short, there is no "absolute" or "best" technology; people develop and use technology at the level of their needs or desires. Technology helps them to live in or adapt to their environment.

How does technology apply to Canada? From what we have noted so far, the answer depends on three further questions: What people? In what place? At what time?

The first people who came to this northern land developed a technology based on the level of their scientific understanding and suited to a land running with rivers, a land of long winters and heavy snows. In response to this environment, Indians and Inuit invented canoes and snowshoes, snowhouses and pemmican, salmon spears and seal-oil lamps. They obtained food by hunting animals, gathering seeds and berries, and growing grains and vegetables. Those who followed wandering herds had to develop a technology that allowed them to travel and take their possessions with them. They made "mobile homes" that they could carry on travois to new hunting grounds. Those who practised agriculture made baskets to collect seeds that they would plant during the next growing season.

Canada has many environments, so the native peoples developed different technologies. There was no stereotype "Indian," so there was no single Indian technology. Woodland inhabitants had a different technology from those of the prairies, which was different still from that of the West Coast. But there was one element that all the native peoples

145

shared. They all developed technologies that enabled them to survive in and adapt to their particular environment.

But not all technologies are developed to enable people to adapt to their physical world. People also develop technologies that allow them to change their environment. The Canada we live in today was produced by technologies that transformed the environment and revolutionized the way people lived. Could there have been a Canada without a railway? What kind of Canada would we live in without the internal-combustion engine, which enables us to harvest wheat in combines, transport goods in trucks, and travel quickly from place to place (except in rush hour!) in automobiles? How would we communicate with each other across this vast country without telephones and cables and radio?

When Wilfrid Laurier became prime minister in 1896, Canada was experiencing important technological changes. The era of Sir John A. Macdonald was passing, and the twentieth century was just around the corner. So by pausing for a moment to examine changing technology, we can develop both a better feeling for Canada's first three decades and for the changes that would transform Canada in the Laurier years.

THE "IRON HORSE"

Perhaps the best place to start is the railway, the most prominent evidence of the technological revolution that marked the beginning of the Industrial Age. Before approximately 1800, most nations in the world relied on agriculture as the basis for their economy. Most of the population in every nation worked on the land, and most of the wealth was in the hands of landowners. This was true not only in colonies like Canada but among leading nations like England or France. Then, in 1776 (to choose a convenient date), James Watt registered his patent for an improved steam engine. The new steam engines, using heat rather than wind or water, drove the machinery in England's textile mills. They also provided power for ships. (Robert Fulton's "steamboat" *Clermont* on New York's Hudson River used a Watt steam engine in 1807.) By the late 1820s and 1830s, they had replaced horses as the source of power for tramways. The tramways, which used wooden rails at first, gradually combined iron rails and steam power to give birth to the railway.

The British developed railways, although, strangely enough, they were more interested in applying the new steam power to water transportation on their extensive system of canals. They could use their technological expertise, however, to manufacture steam engines and export them to countries like the United States, Canada, Argentina, or Russia, where the railway locomotive would be even more useful than in Britain. Locomotives and railways could be used not only to parallel existing water routes, but also to cut through natural physical barriers. In Canada, for example, railways were used to overcome barriers like

The first practical steam engine was a pump to drain water from coal mines. It was invented in 1698 by Thomas Savery.

The Dominion government not only paid part of an immigrant's ship and rail fares and supplied homestead land but, on occasion, also provided temporary housing facilities. Here, in the village of Saskatoon, army tents were loaned to the Barr Colonists, the group of English families that founded Lloydminster, Saskatchewan.

the Canadian Shield or the Rocky Mountains. In fact, the "iron horse" overcame the great distance across Canada and helped to create a Dominion from sea to sea.

If you stop to think about it, it was the iron horse that maintained the political division of North America as two nations rather than one. The building of the American transcontinentals after the Civil War tied together many diverse regions in the United States — the Atlantic Coast, the Mississippi Valley, the Great Plains, the Pacific Coast. Each of these had been linked historically with neighboring colonies in British North America — New England, for example, with Nova Scotia and New Brunswick; California, with Vancouver Island and British Columbia. Before these railways were built, there was natural regional communication and trade. But with the construction of the United States transcontinentals, a new force came into play. British Columbia, for example, could be linked not only naturally with California, but also, via the railroads, with the manufacturing centres of the eastern United States. If Canadians were to maintain their independence in the face of the advantages created for Americans by railroads, they would have to answer with railways of their own. So the building of the Intercolonial and Canadian Pacific railways took on added significance for Canadian independence. As the historian C. P. Stacey noted, the Intercolonial linked the Maritimes with central Canada, overcoming the magnetism of markets in the New England states. And the Canadian Pacific bound the Canadian West to central Canada, rather than to Chicago and the industrial heartland of the United States. In this sense, railways provide a striking example of technology being used to create and develop a political environment that would help guarantee the continued existence and success of Canada.

In the late nineteenth century, political, economic, and even social

The first U.S. transcontinental, the Union-Central Pacific, was completed in 1869.

147

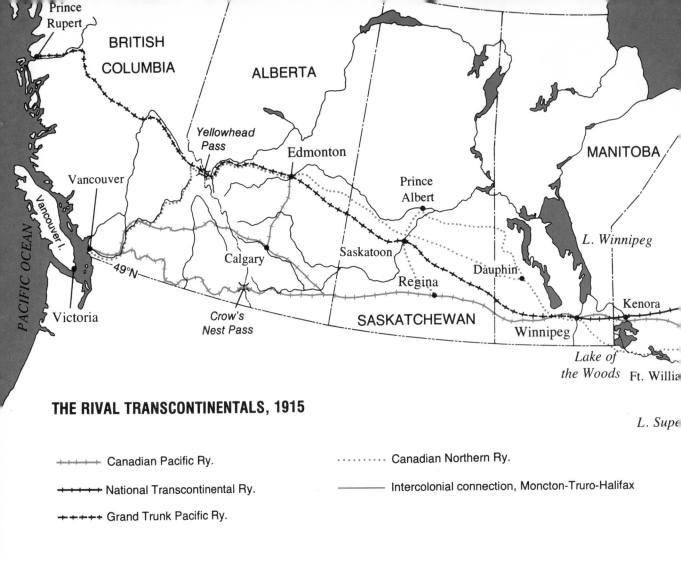

THE RIVAL TRANSCONTINENTALS, 1915

+++++ Canadian Pacific Ry.

·········· Canadian Northern Ry.

+++++ National Transcontinental Ry.

———— Intercolonial connection, Moncton-Truro-Halifax

+++++ Grand Trunk Pacific Ry.

activities centred on railways. Agricultural and industrial products, necessities and luxuries were shipped by rail. Farm families went on picnics by rail, immigrants moved west by rail, and the wealthy used private and luxurious railway cars for personal and business appointments. Small towns in Ontario and Quebec paid railway companies to establish lines and stations. Throughout the countryside, the distant wail of the steam whistle was proof that the economy was humming along. By the 1890s, Canada had developed a coast-to-coast rail system, thanks to three major railway companies — the Grand Trunk, the Intercolonial, and the Canadian Pacific. There were also hundreds of little lines.

The next stage in railway development began in the West, this time under the leadership of two promoters, William Mackenzie and Donald Mann, who were out to capture developing prairie markets. Their first step was to take over the charter of the Lake Manitoba Railway and Canal Company. The proposed line, which was to run from Gladstone

The charter included a land grant of 1480 hectares per kilometre.

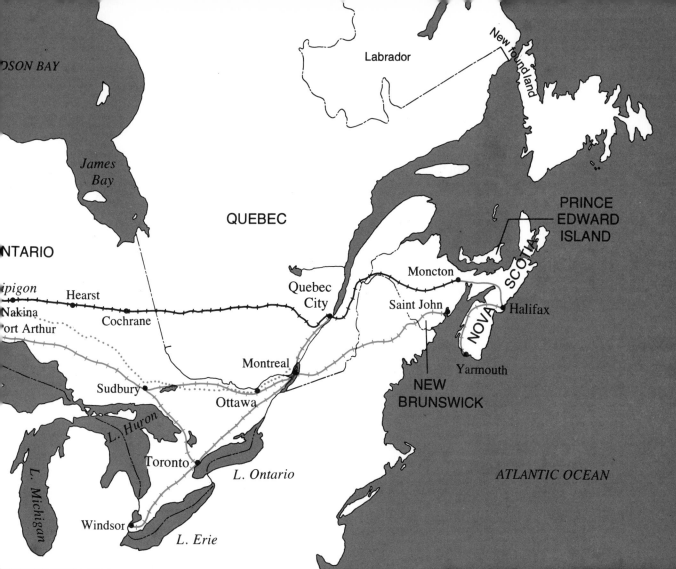

(on the Manitoba and North Western line) to Dauphin, would open a whole new area to settlement. A little later, Mackenzie and Mann, with the backing of the Manitoba government, took over the charter for a railway from St. Boniface (Winnipeg) to the Lake of the Woods. This "Muskeg Special" was then extended to Port Arthur, providing Manitoban farmers with an alternative to the CPR for grain shipments to Lake Superior. With the addition of many small branch operations in Manitoba, this line made their railway a major competitive threat to the CPR. Then, in 1901, the Canadian Northern Railway Company, as Mackenzie and Mann had renamed their system, announced its plan to become a transcontinental line. Its plan was to push from western Manitoba through Humboldt and North Battleford and on to Edmonton (very close, in fact, to the original route planned for the CPR). By continuing to lay track westward and by picking up a few lines in the east, the Canadian Northern could become Canada's second transcontinental railway.

But, in 1902, Prime Minister Wilfrid Laurier decided on another approach to a second cross-country line. He tried to get the Canadian Northern to co-operate with the Grand Trunk in the operation of a trans-Canada railway system. (The Grand Trunk was very interested in getting a share of the traffic to and from the West.) Such co-operation would have been very sensible, combining the western-based Canadian Northern with the eastern-based Grand Trunk. But neither company was prepared to accept anything less than complete control over the proposed system, so the idea fell through. Laurier then had to choose between the Canadian Northern and the Grand Trunk. He chose the latter. His final plan was a combination of public and private enterprise. The new transcontinental would consist of two major sections. One, the National Transcontinental, would be built for and owned by the Canadian people. It would run from Moncton, New Brunswick, north and west to Quebec City, and then due west through the rough, uncharted terrain of northern Quebec and Ontario to Winnipeg. The other section would be built and owned by the Grand Trunk Pacific Railway Company, a subsidiary of the Grand Trunk. It would follow Sandford Fleming's original surveyed route for the CPR: west from Winnipeg through Saskatoon, through Edmonton and the Yellowhead Pass, and on to the Pacific Ocean at Prince Rupert. The Grand Trunk would have the right to operate on the government section of the line for fifty years, paying 3 per cent of the cost of construction as its annual rental. Laurier's scheme met with considerable opposition within his own cabinet (his minister of railways and canals resigned over the issue) and also within the Liberal Party. But, insisting that "Canada cannot wait," Laurier browbeat his cabinet members and his fellow Liberals into submission. In 1903, he rammed his railway bill through Parliament, just as Macdonald had rammed through the CPR bill.

Construction proceeded on *both* the Canadian Northern and the National Transcontinental-Grand Trunk Pacific. Each line competed for the best routes and sometimes, as in the Yellowhead Pass area, came within metres of each other. The Grand Trunk Pacific reached Prince Rupert in 1914; the Canadian Northern reached Vancouver, by way of the Thompson and Fraser River valleys, in 1915. This gave Canada about 48 000 kilometres of railway track, one kilometre for every 155 inhabitants. (There were 250 people per kilometre of track in the United States, and 1250 per kilometre in Great Britain.)

Not only had Canada built railways, it had *over*built them. The costs to the Canadian treasury made the Canadian Pacific expense look small in comparison. CPR costs were about $230 million; the combined cost of the Canadian Northern, the Grand Trunk Pacific, and the National Transcontinental was almost $580 million. And this was not the worst of it. As construction costs mounted and railway revenues stagnated, and as Canada faced generally increasing expenses during the First World War, both the Canadian Northern and the Grand Trunk Pacific faced

The actual construction was undertaken by the Grand Trunk.

certain bankruptcy. The Canadian government, however, could not permit either line to fail, both because of its own investment and because Laurier had persuaded many provincial governments to invest in these railway enterprises. In the end, it was decided to nationalize the railroads, that is, the federal government would take them over and run them. The Canadian Northern became the property of the Dominion of Canada in 1917, as did the Grand Trunk Pacific *and* the Grand Trunk itself in 1920. In 1923, these railways and the National Transcontinental and Intercolonial were joined together to form the publicly-owned system called Canadian National Railways (CNR).

The burden of debt created by excessive railway building during the first years of this century is with us today. But the nation did get something for its money. Many new regions were opened up to mining exploration and settlement. For many families on the prairies, the transcontinentals and their branch lines meant much easier delivery of their grain.

One of the great ironies of the expensive flurry of railway building was that it occurred just as a new technology was beginning to capture people's imagination and start a major transformation of society. If the automobile had been put into mass production twenty years earlier, the railway builders would perhaps have joined together to compete against the automobile and truck, rather than competing among themselves.

The debt still outstanding in 1976 was $2¼ billion. The interest that the CNR paid on this debt in 1976 was $120 million.

THE "HORSELESS CARRIAGE"

If you could be taken back in time to the 1890s, you would soon notice the absence of automobiles. There might be one or two "horseless carriages" in a big city, for the internal-combustion engine had certainly been invented, but only a very few wealthy or adventurous people owned cars. Not that Canada was much behind the rest of the world in the development of the automobile. In 1867, Henry Taylor of Stanstead,

Roy Mitchell Photography

The owner of this Model 490 Chevrolet must have wanted music fairly desperately to have made such elaborate arrangements. Note the several metres of wire rigged up as an aerial on the roof and the crystal radio set mounted on the running board.

151

An entire community named Ford grew up outside Windsor, Ontario, to assemble Model Ts for the Canadian market. Here, this famous, four-cylinder automobile stands next to a streetcar, equipped with a "cow-catcher" for unwary pedestrians. Note the Model T's narrow tires, its vertical windshield, and high road clearance, which was very useful on muddy or deeply rutted roads.

Ford factories turned out millions of Model Ts — dreadful in design, bone-rattling to ride in, but at a price the average American and Canadian could afford.

Quebec, built Canada's first steam carriage. In Ontario in 1893, William Still and Frederick Featherstonhaugh built Canada's first electric car. In 1897, Dr. H. Casgrain of Quebec City took the front wheels off his automobile and replaced them with skis, creating what was probably the first snowmobile. And in 1897, George Foss of Sherbrooke, Quebec, built Canada's first gasoline automobile. Its performance was excellent: about eighteen kilometres to the litre!

But, in the 1890s, for nearly all local or short-distance travel, the horse still provided the main means of transportation. Throughout Canada, there was a "horse technology." Instead of garages, there were stables; instead of service stations, livery stables; instead of automobile designers and salespeople, horse-breeders and horse-traders. And instead of automobile exhausts, there was the particular kind of pollution generated by horses, which made dirt and gravel roads particularly dangerous for men's shoes and women's long skirts.

We have noted how railway technology enabled the Canadian government to respond quickly to the Northwest Rebellion, in far less time than it had taken troops to go from central Canada to the Red River in 1870. And we have seen how the use of this technology produced major effects on the political environment. In the same way, the use of horses for transport helped determine the social environment in the 1890s.

In the Age of the Horse, distances were longer in one way and shorter in another. Either way, the difference can be explained by the time it took to cover distances. Take a convenient distance, say thirty kilometres. On a good road, without too much traffic, an automobile can easily cover that distance in about half an hour. It would take a horse at least five hours. For prairie farmers who had to haul their grain thirty kilometres to a rail line, in horse-drawn wagons, the round trip took all day. (No wonder Western farmers wanted more branch lines!) So, measured this way, distances were longer because it took longer to get where you were going. But distances were also shorter. Think of doing the following activities, first in an automobile and then on horseback, allowing only half an hour for each activity: going shopping; going to a hockey game; going to work. How far would you be able to travel by automobile (or bus or truck)? How far on horseback? In the age of horse technology, how far away from your work could you live? How far outward could towns spread? Measured this way, distances were shorter because your business and social environment was limited to how far you could travel on foot or by horse. The idea of large cities with sprawling suburbs was impossible until the age of the internal-combustion engine, which enabled people to drive longer distances to work or shop or go to a hockey game. It was motorized-vehicle technology that helped transform Canada from a nation of farming communities and rural towns into a society of city dwellers and suburbanites.

A NEW KIND OF POWER

During the 1890s, Canada participated in another technological development that would change its future. This was the generation and use of electricity. Just think of life in the pre-electric age — no electric lights, no radio, no television, no electrical appliances, no stereo, no electronic computers — and you will appreciate how significantly this technology transformed the environment.

Two developments in the field of electric power are particularly interesting. The first of these has to do with the name many Canadians use for electricity. Most early generating plants used coal to raise steam to drive the turbines which generated electricity. This was the case, for example, in Alberta's first generating plant, started in 1888, in Calgary. But throughout the country, engineers began to take advantage of falling water to generate electricity, and so Canadians began to speak of "hydro-electric power." In time, this was shortened to "hydro." In Canada, most people use expressions like "hydro lines" and "paying the hydro bill." It is a peculiar Canadian term, used in both official languages.

Some of the most easily available supplies of falling water were to be found in the rivers on the edges of the Canadian Shield. In Quebec particularly, where these rivers were often close to population centres, several companies combined the generation of hydro-electric power with the production of pulp and newsprint. They sold the newsprint to U.S. newspapers and the extra electricity that was generated to customers in the Province of Quebec. The development of the pulp-and-paper industry, along with new sources of hydro power, began a transformation of Quebec society. Many jobs were created for loggers and workers in pulp mills, and the new power sources helped new secondary manufacturing industries to get started. One interesting effect of this hydro development and industrialization was that fewer

"Hydro" comes from the Greek word for water.

In 1884, electric arc lights were installed on Toronto streets.

In 1892, Winnipeg replaced horse-drawn tramcars with electric streetcars, as did other cities, such as Halifax in 1896.

153

One of Mackenzie's associates was Henry Pellatt, probably best remembered for building Toronto's Casa Loma, which was part of a railway promotion scheme.

One of Holt's associates in Calgary was a lawyer who also handled CPR interests, a former New Brunswicker named R. B. Bennett.

A similar development occurred in Winnipeg in 1906, when the publicly owned Winnipeg City Hydro was formed. It operated in competition with Mackenzie's privately owned company. For years, its rates were the lowest in North America.

Alexander Graham Bell was born in Scotland in 1847.

young French-speaking Canadians left Quebec to seek jobs outside the province. In fact, skilled French Canadians began to return to Quebec from the New England states to work in the newly developing industries.

Another important development concerned the ownership of hydro generating and transmission facilities. During the 1890s, wealthy financiers got control of electric companies, and they were determined to extend that control until, among them, they had monopolized the production and supply of electricity. For example, one of the men behind the Canadian Northern, William Mackenzie, owned a large part of the Electric Development Company in Toronto and of the Winnipeg Electric Street Railway Company. Herbert Holt, another of Mackenzie's associates, owned a large part of the Montreal Light, Heat, and Power Company, and, when it was organized in 1909, of the Calgary Power Company Limited. These millionaire financiers could have created a monopoly situation had they not encountered a very important movement that changed the whole nature of utilities like hydro. In Ontario, for example, smaller businessmen from centres outside Toronto feared that any monopoly would make hydro power too expensive to use in their factories and businesses. Led by the former mayor of London, Ontario, a man called Adam Beck, they argued for public control of the hydro utility and were finally successful in their campaign. In 1905 the Hydro-Electric Power Commission of Ontario was established as a public utility. Its modern name, Ontario Hydro, sums up the two great Canadian advances in the provision of electric power — the use of water resources and the idea of public ownership and control.

WIRES AND WAVES

There were two other technological developments at this time that also transformed our environment. Like the automobile, they made distances shorter; but these inventions made it possible to shorten distance without having to travel. People in one place could reach people thousands of kilometres away — by telephone and radio. Canada and Canadians participated in the early development of both telephone and radio communications.

Canadians and Americans argue about where the telephone was invented, for Alexander Graham Bell, the inventor of the telephone, worked both in Canada and the United States. He came to Canada in 1870, opened a school for teachers of the deaf in Boston in 1872, returned to Canada in 1874 because of ill health, and then, in 1876, demonstrated his telephone apparatus in the United States. Perhaps Bell's own words will help settle any argument about *where* the telephone was invented. In 1911, the inventor explained, "in the summer of 1874, during my visit to my father's house in Brantford, Ontario . . . the

Bell Canada Telephone Historical Collection

thought of the membrane telephone was elaborated. So that the conception of the telephone originated in Brantford in the summer of 1874." Bell's invention soon began to have its effects. In 1877, Prime Minister Alexander Mackenzie had a telephone installed in the Department of Public Works and linked to another at Rideau Hall, the Governor General's residence. Long-distance lines were installed between Toronto and Hamilton in 1882, and between Montreal and Ottawa in 1885. So by the 1890s telephone wires, together with hydro lines, were producing that peculiar urban jungle of trees and vines — poles and wires — in many Canadian cities.

Alexander Graham Bell continued much of his work in the United States, but after a visit to Cape Breton Island in 1885, he decided to build an estate there, near Baddeck. From Baddeck, he and his four associates in the Aerial Experimental Association (AEA) continued to experiment, this time in technologies that really belong to the twentieth century. On February 23, 1909, J. A. D. McCurdy flew the Association's aircraft, *Silver Dart*, about two kilometres over Baddeck Bay, the first flight by a British subject in the British Empire. Bell and another member of the AEA group, Casey Baldwin, also worked on hydrofoil ships. By 1919, their "HD-4" was reaching speeds of over 114 kilometres per hour. These and Bell's other important inventions are displayed in the Alexander Graham Bell Museum in Baddeck.

On Signal Hill, in St. John's, Newfoundland, on December 12, 1901,

Alexander Graham Bell's hydroplane (seaplane) moored at Baddeck, Nova Scotia, sometime about 1912. It was in 1912 that the first hydroplane flight in Canada was made. The event occurred at the Lake Erie resort of Port Stanley, Ontario, in a Burgess-Wright seaplane flown by Walter R. Brookins.

the first transatlantic wireless message was received. It consisted of three "dots," Morse code for the letter "s," and it was sent from Cornwall, England, by Guglielmo Marconi, who is generally considered the inventor of radio. But this transatlantic message, even though wireless, was still "telegraphy" — the transmission of signals. It was not "radio telephony" — the transmission of *sounds through the air*. The credit for the invention of radio telephony and the first radio broadcast belong to a Canadian.

Reginald Aubrey Fessenden was born in 1866 in East Bolton, near Sherbrooke, Quebec. As a young man, he travelled to the United States, where he worked for both Thomas Edison and George Westinghouse. All the time he was working for these men, and while later employed by the U.S. Weather Bureau, he was experimenting with the possibilities of radio transmissions, but his early efforts were overshadowed by Marconi's success with wireless telegraphy. Fessenden was convinced that Marconi's basic theory was wrong. Marconi understood wireless transmissions to be like the crack of a rifle, with the electric spark of a wireless transmitter shooting out violent impulses that could be picked up by receivers. Fessenden, on the other hand, accepted the theories of Heinrich Hertz, the German scientist who had discovered that wireless impulses could go through solid materials, a wall or building, for example. The Canadian inventor worked on the idea that electrical impulses were like ripples in a pond after a stone has disturbed the surface of the water. Electrical impulses, like pond ripples, could be continuous. So instead of turning the electricity on and off by closing and opening the keys of a telegraph machine, Fessenden believed that the electrical impulse should be turned on all the time — that it should be continuous. By modifying this continuous electrical impulse, real *sounds* could be transmitted instead of Marconi's little dots and dashes.

The term "hertz" meaning "cycles per second" is named after him.

156

A pen-and-ink drawing of Titanic survivors queuing up to thank their savior, Signor Marconi.

On the night of April 14-15, 1912, the luxury liner Titanic sank near the coast of Newfoundland, with over 1500 passengers and crew. Twenty minutes later, a Cunard liner, alerted by the doomed ship's wireless operator, picked up the 700 survivors.

Not only was Fessenden right about radio, but he was right a year before Marconi transmitted the first transatlantic wireless message in 1901. On December 23, 1900, Fessenden spoke into a microphone, to an assistant eighty kilometres away: "One, two, three, four. Is it snowing where you are, Mr. Thiessen? If so, telegraph back and let me know." Thiessen telegraphed back that it was indeed snowing. The first radio message had been transmitted.

From here on, however, bad luck dogged Fessenden. Marconi's successful transatlantic transmission captured public attention and convinced everybody that his theory was right. What could a young, unknown inventor do against all the acclaim given Marconi? His request for research funds was rejected by the Canadian government (which gave financial support to Marconi).

Reginald Fessenden at work in his studio. His life was a perpetual struggle for recognition of his various inventions, which involved lawsuits with former partners who had sold his patents to American companies. When he died, his achievements were unknown to Canadians and Americans.

157

Confederation Life Collection

The Public Archives of Canada

Left: It was in 1866, in the Newfoundland outport of Heart's Content, that the Old World and New World were first linked by telegraph. After the expenditure of millions of dollars and several unsuccessful attempts at laying a cable on the floor of the Atlantic Ocean, a telegraph line was finally brought ashore.

Right: Guglielmo Marconi's Station XWA (now CFCF) in Montreal. Marconi (and Canada) can claim a radio "first." It was from this station, on May 20, 1920, that North America's first scheduled radio broadcast was made: a music program relayed to a meeting of the Royal Society of Canada in Ottawa.

Fessenden's company was supported by Sir Robert Borden and other prominent Canadians.

Despite his disappointments, Fessenden continued to work on radio transmission via continuous electromagnetic waves. His National Electric Signalling Company built two radio towers for transatlantic transmission — one at Brant Rock, near Boston, and one at Machrihanish, in Scotland. In July 1906, he formed the Fessenden Wireless Telegraph Company of Canada so that he could transmit messages between Canada and Europe. Then, in November 1906, he received news from his engineer in Scotland that startled him. According to this letter, "I was listening in for telegraph signals from Brant Rock when to my astonishment I heard instead of dots and dashes, the voice of Mr. Stein telling the operators at Plymouth how to run the dynamo . . . as clearly as if he were in the next room." Fessenden's equipment had transmitted, unintentionally, a voice message across the ocean! And then an accident. A storm destroyed the tower at Machrihanish the very next month. And then another disappointment. Marconi had been given exclusive rights to build wireless stations in Canada. This meant the end of Fessenden's Canadian company. But not the end of Fessenden. He would prove that he was the real inventor of radio.

On December 24, 1906, he gave an unexpected Christmas present to one of his customers, the United Fruit Company (UFC), which had installed wireless systems on its boats. From his Brant Rock transmitting station, Fessenden sent out a radio program to UFC ships in the Atlantic. He made a short announcement, played a phonograph record, and then, to complete the program, played "O Holy Night" on his violin. The broadcast was received — and radio was born.

Fessenden has never received due recognition for his invention, but history and science have proved that he was right. Had he been able to sell his ideas, the name Fessenden would have the meaning today that Marconi has.

The end of the nineteenth century witnessed so many new ideas and inventions in Canada that it would be impossible to list them all. But here are a few. James Naismith of Almonte, Ontario, invented basketball. John Connon of Elora developed the world's first panoramic picture camera. And John Joseph Wright of Toronto built and sold the world's first electric streetcar in 1883. All these inventions edged Canada toward the modern age we know today. New technologies and new industries began the change that was to transform Canada from a rural into an urban nation. But, in the 1890s, agriculture still gave Canada its muscle, and it was in agriculture and food production that some of the most important new scientific discoveries and new technological developments were applied.

PUTTING BREAD ON THE TABLE

Before considering some of the developments that helped turn Canada into one of the world's granaries, it helps to know the stages involved in growing grain.

To produce grain for use, there are five steps to be considered: preparing the land (after it has been cleared), including ploughing and breaking up the big lumps; sowing seed (and hoping for enough rain, no hail, no early frosts); cutting the ripe grain; gathering the stalks of grain together; and, finally, threshing — separating the kernels of grain from the chaff (the outer covering) and the straw. Every farmer since the beginning of history has had to follow these steps.

Most of the early farmers in Canada used the traditional methods. With oxen and a wooden plough, they prepared the soil. Seed was thrown out by hand — broadcast. To cut grain, farmers in New France used sickles or scythes. By the early nineteenth century, most Canadian farmers used a modified scythe called a cradle, which cut grain so that it was easier to pile in rows. The grain was then tied together into sheaves. After drying in the field, the stooks of grain were stored in a barn or shed, and threshed during the winter months. To separate the kernels from the chaff and straw, a jointed stick called a flail was used to beat the grain. (Sometimes, oxen walked around on the grain, but this left the kernels very dirty and was not the best method.) After flailing, the grain was winnowed by throwing it into the air and letting the wind blow the lighter chaff away from the heavier kernels. Then the threshed grain was stored, used for animal feed or milled for flour.

Stalks of grain were used to tie the sheaves together.

These were the basic methods that men and women had used for centuries. There had been improvements in farming throughout this Agricultural Age, which prevailed until the end of the eighteenth century. But from the middle of the 1600s to the late 1700s, improvements

159

*Near Gleichen, Alberta,
the Reeves Company
demonstrates its new
steam tractors.*

quickened and many important changes began to take place. English landowners and farmers began growing clover for hay, because they discovered it restored the soil. (It puts nitrogen back into the earth, which is important for the production of strong grain stalks.) They developed new systems of crop rotation, which increased their yields and helped preserve the soil. They also improved their livestock, breeding stronger, faster horses, and bigger cattle and sheep. This Agricultural Revolution was most important, for it enabled England to feed those who left the farms to work in factories during the early Industrial Revolution. From England, these practices spread throughout the Western world, so that in France, Germany, and the United States food production increased. As the Industrial Revolution progressed in the nineteenth century, many other developments affected agriculture. These included the use of steel, chemicals, and, in a limited way, steam engines.

Perhaps the most striking thing about technological development in the nineteenth century was that agriculture was no longer leading the way. Rather, it was taking advantage of new inventions and techniques that were first applied in manufacturing. As much as any other factor, this use of industrial technology in agriculture marks the difference between the Agricultural and the Industrial Age.

How did these technological advances affect Canadian agriculture? By the middle of the nineteenth century, several steps in grain growing and harvesting had been mechanized (that is, machines did the work that human muscle power had formerly done). For example, seed was now generally sown with a seed drill, a machine that used tubes or discs to plant the seed in rows and cover it with a thin layer of earth. Scythes and cradles had been replaced by a mechanical reaper. This machine used a long-toothed knife that worked back and forth, much like an electric hedge clipper, to cut the ripe grain. The reaper could take the place of as many as thirty or forty men with scythes. (This was important when many farmers' sons and farm laborers were leaving to go to the California

The John Deere Company was a famous name in agricultural machinery. Here, its binders, hitched to gasoline-driven tractors, are making short work of a grain field in 1911.

and British Columbia gold rushes, to work on railways, or to seek and settle new farms for themselves.) A threshing machine had been developed that replaced the earlier flailing and winnowing operations, saving time and increasing production. All these new machines were horse-drawn or horse-powered. Seed drills and reapers were pulled by horses. Threshing machines were powered by horses turning a capstan, or walking on endless belts or treadmills.

The Scots had developed many of the earliest farm machines, but by the 1850s, Americans had taken over the design and manufacturing of agricultural equipment in North America. They produced most of the machinery used on Canadian farms. When Canadian manufacturers started to build farm machinery, they had to pay the American manufacturers a licence fee for the right to use their machine designs. As the market for implements grew, Canadian manufacturers aimed at control of the Canadian market. This was one of the reasons why manufacturers and business supported Sir John A. Macdonald's National Policy, with its tariffs to protect Canadian manufacturers and reduce foreign competition. It was also the reason why many farmers, particularly those in the West, were opposed to tariffs; they believed that without tariffs they would be able to import farm machinery cheaper from the United States.

In the 1860s another new industrial development gave North America another advance in agriculture. The new Bessemer process, with its precise control of the amount of carbon mixed with iron, enabled manufacturers to produce steel cheaply. Thanks to the production of inexpensive steel, new hard ploughs could be mass-produced, and the tough sod of the Great Plains could be broken and the land sown to wheat. From the 1870s on, both in Canada and in the United States,

Some Canadians did not bother to obtain a licence; they merely copied the designs and started producing.

161

thousands of hectares of new land were broken up by the new chilled-steel ploughs, and North American grain growers began to take over markets in Europe. Steel was put to another important use in agriculture in the 1870s. In 1874, barbed wire began to be mass-produced, with very significant effects for farmers. In eastern Canada, wire could be used for fences, instead of stone or cedar rail, which farmers had used previously. And in western Canada, where neither stones nor rails were easily available, barbed wire meant that prairie lands could be fenced off.

Despite the improved farm machines, one stage of the grain harvesting process remained unmechanized: tying the grain stalks together to make sheaves. The first step toward mechanization came with reapers that laid the cut grain in rows, by letting it fall on a wide moving belt behind the blades. (People still had to walk along behind the reaper to pick up the grain and tie it in sheaves.) The next step was two men riding on the reaper and binding the grain into sheaves by hand. Then an automatic grain binder was developed, but it used wire to bind the sheaves, and this made trouble for threshing machines and for cattle. (Cattle often swallow all sorts of metal hardware, so that a magnet has to be put down their throat to draw up the pieces of metal.) Finally, about 1877, a man called John Appleby invented a mechanical knotter that used binder twine to bind the sheaves. Now, the whole process of cutting the grain and making sheaves had been mechanized. (The binder itself was still horse drawn, but it saved a huge amount of human muscle power.) Once the grain sheaves were bound, they were piled, head up, in stooks, so the grain would dry. At this point, there was another hitch in the harvesting process. The farmer had to get the grain off the field and threshed before fall rains, or even snow, ruined the crop.

Threshing, the most hectic and exciting time in a farm family's life, meant big machines and a gang of workers going at it from early morning to late night. Sometimes, farmers helped each other out by taking a team of horses and a wagon to help with a neighbor's threshing, and then having the neighbors help them with their teams and wagons. But, usually, they hired a whole threshing outfit — men and machines.

A few miles south of Edmonton, Alberta, a threshing gang takes a brief rest from its labors. Many members of these gangs came from eastern Canada on special CPR "harvest trains" to work the Western grain fields for a couple of dollars a day and keep.

The threshing crew were the five men who ran the threshing machine (separator plus steam engine). The gang were all the men who worked in the threshing operation.

162

The first crop in a new land. This farm family owed part of its success to a man called Charles Saunders. Although his only real interest in life was playing the flute, Saunders had been badgered by his father into accepting the position of Dominion Cerealist in 1903. In his work of improving Canadian grain and developing new varieties, he discovered a cross between Hard Red Calcutta and Red Fife wheats. He tested this on the government's experimental farm near Ottawa and found it gave a greater yield per bushel of seed, it was stronger and more disease-resistant, and most important for the prairie climate, it matured within 100 days. By 1920, about 90 per cent of all Canadian prairie wheat was this new variety — Marquis.

The threshers moved from farm to farm, sometimes with a big gang of men who worked on the stook-wagons that brought the grain to the separator, or threshing machine. (Only very rarely did farmers own their own separators.) The steam-driven threshing machine was a huge dinosaur-like affair, which gobbled the sheaves thrown into it and separated grain from straw, funnelling the grain into bins or wagons and spewing the straw out into stacks. It took a crew of five to operate the monster. There was the boss, who during the threshing season got little or no sleep; the separator man, who cunningly oiled the moving parts and seemed like a sorcerer to little children; the engineer, who was in charge of the steam engine; the fire-man, who was also the crew's alarm clock; and the tank-man, who had to make sure the steam engine always had enough water. (Sometimes the water had to be pumped from a river or slough.)

The fire-man started the threshing day, rising at four o'clock in the morning to "get up steam." The men started work early in the morning, but not before the women. They had to be up to feed the threshers, and the men ate like horses. A gang of twenty could eat six or seven dozen eggs for breakfast, together with mountains of potatoes and a loaf of bread per man. And the bread did not come factory-baked from the supermarket; it came fresh-baked by the farmer's wife. (And if the same twenty men had pie for dessert, she also had to bake eight or ten pies.) There was not much conversation around the table: if a person talked too much, he did not get enough to eat. Children usually ate with the farm women; it was a great day in a little boy's life when he could sit at the table and eat with the men.

Threshers got to know where the food was good. They would use lanterns and work far into the night, just to get away from a household where the cooking was bad. Work done, in the middle of the night they would move on to another farm, where they knew they could count on good cooking. The women might be gratified by such a compliment to

163

their cooking, but it was a mixed blessing, because it meant more work. And the women hated rain at harvest probably even more than the men, because it meant more potato-peeling and more cooking and more dishwashing, as the men waited to get back out to the fields.

Threshing was a long, hot, dirty, smelly job. The engine and separator crew got up early in the morning, worked all day, and dropped like stones into their beds at night (sometimes in a sleeping caboose attached behind the separator). Baths were few and far between, and by the end of a threshing season the crew were a grimy lot, and the dirt and odor of the caboose defied description.

Perhaps all the dirt and trouble and excitement were an inevitable part of the 1890s boom in agriculture. Western Canada was turning into a world granary, its first-class wheat taking over markets in Britain and Europe. Unfortunately, all the technological improvements in agriculture had not done a thing to control the weather. Grain growing was still a hazardous operation, particularly when early frosts destroyed a promising crop of wheat. Of all the kinds of wheat in Canada, the most popular was Red Fife. Although it was actually a Polish wheat, it had been promoted in Canada by a Scotsman called David Fife, who had a farm near Peterborough, Ontario. Red Fife, however, took too long to ripen to be completely dependable for the short Canadian prairie growing season. A new wheat was needed — one that would mature in one hundred days or less. And it was found when Red Fife was crossed with Hard Red Calcutta Wheat in 1892, although at first the new wheat went unnoticed. This was the wheat the prairie farmers needed, but more than ten years were to pass before it was "rediscovered." When the man — Charles Saunders — and the wheat — Marquis — finally connected, Canada was on its way to becoming one of the world's largest wheat producers.

One other aspect of western agriculture should be noted — the cattle ranching industry in southern Alberta. Reverend John McDougall and the NWMP had brought in a few cattle in the early 1870s, but ranching got its real start in the 1880s. Senator M. H. Cochrane of Quebec, a long-time cattle breeder and owner, established the Cochrane Ranche Company. In 1881, 12 000 head of cattle were driven north to Alberta from Montana. The first two years for the Cochrane Ranche were almost a disaster. Bad treatment on the drive north and hard Alberta winters had killed all but 4000 of Cochrane's original herd. Slowly, however, from this small start, ranching became established in southern Alberta.

The early days of ranching were uncertain, as they can be today. There was always the question of whether the warm Chinook wind would come in January and melt the snow so that the cattle could feed on the range. (In 1886, the Chinook failed, and in spring dead cattle lay everywhere.) There was the question of what breed of cattle was best for the West. (The answer came in the white-faced Herefords, still the symbol of western ranching.) And there was the hard life on the range, which bred its own kind of uncertainty — and humor. A man called

In 1911, at the New York Land show, Marquis won top prize as the best wheat in North America.

It has been estimated that by the 1920s Marquis wheat was contributing an extra $100 million to prairie farm income annually.

The "Big Four" ranchers were George Lane, Pat Burns, A. E. Cross, and John Ware.

164

In the 1870s and 1880s, the HBC brought furs out of the North-West Territories by employing trackers to pull scows up the Athabasca River. The fur bales were eventually loaded on wagons and taken to the nearest railhead, Calgary. By the 1890s, marine engines had been hauled into the Territories by wagon and scow, and steamboats had been built for service on the Athabasca and Mackenzie rivers.

Kamoose Taylor opened the Macleod Hotel in Fort Macleod and posted these "Rules and Regulations" for his guests:

> "Spiked boots and spurs must be removed at night before retiring."
> "Towels changed weekly. Insect powder for sale at the bar."
> "A deposit must be made before towels, soap or candles can be carried to rooms. When boarders are leaving, a rebate will be made on all the candles or parts of candles not burned or eaten."
> "No kicking regarding the quality or quantity of meals will be allowed; those who do not like the provender will get out, or be put out."
> "To attract attention of bell boy or waiters, shoot a hole through the door panel. Two shots for ice water, three for a deck of cards, and so on."
> "All guests are requested to rise at 6 a.m. This is imperative as the sheets are needed for tablecloths."

*   *   *

With all this progress in agriculture and the revolutionary changes in technology, the 1890s and early 1900s wrought a major transformation in Canadian life. How did the new government of Wilfrid Laurier meet the challenge of leading this changing Canada?

STUDY 5

1. Summarize your understanding of the meaning of technology.
2. Turn a map of North America so that west is at the top. Draw a sketch map of this view of the continent.
   (a) Which city is in a better position to tap the interior of the continent — Montreal or New York?
   (b) Why did the Grand Trunk seek a terminus at Portland?
   (c) With which eastern United States railways did the Grand Trunk have to compete?
   (d) Mark on your map two U.S. transcontinental railroads (with, if possible, their dates of completion).
   (e) What is the importance of Chicago in North American railway networks?
   (f) What did the completion of the United States transcontinentals mean for Canadian railway building?
3. In the late nineteenth century, what other technologies could Canada have used to tie the country together?
4. Talk to someone who can remember what it was like to live in a world of horses. What were horses used for? What were their advantages and disadvantages?
5. Ask your parents (or grandparents) about their first experiences with (a) electricity (b) telephone (c) radio and (d) television. Compare the dates you gather with your classmates. How do you explain the differences in dates?
6. Why, in your opinion, did Reginald Fessenden not receive the public recognition given Guglielmo Marconi?
7. Grain farming remains one of the most important elements in the Canadian economy, so it might be helpful to check out the meaning of these words: sowing (and broadcasting); reaping; gleaning; flailing and winnowing; binder and binder twine; threshing.
8. What breeds of cattle were successful in western Canada?
9. Try to determine how many hectares are required to raise one cattle-beast (a) in Alberta and (b) in eastern Canada. Explain the difference. What does this mean for the size of a ranch in Alberta and a farm in, for example, Ontario?
10. Outline a day in the life of a Canadian farm family in the 1890s. How does it differ (a) from the life of a farm family today and (b) from your own daily schedule?
11. Why would you like to live in Canada in the 1890s? Would you rather live in Canada today? Why?
12. Choose from this chapter the technological development that you think has most significantly affected the Canadian environment. Explain your choice.

unit 2

Crisis and Change

the Laurier Years: 1896–1911

In August 1896, George Washington Carmack arrived at the NWMP post in the town of Fortymile in the Yukon Territory. Carmack was excited. He and two Indian companions, Skookum Jim and Tagish Charlie, had just discovered a rich stretch of gold-bearing gravel in Rabbit Creek — later renamed, appropriately, Bonanza Creek — a tiny tributary of the Klondike River. After staking out a 300-metre claim, he had rushed to the police post to register his find. This was the beginning of the Klondike Gold Rush. By the summer of 1897, the word had begun to leak out, and a number of gold-seekers reached the area. But it was not until 1898 that the largest wave of all hit the Yukon. From all parts of the world came men and women, lured to the Canadian north by the fantastic dream of chancing upon the rich mother lode. Week after week, boatloads of enthusiastic adventurers entered the Lynn Canal, a long inlet on the north Pacific coast. Their destination was Dawson City, a frontier shanty town at the mouth of the Klondike River that grew in a couple of years into a city of 30 000.

A few lucky ones found gold. Some, like the unfortunate sourdough in Robert Service's poem "The Cremation of Sam McGee," perished in the frigid Yukon wilderness. Others, like Service's "Dangerous Dan McGrew," were unable to resist the fatal attraction of cards, whisky, and women in the gambling dens. Fortunately, compared to San Francisco during the California Gold Rush of 1848, there was little crime and violence in Dawson City. In Canada, the law reached the frontier in advance of settlement. A NWMP detachment was waiting for the rush of prospectors in 1898.

The "Trail of '98" was littered with tales of tragedy and heroism, greed and selflessness. Through the verses of the Canadian poet Robert Service and the short stories of the American writer Jack London, the whole world heard about the fabulous Klondike. But there was more glamor than gold in the Yukon. After reaching their production peak in 1903, the mines rapidly declined. Within a few years, Dawson City was once again a small town.

A LIBERAL PRIME MINISTER

The Carmack discovery took place just three days before Wilfrid Laurier entered the House of Commons for the first time as prime minister. Two years later, at the height of the gold rush, Laurier faced his first serious

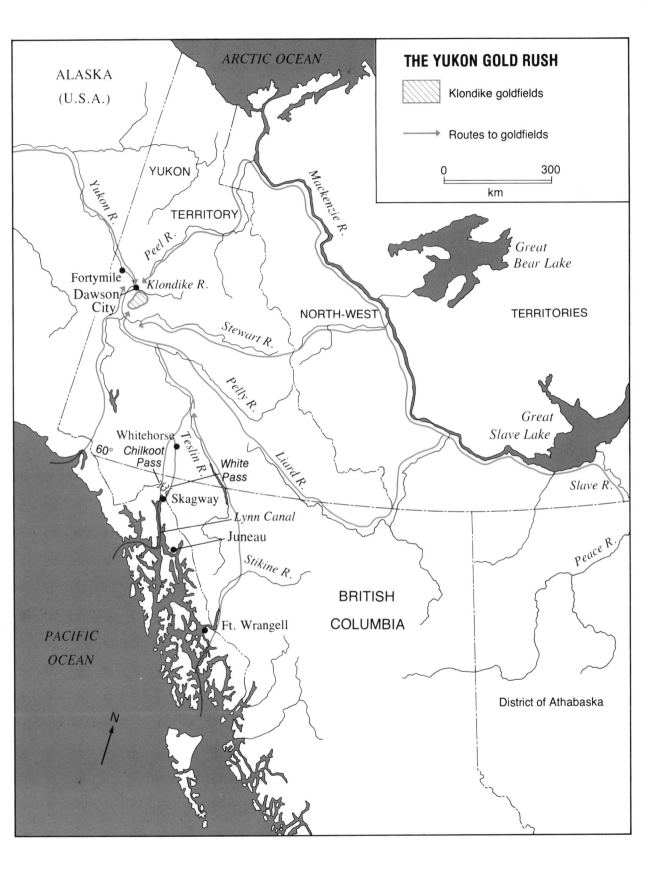

Klondike goldfields

Routes to goldfields

0   300
km

ALASKA
(U.S.A.)

ARCTIC OCEAN

YUKON

TERRITORY

Yukon R.

Peel R.

Mackenzie R.

Great Bear Lake

Fortymile
Dawson City

Klondike R.

Stewart R.

NORTH-WEST

TERRITORIES

Pelly R.

Whitehorse
60°
Chilkoot Pass

Teslin R.

White Pass

Liard R.

Great Slave Lake

Slave R.

Skagway

Lynn Canal

Juneau

Stikine R.

BRITISH

COLUMBIA

Peace R.

Ft. Wrangell

PACIFIC OCEAN

N

District of Athabaska

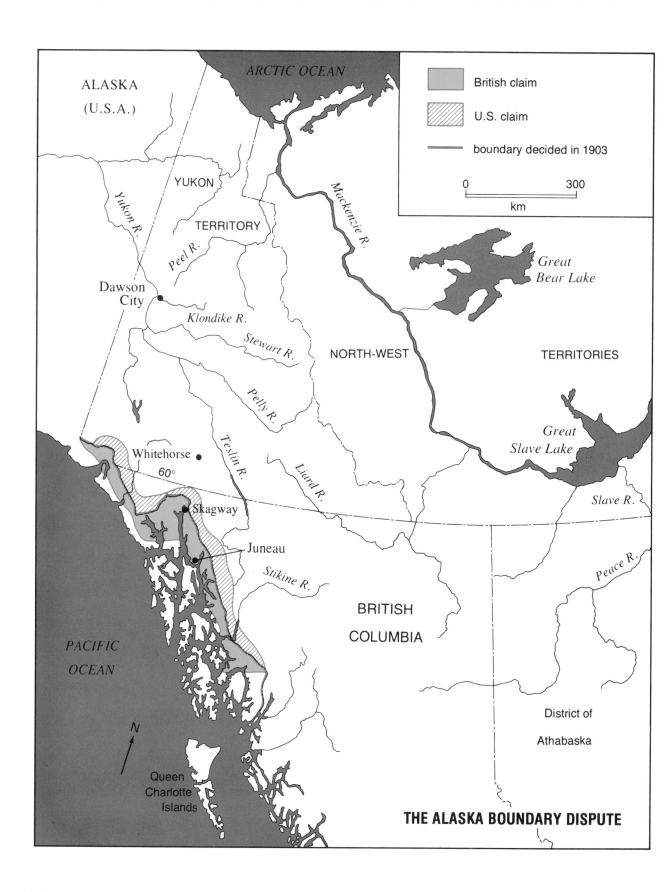

THE ALASKA BOUNDARY DISPUTE

FROM Nº 8 EL DORADO.
PROPERTY OF CHAS. LAMB.
VALUE $315⁰⁰

SCHMIDT L. & LITH CO. S.F.

DISCOVERER.
GEO. W. CARMACK

THE LARGEST GOLD NUGGET.
FOUND IN EL DORADO CREEK Nº 35 BY M KNUSTON
WEIGHT 35 OUNCES VALUE $530⁰⁰

courtesy of Canadian Pacific

The April 1, 1898, issue of The Klondike News, *published in Dawson, N. W. T., framed George Washington Carmack between the silhouettes of two massive gold nuggets. The one on the left was valued at $315 and that on the right, weighing 1000 g, at $530.*

problem in foreign relations. The United States had purchased Alaska from the Russians in 1867. For years there had been disagreement between Canada and the United States over the border that separated southern Alaska and the neighboring Yukon Territory. The exact location of the border between Canada and the Alaska Panhandle, a narrow strip of land stretching southward along the Pacific Coast, had never been settled. And nobody seemed to know or care until the sudden rush of prospectors into the disputed area. Were they crossing Canadian or American soil? Which country had the right to police the gold route? Before tempers broke, Great Britain convinced the two disputing nations to let a tribunal (a court) decide the matter. Britain and the United States would each name three members, all of them guaranteed to be "impartial jurists of the highest repute."

Of the three members representing Canada, two were Canadian and one, Lord Alverstone, was the Lord Chief Justice of England. After months of examining maps and listening to arguments, the six men agreed to vote. Lord Alverstone cast his ballot with the Americans. He reasoned that the Americans had a better claim, both historically and

The Canadian members were Sir Louis A. Jetté, lieutenant-governor of Quebec, and A. B. Aylesworth, a Toronto lawyer.

171

legally. However, the Canadian delegates felt betrayed and refused to sign the agreement, which, in 1903, drew the boundary through the Alaska Panhandle on a line that was very close to the one demanded by the Americans. Their refusal was supported by most Canadians, who felt, in Sir Charles Tupper's words, that "The whole course of British negotiations with the United States is marked with a line of gravestones under which Canadian rights are buried."

When he took office, Laurier's most pressing problem was the issue that had dominated his election campaign in 1896. He had promised to use the "sunny ways" of conciliation to solve the religious and language conflict in the Manitoba Schools Question. By the end of that year he had worked out the details of an agreement with the provincial government. This laid down that only a single public school system would be allowed, but any religion could be taught by any denomination in Manitoba classrooms at the end of the regular school day. When there were at least ten pupils whose language was French, a bilingual teacher would be provided. As a compromise, the agreement had the usual effect; it antagonized both sides in the dispute. In particular, the Roman Catholic bishops in Quebec were extremely upset. Only when the Pope sent a special representative to Quebec to talk the matter over with them did they grudgingly accept the decision.

For background information on the Manitoba Schools Question, see pp. 131-132 and 139-140.

Laurier was greatly impressed by the chief spokesman for the Manitoba government during the negotiations on schools and schooling. He was Clifford Sifton, a determined and successful lawyer who was convinced that Canada was one of the last lands of opportunity in the world. He had learned this through personal experience: shrewd real-estate ventures had made him a wealthy man. He had entered Manitoba politics as a Liberal, winning a seat in the provincial election of 1888. Recognized for his administrative skills, he soon became an important politician who took the lead in defending his government's position on the Manitoba Schools Question. Laurier offered and Sifton accepted the position of minister of the interior in the Liberal cabinet.

Clifford Sifton, 1861-1929

The choice was ideal for Laurier and the Liberal Party, for Sifton, and for Canada. Sifton helped to make wheat king of the Canadian economy. From a total production of roughly 220 000 tonnes in 1896, it jumped to just over 700 000 tonnes in 1901, then skyrocketed to just over 2 000 000 in 1911. By 1914, even with the impressive output of industry, wheat accounted for one-third of the value of all Canadian exports. And the way Sifton did this was by opening Canada's western lands to massive settlement.

"THE LAST, BEST WEST"

Between 1901 and 1911, Canada's population rose from 5 371 000 to 7 204 527, an increase of 35 per cent. This phenomenal growth was

172

FREE FARMS FOR THE MILLION

DOMINION OF CANADA

EXPERIMENTAL FARM, BRANDON, MANITOBA, CANADA.

EXPERIMENTAL FARM, INDIAN HEAD, NORTH WEST TERRITORY

RED RIVER VALLEY.
Saskatchewan Valley,
THE GREAT FERTILE PLAINS
and British Columbia
CONTAIN
LARGE AREAS SUITABLE FOR GRAINS OR GRASSES

VAST MINERAL RICHES
GOLD, SILVER, IRON, COPPER, SALT, PETROLEUM, ETC. ETC.

Immense Coal Fields,
ILLIMITABLE SUPPLY OF CHEAP FUEL.

Railway from Ocean to Ocean.

SEE REPORTS OF BRITISH TENANT FARMERS WHO VISITED CANADA IN 1890.

CLIMATE THE HEALTHIEST IN THE WORLD.

CANADA HAS 5 Experimental Farms
representative of the whole settled area of the Dominion, instituted for the advancement of Agriculture.

CENTRAL EXPERIMENTAL FARM, OTTAWA, CANADA.

EXPERIMENTAL FARM, NAPPAN, NOVA SCOTIA.

EXPERIMENTAL FARM, AGASSIZ, BRITISH COLUMBIA.

FREE FARMS OF 160 ACRES
Given to every Male Adult of 18 years and over, in the great Fertile Belt of
MANITOBA, CANADIAN NORTH-WEST AND BRITISH COLUMBIA
Deep soil, well watered, wooded, and richest in the world—easily reached by railroads. Wheat—average 30 bushels to the acre, with fair farming.
VAST COAL FIELDS AT CONVENIENT DISTANCES.
GRANTS FROM 100 TO 200 ACRES ARE OFFERED IN OTHER PARTS OF CANADA.
Further and full information, in pamphlets and maps, given free on application by letter (within the Dominion, post free.) addressed—
Or to HIGH COMMISSIONER FOR CANADA,
17 Victoria Street, London, S.W., England.
DEPARTMENT OF THE INTERIOR,
OTTAWA, CANADA.

The Public Archives of Canada, C 63478

This government advertisement, widely circulated in farming districts in Great Britain, offered quarter sections of free land "in the great Fertile Belt of Manitoba, Canadian North-West and British Columbia." It listed various other attractions: "Deep soil, well watered, wooded, and richest in the world — easily reached by railroads"; "Wheat — average 30 bushels to the acre, with fair farming"; "Canada has 5 Experimental Farms . . . instituted for the advancement of Agriculture"; and "Grants from 100 to 200 acres are offered in other parts of Canada."

caused by immigration. In 1896, it was a mere trickle — 17 000 immigrants. By 1900, an almost endless stream of people was flowing into Canada from the United States and Europe. By 1911, immigrants were arriving at an average rate of 1100 a day. Most of them were lured to Canada by the government's offer of free western land — a quarter section (sixty-five hectares) — and an option to purchase an additional sixty-five hectares at a very low price. The only condition was that the immigrant live on the land and develop it for three years. At the end of

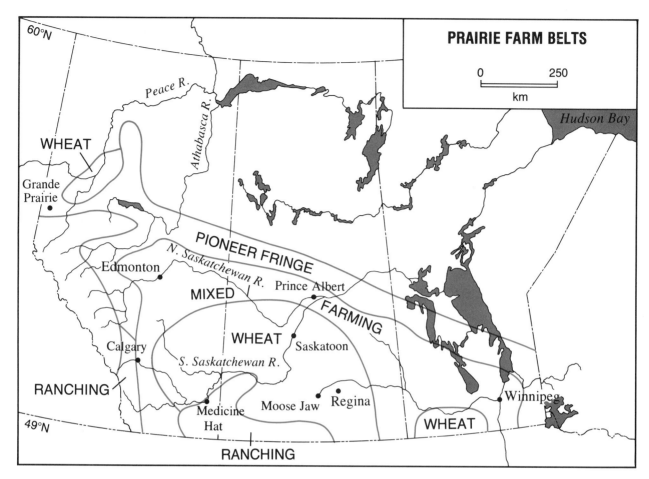

PRAIRIE FARM BELTS

0 ————— 250
km

that time, by agreeing to become a British subject, he or she could secure title to the property.

The policy of granting free land to immigrants had been established by the Macdonald government in the Dominion Lands Act (1872). Until the Liberals came to power, there had been few takers. The worldwide depression years of the 1870s, 1880s, and 1890s had reduced the number of immigrants crossing the Atlantic. Most of those who did decided to settle in the American West. But, by 1896, the productive land west of the Mississippi had been taken up and the American frontier had been closed. Sifton realized that he could turn the closing of the American frontier to Canada's advantage. To the landless masses of Europe and Great Britain living in poverty and to those who rejected religious or political domination, North America would seem like a paradise. Sifton intended to dip into this human reservoir to find the people to fill the prairies. But he was not prepared to open the immigration gates to all. The minister of the interior had his own very clear definition of the ideal settler. He or she must have had farming experience, be willing to work, eager to save and, above all, be hardy. It would also be useful for the settler to enter Canada with some money because the land was the only government help he or she would receive. Yet certain purchases were essential: a team of horses ($250), a wagon ($30), and a plough ($20). In addition, settlers needed a cow, a few pigs and chickens, and such implements as hoes and shovels.

The land was there, hundreds of thousands of hectares of arable soil. The problem was to encourage the "right" people to come to Canada to take possession of it. To do this, Sifton was prepared to spend money, and in the best North American tradition this meant promotion and advertising. During his ministry (1897-1905), millions of pamphlets were distributed throughout the United States, Great Britain, and Europe. Their titles varied — "The Wondrous West," "The Last, Best West," "Land of Opportunity" — but their purpose was always the same. They were designed to sell Canada to the world. In glowing terms they described the land, the opportunities, and the conditions of entry. There was, of course, an occasional tendency to exaggerate, as in this verse from a poem, "The Land of the Sugar Maple Tree," which was reproduced in a pamphlet entitled, "The Last West: The Latest Gift of the Lady Bountiful":

> Oh we are a mighty nation
> And prolific with wheat kings,
> We are filled with jubilation
> That wealth and comfort brings.

Sifton made a point of sending agents to open offices in several American states where many Canadians who had left their native land during the dreary 1870s and 1880s had set up homesteads. The idea of selling at high prices property they had once bought cheaply appealed to large numbers of them and to their American neighbors. In this way, several hundred thousand Americans came to Canada. And they made good settlers. They were already familiar with the language, business methods, agricultural techniques, and soil conditions. Sifton reasoned that they would have little trouble adapting to life north of the 49th parallel. He welcomed them. Other Canadians were not so sure, as this satirical verse from the *Grain Growers' Guide* in 1911 suggests:

> The Yankees in the land abound
> For Uncle Sam gets all around.
> And with his push and grit and go
> Is sure to make the country grow.

Americans and former Canadians may have been rather easy to entice to the prairies because of the relatively short distance that separated them from the new promised land. Britons needed even less prodding. A few may have come to counter the wave of American immigrants and keep Canada British, but most of them were escaping from crowded cities, poor-paying jobs, or the ranks of the many unemployed. They responded to an intense propaganda campaign that Canadian government officials launched from their main office in London. In addition to pamphlets mailed to adults, medals were offered to school children for

175

the best essays on Canada; wall maps of the Dominion were donated to thousands of classrooms. One of the many promotion efforts was a horse-drawn wagon, painted in brightest red, which toured the British Isles. The wagon was two-tiered. On the first level was a display of Canadian fruits preserved in alcohol-filled bottles. Above it were samples of various cereals, wild grasses, and stuffed prairie chickens. It must have looked like something from a Buffalo Bill Wild West Show or a Barnum and Bailey Circus, yet wide-eyed Britons were obviously attracted to it and other showpieces used by Sifton's agents. During the Laurier years, almost a million English and Scots people migrated from Britain to Canada.

Sifton's search for immigrants from continental Europe was sometimes difficult because many European governments were opposed to emigration. To get around this, Sifton made a secret arrangement with the North Atlantic Trading Company, an organization of German steamship agents. It was their job to persuade immigrants to come to Canada. For each new arrival on Canadian soil, an agent was paid a commission by the ministry of the interior.

The result was that tens of thousands of hopeful settlers came from central Europe, mostly from Russia and the Austro-Hungarian Empire, a hodge-podge of ethnic groups, languages, religions, and social customs. At Quebec City and Montreal, bewildered immigration officials recorded little-known groups of newcomers: Ruthenian, Galician, Serbian, Croatian, Bulgarian, and Bukovinian.

Of a total of about 600 000 immigrants from central and eastern Europe, the most numerous were the Galicians, Ruthenians, and Bukovinians, who are generally grouped as Ukrainian. Most of the more

Using a method that was very common in their Russian homeland, Doukhobor women team up to haul a plough through the tough prairie sod.

Provincial Archives of Alberta

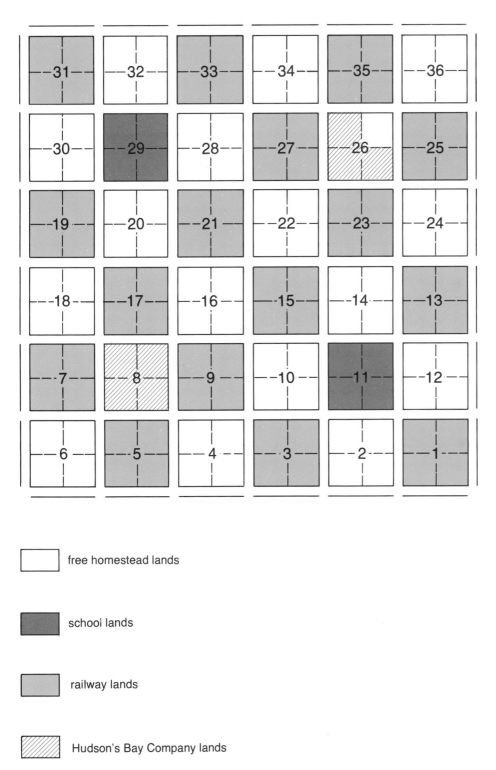

31	32	33	34	35	36
30	29	28	27	26	25
19	20	21	22	23	24
18	17	16	15	14	13
7	8	9	10	11	12
6	5	4	3	2	1

Beginning in 1871, the rectangular survey system was used to divide prairie land into square-mile sections and then into quarter sections of 160 acres each. Thirty-six square-mile sections made up a township.

In every township, Sections 11 and 29 were sold by auction to raise money for education; Section 8 and three-quarters of Section 26 (the whole of 26 in every fifth township) were given to the HBC. In many townships, the odd-numbered sections were land grants made to encourage railway building. In the case of the CPR, for instance, the railway had the right to claim (and then sell) the odd-numbered sections in townships lying in a belt 24 miles on either side of the main line between Winnipeg and the Rockies.

Every mile in each township allowance was made for roads running east-west and, every two miles, for roads running north-south.

- ☐ free homestead lands

- ■ school lands

- ▨ railway lands

- ▨ Hudson's Bay Company lands

A TYPICAL PRAIRIE TOWNSHIP

Immigrant families — wives and mothers, in particular — learned to cope with deplorable living conditions. This one-room tenement in Manitoba shows the typical home of the urban poor in the early years of the twentieth century.

than 100 000 Ukrainians who arrived during the Laurier era were prime examples of Sifton's famous statement of the type of people needed to seed and harvest the West:

> I think a stalwart peasant in a sheepskin coat, born on the soil, whose forefathers have been farmers for ten generations, with a stout wife and a half-dozen children, is good quality.

Although many of them settled in blocs in remote rural regions, where they opened up undeveloped farmland, others moved into cities such as Winnipeg. Here, they soon found flaws in the promised land. They had to accept poorly-paid jobs as unskilled laborers and were obliged to live in crowded, unsanitary rooming houses. Many of the newcomers from Europe were subjected to the abuse of Canadians, who resented their foreign dress, language, and customs. In schools, immigrant children were sometimes ridiculed or set upon by their fellow students. Parents had to suffer the indifference, contempt, or hostility of storekeepers, co-workers, and neighbors. The result was the formation of ghettos — whole neighborhoods where persons of a particular ethnic group congregated.

One Canadian, a Methodist minister named J. S. Woodsworth, was alarmed by the spread of ethnic prejudice. In his position as superintendent of the All Peoples' Mission in Winnipeg, he worked with immigrants, learned their problems, and tried to help them adjust to their new life. In his book *Strangers Within Our Gates*, he describes the reaction of the average Canadian to the "foreigners":

> . . . he thinks of them as the men who dig the sewers and get into trouble at the police court. They are all supposed to dress in outlandish garb, to speak a barbarian tongue, and to smell abominably.

There was little attempt to hide the unfriendly feeling that greeted many immigrants. Ethnic prejudice was expressed openly, even in the House of Commons, where one Member of Parliament angrily complained that "Canada is today the dumping ground for the refuse of every country in the world."

If some Europeans were refused jobs or physically attacked, this was mild compared to the treatment given many Asiatics. During the construction of the CPR, Chinese laborers had been brought to British Columbia. They were hard workers, rarely got in trouble with the law and, because they had little choice, often worked for low wages. As more Chinese, and then Japanese, began to arrive in the province, feeling against them grew. Giving in to this popular prejudice, Parliament passed a law in 1903 that imposed a tax of $500 on each Chinese immigrant. Typical of the attitude of the times was a statement made by R. B. Bennett, a lawyer-politician who later became prime minister of Canada: "We must not allow our shores to be overrun by Asiatics, and become dominated by an alien race. British Columbia must remain a white man's country."

THE BOOM IN MINING AND LUMBERING

The rapid growth of the Canadian West was only one of the sweeping changes taking place during the Laurier years. They came at the end of more than two decades of near economic stagnation. Indeed, just as Laurier entered office, world economic conditions began to change. International trade picked up, and Canadian raw materials were in demand. As jobs became available, prosperity replaced depression. Pessimism gradually disappeared as faith in Canada's future returned. Noting this rebirth of confidence, Laurier expressed it in very optimistic terms: "The nineteenth century was the century of the United States; the twentieth century will be the century of Canada."

The bustle and vigor in Canada at the turn of the century seemed to justify Laurier's boast. One of the most visible signs of the economic upturn was railway expansion. When the first wave of immigrants arrived in Canada, the CPR was the only railway link with the West. A few years later, Mackenzie and Mann's Canadian Northern Railway had

For details, see
pp. 148-151.

linked the northern prairies with Lake Superior. Some years later still, the Canadian Northern and the Grand Trunk were engaged in a race to see who would be the first to lay rails all the way to the Pacific. Some people thought the prime minister mad to allow all this construction, some of which was paid for by funds from both federal and provincial governments. But in the election of 1904, most Canadians seemed to agree with Laurier's reply to his critics: "We cannot wait because time does not wait. We cannot wait because in these days of wonderful development, time lost is doubly lost."

Fanning out from the new rail lines like rivulets from a river in flood were hundreds of branch lines. They linked formerly out-of-the-way towns to large cities and transported products and passengers to communities that mushroomed along the routes. It was during the construction of one of these lines, the Temiskaming and Northern Ontario Railway (T.N.O.), that a man threw a hammer aimed at a fox, hit a rock instead, and put Cobalt on the map of Ontario. Alfred La Rose, a blacksmith employed by the T.N.O., bent over to examine a strangely colored piece of rock dislodged by his hammer. The rock was a hunk of rich silver ore.

It was impossible to conceal the good news. Within a short time, an army of excited prospectors was hacking a way through the thick pine forests to stake out claims. Unlike La Rose, most of the prospectors returned empty-handed and dispirited. Only a handful were lucky enough to strike it rich. The profits eventually realized from this rich lode of silver were huge. They went, not to the prospectors who had forged the way, but to a small group of investors in Toronto and Montreal. These financiers had put up the capital to form several mining corporations that bought out the claim holders.

Cobalt was founded shortly after La Rose's discovery in 1903.

Placer mining was a method of recovering minerals — notably gold — from deposits of sand and gravel. The inside of the sluice box was lined with corduroy or some such ridged material, to which minerals stuck as the water drained through the box.

The Department of Mines and Petroleum Resources, British Columbia

In the long run, the profits from silver were dwarfed by those from copper and nickel. Twenty years earlier, dynamite blasts that cleared a roadbed for the CPR had uncovered an immense lode of copper near the modern town of Sudbury, Ontario. Careful examination of the ore revealed that the copper was mixed with nickel. At the time, there were few uses for nickel and no one knew how to separate it from the copper. By the beginning of the twentieth century, scientists had found such a technique — and also an important use for nickel. It was valuable for toughening steel, particularly the steel from which was made the armor plate on the battleships of European navies and the artillery shells used by European armies. International demand for nickel renewed interest in the copper-nickel mine. By the time of La Rose's silver find, Sudbury was on its way to becoming the "Nickel Capital" of the world. Eventually, Canadian mines would produce 90 per cent of the world's supply of nickel.

During the Laurier years, minerals were discovered in several parts of the nation: silver, lead, and zinc in the Kootenay region of British Columbia; coal in Alberta and Nova Scotia; and asbestos and cement in Quebec. But it was Ontario with its gold, silver, nickel, and copper mines that led both in variety and amount. Nearly one-half of the total Canadian profits from mining came from this province.

Mining was an expensive business. Large amounts of money were needed to locate productive ore-bearing sites, to purchase machinery for extraction and refining, and to pay for labor and transportation. Lumbering, one of the earliest industries in British North America, was less costly. And it proved to be a very profitable enterprise for lumber companies.

In the first decade of the twentieth century, the most valuable timber came from the white pine. The forests of New Brunswick had been stripped of most of their great stands of this species of pine, but there were still thousands of square kilometres of these trees in northern Quebec and northern Ontario. Before the outbreak of the First World War, the saw and axe had felled the finest of them. Small mountains of sawdust rimmed lake shores and bays, all that remained of the trees that helped to build the growing cities of Quebec and Ontario.

The forests of Ontario, Quebec, and New Brunswick yielded valuable pulpwood. Many of the rivers of these three provinces were clogged with hemlock and spruce booms heading to the pulp-and-paper mills. Eager to meet the mammoth demands of the American market for newsprint, the pulp-and-paper industry grew at a spectacular rate. By 1910, Canada had become the world's leading exporter of newsprint.

The spread of western settlement was a boon to the lumber industry in British Columbia, which attacked the vast forests of Douglas fir, spruce, and cedar that covered the Pacific slopes. It also supplied an expanding market in the Orient and in the United States. This, of course, was the age of wood: poles were needed for telegraph, hydro,

The Royal Navy used New Brunswick pine and oak for the masts and hulls of many of its ships during the Napoleonic Wars.

Many of the pulpwood forests were near rivers from whose falls came the electrical power to drive the machinery in the paper mills.

and telephone lines; ties for railways; and props and beams for mine shafts and buildings. Sawn lumber was in great demand for houses, roofs, flooring, and furniture.

Timber and pulp-and-paper companies boosted the Canadian economy by bringing into the country much needed capital investment, which produced employment for Canadian workers. But lumber companies often acted irresponsibly. Little or no attempt was made to plant new trees to replace those cut down and carted away. And there was considerable waste. Since these companies cut down trees of all sizes, they often discarded the smallest and these, together with the trimmings of larger trees, were left in heaps of slash.

THE TARIFF ISSUE

The election of Laurier in 1896 coincided with the gradual return of good times. The causes lay beyond the borders of Canada. Since the early 1870s, the world economy had flip-flopped from recession to mild recovery and back again to recession. During the 1890s, a trend developed toward steady recovery. One sign of this was a revival of world trade. Nations in Europe and the United States began to purchase raw materials from Africa, Asia, South America, and Canada. Britain, France, Germany, and the United States bought huge quantities of Canadian wheat, lumber, pulp and paper, nickel, copper, zinc, gold, and silver.

Every nation sells its products to two different sets of customers: those in the domestic or national market and those in foreign markets. Canada's small population does not provide a large enough domestic market to maintain many industries. To survive, these industries have had to export their products to other countries. There are, broadly, two main types of industry. *Primary industry* produces the raw materials that come from natural resources, for example, timber and minerals. *Secondary industry* processes or refines the raw materials into semi-finished goods (lumber, steel) or finished products (furniture, stoves). Each stage in the production of goods requires workers and materials. So, secondary industry provides more jobs than primary industry, and the finished goods it produces cost more than raw materials or semi-finished products. For these reasons, the development of secondary industry is important in the growth of a country. At the turn of the twentieth century, Canada had fewer secondary than primary industries. Many of the finished products sold in Canada were imported from abroad, chiefly from Great Britain and the United States. Foreign manufacturers were buying cheap raw materials in Canada and selling them back to Canadians in the form of high-priced manufactured products. Unless more Canadian businessmen took the risk of investing their money in the manufacture of furniture, clothing, shoes, and other types of finished goods, Canadians would be compelled to buy many foreign-made goods.

13G6149. Boy's Sailor Suit, made from a splendid quality of soft fin- shed mported serge in navy blue, which will keep its color. The blouse is made neat fitting, with arge sailor collar, trimmed with white braid, and shield in front. Pants have plain bottoms, and ined throughout. This is a splendid wearing suit, and looks dressy. To fit boys 3 to 8 years. State age of boy. Price.. **2.00**

40-7590. Child's Coat of Im- ported Cheviot, loose fitting box back; fancy shaped collar of self material trimmed with con- trasting shade; patch pockets and shaped cuffs trimmed to match collar; unlined. Navy or red: 4 years, **2.50**; 6 years, **2.75**; 8 years, **3.00**; 10 years, **3.25**; 12 years, **3.50**.

Women's "Eatonia" Comfortable Low Heel 3.00

20B141. Made from fine import- ed Dongola kid, Goodyear welt- ed soles, low broad heel, patent tip, dull kid top, Blucher cut.

Sizes 2½ to 7.

3.00

Be sure to give size wanted.

3.00

The Superior Electric Iron is neatly finished and con- venient to handle. The ironing face is heavily plat- ed giving a smooth working surface. Heat is evenly distributed over the entire working surface, even the point being always hot. The Superior Iron comes neatly packed in a box, complete with grooved stand and six foot attachment cord with spring coil to take up slack. Price, complete .... **4.50** This iron can be used on voltages ranging from 105 to 114.

CARPET SWEEPERS

26G572. EATONIA Ball-Bearing Carpet Sweeper. The newest improved Sweeper manufactured, perfect in every detail, oak, mahogany or walnut finish. Fitted with best quality brush and new improved iron screw handle, japanned trimmings, each **3.00**

26G573. Bissell's Sweepers, according to grade, each **2.00 3.50 4.00**

In the early years of the twentieth century, when most Canadians lived on farms or in small towns and did not travel far beyond their community, Eaton's Catalogue brought a whole department store onto every kitchen table. The catalogue provided more than a commercial service. It helped immigrants learn how to read. It gave people in remote settlements contact with the "outside world" by showing them what "folks" were wearing and what appliances they were using. And when it had performed all these services, the catalogue still had one last use in the outhouse.

There had always been some secondary industry in Canada. Even before Confederation, there were textile mills, shoe factories, and furni- ture companies, some of which employed several hundred employees. Yet, as late as 1900, the average Canadian factory employed few more than five workers. These small industries were at the mercy of manufac- turing giants in the United States and in Great Britain, which could produce and sell goods more cheaply than Canadians could. Since John A. Macdonald's time, the Conservative Party had used the protective tariff as the keystone of its National Policy. As a result, manufacturers and most factory workers, whose jobs were made possible by the tariff, generally supported the Conservatives at election time.

Every Canadian had some reason to love or hate the tariff, but the

For the tariff and National Policy, see pp. 79-81.

For information on tariffs, see pp. 48-49.

strongest opposition came from the farmers, because the tariff forced them to pay high prices for agricultural tools and machinery and many other necessities made in Canada. They complained that the tariff led to inefficiency and high costs. If manufacturers could count on the protection of the tariff, they could afford to be careless in the manufacture of their product. If, instead, they were forced to compete with foreign manufactures, they would have to find ways to produce more efficiently, and thus more cheaply. Farmers bitterly complained that the tariff was, in effect, a subsidy to Canadian industry. Not surprisingly, most of them supported the Liberal Party, which for years had promised to eliminate many tariffs and lower others if elected to office.

By 1896, the Liberals had been beaten too many times at the polls on the tariff issue. Although they still advocated freer trade (lowering but not eliminating tariffs), they no longer talked about unrestricted reciprocity. With the exception of a few minor changes in certain tariffs, Finance Minister W. S. Fielding's first budget in 1897 made it clear that the Liberals had decided to maintain their opponents' National Policy.

For the next dozen years, Laurier's tariff policy assured him the support of Canadian business leaders. There were periodic rumblings of discontent among farmers, who resented what they regarded as Liberal treachery, but his economic policy was never seriously challenged. Even the farmers' complaints were muted in the summer of 1910, when Laurier made his first extensive tour of the Prairie Provinces. (Western wheat, other grains, and meat were selling in enormous amounts in Europe.) It was a triumphal trip for the Liberal leader. At whistle stop after whistle stop, he was greeted by hundreds of smiling, flag-waving people who had come long distances on country trails to see and listen to the tall, always elegantly dressed gentleman with the handsome mane of silver hair and the courteous, gentle voice. The prime minister's train pulled in to numerous towns that had been founded because of his immigration policy and had prospered because of his economic policy. Laurier was at the height of his career.

Among the crowds at railway stations in towns and cities were delegations of farmers, who politely handed Laurier petitions demanding tariff reductions. The requests were less surprising than the number of them and their degree of opposition to Liberal policy. To prove their determination, nearly one thousand western farmers marched into the House of Commons just before Christmas that year to present a lengthy petition to the government. Its message was simple: lower tariffs or lose votes. (It also listed other complaints, particularly the high railway freight rates and the fees charged by grain elevator storage companies, all of which reduced the profits on wheat sold overseas.) Why not eliminate all tariffs, Canadian and American? Then, wheat could be easily sent across a border behind which growing American cities needed the cheap bread made from Canadian wheat.

At this point, fate seemed to favor Laurier. In October, President Taft of the United States had proposed a total review of Canadian-American trade policy. The suggestion was unmistakable, if surprising. Americans, like Canadians, had for many years been protected by a high tariff wall, but they now might well tear it down. Laurier did not hesitate. Early in 1911, Fielding led a Canadian delegation to Washington to discuss terms, which turned out to be much more favorable than Laurier had dared to hope for. The United States proposed that the natural products of agriculture, forestry, fisheries, and mining be allowed to cross the international boundary duty-free. And tariffs on a number of manufactured goods would be lowered.

The Liberals moved quickly to accept the American offer, which met exactly the demands of the representatives of the grain growers' associations who had invaded the Commons. They expected some opposition from business but felt they could overcome it. After all, there would still be tariffs, though somewhat reduced, on American manufactured goods. When Laurier proudly announced the proposed reciprocity agreement in the House of Commons, the Conservative opposition was stunned. Tory Members of Parliament from the West were especially caught off balance. How could they oppose a policy so desperately wanted by their constitutents?

NATIONALISM

Swift passage of the bill to reduce Canadian-American trade barriers was important to Laurier, especially in 1910-1911. But another equally serious problem, Anglophone-Francophone relations, was threatening

In 1902, in honor of the coronation of King Edward VII and Queen Alexandra, Canada erected this arch in London, England. The message on the other side of the arch read, "CANADA: FREE HOMES FOR MILLIONS: God Bless the Royal Family." Loyalty to the Crown and promoting immigration could obviously be combined to good effect.

185

Germany became a nation in 1871; Italy, in 1861.

Spanish American colonies in South America won their independence in the first half of the nineteenth century.

Canadian unity. The problem stemmed from different views of what it meant to be a Canadian. The nineteenth century was the beginning of an age of intense nationalism, a strong feeling that all persons who shared the same language, customs, and traditions (and sometimes religion) belonged together within a certain geographic and political area called a nation. Nationalism was a powerful force that generated the will and the strength to form the nations of Germany and Italy in the latter half of the century. It inspired people sharing a common nationality, who lived under foreign rule, to rise up in bloody revolution to win the right to govern themselves. However, in its most narrow form, known as jingoism or chauvinism, it led to the dangerous practice of believing that one's own nationality was superior to all others.

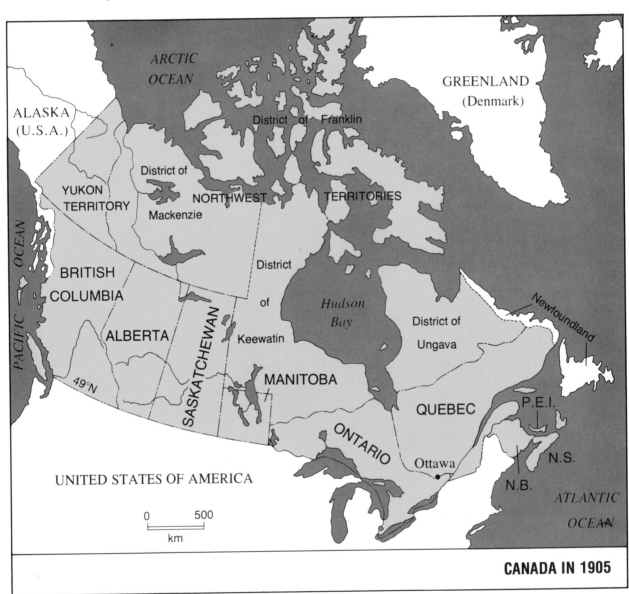

CANADA IN 1905

Confederation had brought together two nationalities in 1867. With the exception of small pockets of population in various regions of the country, the French had concentrated in the Province of Quebec. As a minority, they were determined to preserve their language, customs, and traditions. Although their ancestors had come from France, Canadian Francophones had almost no contact with their mother country, and few French people immigrated to Canada. Francophones were a cultural group with roots deep in the soil of Canada. Their heritage was Canadian and they thought of themselves as Canadians.

The British, who outnumbered the French by about two to one, had spread themselves throughout Canada. The major cultural group, they were different in outlook. Many English, Irish, Scottish and Welsh immigrants who came to Canada thought it natural and right to support their mother country in various matters. Most Canadian Anglophones looked to Great Britain for military and economic support in return for their willing pledge of allegiance. (At this time, all Canadians were British subjects, and it was not until 1947 that Canadian citizenship was established.) Few were much concerned by the question of political independence. The nationalism of Anglophones was, therefore, double-edged. It embraced both love of Canada and devotion to Great Britain and its Empire. It was a sort of British-Canadian nationalism.

These different views of nationalism inevitably caused conflict between Francophone and Anglophone. To reduce friction, if not to avoid a head-on collision, Laurier tried to steer a course between them. For a time, his patient, skilful manoeuvering managed to balance their contrasting opinions on national issues. He was able to persuade both sides to give in a little on questions that separated them. His role as peacemaker was well established at the start. Many Canadians, both in Quebec and elsewhere in the nation, applauded his resolution of the Manitoba Schools Question via his "sunny ways" of conciliation. Unfortunately, argument over education and language was not disposed of by the Manitoba dispute. Eight years later, it appeared again to challenge Laurier. This time the results were different.

The federal government had promised that the North-West Territories would be given provincial status after the 1904 election. The Autonomy Bills of 1905, legislation that was to create the provinces of Saskatchewan and Alberta, produced a bitter political controversy that is sometimes referred to as the North West School Question. Clause 17 of these bills was the principal source of trouble. It was framed to provide a twin system of state-supported schools, one English-speaking and Protestant, the other French-speaking and Catholic. Such a system had been authorized under the North-West Territories Act of 1875, but the majority of the Territories' residents were Anglophones and they wanted a single system, with no denominational schools. Encouraged by the example of Manitoba in holding out for control of education, the Territorial legislature had, in 1892 and 1901, gradually established a

In 1875, most of the settlers in the N.W.T. were living in the areas that became Alberta and Saskatchewan.

187

uniform, non-denominational system with common courses of study, common textbooks, and an approved standard of teaching and school inspection. Roman Catholics were allowed to organize their own schools — if they paid for their upkeep in addition to the taxes they had to pay to maintain the uniform system of schools in the Territories. Also, French was no longer accepted as a language of instruction.

The Autonomy Bills came under fierce attack, not only from the Tory opposition but from members of the Liberal cabinet. One of them, Clifford Sifton, raced back from a vacation abroad to submit his resignation in protest against Laurier's support for minority rights. Few politicians were ready to accept this policy. Laurier had to back down and change Clause 17 to give the new provinces complete control of education. It was a serious setback for the prime minister, and one which lost him respect and support. As someone remarked of the whole episode, "the storm blew over but the wreckage remained." Long after the passage of the Autonomy Bills, many Anglophones continued to resent his attempt to permit the official spread of separate schools.

Laurier had expected some counter-complaint from Francophone Roman Catholics, but he was amazed by its intensity. He was particularly surprised that one of his fiercest and most influential Quebec critics was a young, promising Member of Parliament called Henri Bourassa, who had originally been drawn into politics by his admiration of Laurier. The grandson of Louis Joseph Papineau, he had inherited some of the old rebel's characteristics: a brilliance in debate, a gift for writing, and an eagerness to wage an argument or a fight based on principle. His chief weaknesses — again inherited from his rebel grandparent — were an unwillingness to see any but his own view of an issue and a fierce impatience to get things done. So Bourassa turned against Laurier for what he called the prime minister's quick surrender to Anglophone prejudices. In the Commons' debate on the Autonomy Bills, he remarked bitterly:

> I regret every time I go back to my province to find developing that feeling that Canada is not Canada for all Canadians. We are bound to come to the conclusion that Quebec is our only country because we have no liberty elsewhere.

IMPERIAL FEDERATION AND THE BOER WAR

The break between Bourassa and the prime minister had really begun several years before when the prime minister was trying to handle the very delicate question of Canada's position within the British Empire.

Laurier had been elected at the height of popularity of the Imperial Federation Movement, an organization formed in the 1880s by a group of patriotic Britons who were eager to strengthen the ties that bound Great Britain to her colonies. At the heart of their plan was the estab-

Sifton's resignation from the cabinet was partly due to resentment. As the minister responsible for the Territories, he felt he should have been consulted about Clause 17 before the Autonomy Bills were introduced in Parliament.

Henri Bourassa, 1868-1952

Papineau had led the Rebellion in Lower Canada in 1837.

The British Empire at that time included Great Britain and Ireland, and the Dominions of Canada, Newfoundland, Australia, New Zealand, and South Africa.

lishment of an Imperial Council in London, to which each colony would send representatives, a Council that would rule the Empire. Laurier kept a wary eye on their scheme because he realized it would reduce the powers of self-government that colonies such as Canada had gradually been gaining.

The strong man of the Imperial Federation movement was the British Colonial Secretary, Joseph Chamberlain, who believed that Canada's acceptance of Imperial Federation would influence other colonies such as Australia and New Zealand. Thus, when Laurier arrived in London in 1897 for the celebration of Queen Victoria's sixtieth anniversary, the famous Diamond Jubilee, the Canadian prime minister was given extra-special attention by Chamberlain. Laurier was royally treated, invited to the homes of the leading members of British society, and even granted the honor of knighthood by Queen Victoria. None of this swayed Laurier, who pledged Canada's loyalty to the British Empire but stubbornly rejected the notion of Imperial Federation. To have accepted Chamberlain's proposals would have encircled Canada in the protective and controlling arms of the mother country. "Canada," Laurier firmly maintained, "is a nation. . . . Canada is practically independent." Laurier wanted the British to understand that Canada's goal was complete independence within the British Empire. "The more the Empire is free, the stronger it will be. . . ."

Bourassa, for his part, still feared that the prime minister would rush to Great Britain's side when called. And the Boer War was proof enough of this. In 1899, two tiny nations in southern Africa, the Transvaal and the Orange Free State, declared war on Great Britain. As this struggle between two foxes and a lion continued, the full might of a powerful

At colonial conferences in 1902 and 1907, Laurier continued to insist that Canada's destiny lay in its own nationhood.

Henri Bourassa's parliamentary career was confined to the years 1896-1899 and 1900-1907. His main career was journalism: editor-owner of L'Interprète, *published in Clarence Creek, Ontario, and co-owner and editor-in-chief of the Montreal newspaper* Le Devoir.

189

courtesy of the Director General Information, Department of National Defence, Ottawa

The first Canadian Navy recruiting poster, 1911. It announced that "Only Strong, Healthy and Well Educated Men and Boys are Required and they Must be of Good Character." The entry age for "Seaman Class Boys" was fifteen to seventeen years. Men were offered jobs as stokers, sick berth attendants, stewards, cooks, engine room artificers, carpenters, plumbers, painters, electricians, and armorers.

empire that commanded the loyalty of millions was pitted against several thousand Boers, almost all of whom were a farming people.

At the war's outset, newspapers and numerous public figures in Canada demanded that troops immediately be sent to assist the mother country. Most Anglophones, mainly those born in Great Britain, supported these demands: it was Canada's patriotic duty to become involved. In Quebec, where feeling was exactly the opposite, Bourassa was one of the leaders of the opposition to any Canadian involvement. He saw the Boer War as an imperialistic "land grab" in which Canada had neither any interest nor right to interfere. Since Canadian soil was not being attacked and Canadian lives were not being threatened, the war was no concern of Canada's. He warned that once troops were sent to aid the British against the Boers, this would be the nation's fate in all future British wars. He begged Laurier to resist the pressure of those — notably in Ontario — who insisted that it was Canada's duty to side with Great Britain. Caught in the middle, Laurier tried to please both sides. He agreed to send a contingent of troops to South Africa, where they would join the British Army. To satisfy Bourassa and his followers, Laurier insisted that each member of the military expedition be a volunteer: no Canadian would be forced to go. He also insisted that the British government assume all financial responsibilities for the Canadian contingent once it reached South Africa.

By the end of the war in 1902, about 7000 Canadians had served in South Africa alongside British units. Anglophone newspapers constantly gave the war front-page coverage, and when the Boers were finally overwhelmed, there were festive celebrations throughout English-speaking Canada. The troops, some of whom had been decorated for gallantry in action, came home to march in "victory parades" and were treated as heroes. The first major war in which Canadians had participated strengthened British-Canadian nationalism. A sense of having participated in a great Empire endeavor was aroused in many who had previously been indifferent to the idea of imperial unity.

Bourassa deplored the Boer War as a national tragedy. By accepting the British call to arms, the prime minister had needlessly meddled in foreign affairs. As war clouds gathered in Europe, Bourassa waited for the next British distress signal. It came in 1909 at the Imperial Conference attended by Laurier.

The prime minister returned from London with the gloomy news that war between Great Britain and Germany was a distinct possibility. The two nations were in the midst of a dangerous armament race, and Great Britain urged the colonies to come to its assistance. The Naval Service Bill of 1910 was Laurier's response. As he had done at the beginning of the Boer War, the prime minister again tried to arrange a compromise. Canada would build its own navy: one squadron to defend the Atlantic coast and another to guard Pacific shores. The Conservative opposition mocked his naval program as weak and half-hearted. Laurier's "tin-pot navy" would be of no value to Great Britain in time of war. Bourassa struck from the other side with equal ferocity. Neither Germany nor any other nation was threatening or would threaten Canada. It was clear to him and to other French-Canadian nationalists that the proposed navy was designed not for protection of Canada, but for use by Great Britain when it went to war. As debate on the Naval Service Bill dragged on, Laurier stated flatly: "If England is at war, we are at war, but if we do have a navy, that navy will not go to war unless the Parliament of Canada chooses to send it there." Despite opposition both within and without Parliament, the Liberal majority passed the Naval Service Bill. Canadian naval bases were established at Esquimalt, British Columbia, and Halifax, Nova Scotia. Five cruisers and six destroyers would be built in Canada. The Royal Canadian Navy had been born.

All this finally broke the slender thread of respect and friendship that linked Laurier and Bourassa. On the day after the passage of the Naval

The British were particularly threatened by the build-up of the German Navy. To keep open vital trade routes, it was essential that "Britannia rule the waves."

191

Service Act, Bourassa told a friend, "Laurier has now driven not one nail in his coffin but many." He vowed to do everything in his power to destroy his former idol. It was a promise Bourassa kept.

THE ELECTION OF 1911

In the late winter of 1910, Laurier was still troubled by the deep emotional disturbances caused by the debate on the Naval Bill. He now hoped that his good fortune in securing such favorable trade terms from the United States in the proposed reciprocity agreement would divert attention to what he believed would be regarded as a great Liberal success. The embarrassment and confusion on the faces of Conservative Members of Parliament as he read the terms of the agreement confirmed his hopes. The Tories could hardly reject it. But Laurier had not counted on the reaction of Canadian industrialists. They reacted quickly. The powerful Canadian Manufacturers' Association, many of the larger Anglophone newspapers, notably those in Montreal and Toronto, who depended on advertisements from business for their financial support, and British-Canadian nationalists from all walks of life sprang to the attack. Suddenly, the Conservative Party was galvanized into action.

The Commons debate on the Liberal reciprocity proposal was much more fierce than Laurier had anticipated. Yet the Liberals were so confident that they adjourned the House to let the still-optimistic prime minister sail to Britain to attend the coronation of King George V. When Parliament convened again in July, 1911, the Conservatives were spoiling for blood. During Laurier's absence, a well-organized campaign directed by the Conservatives and influential industrialists had reached every corner of the nation. Politicians, industrialists, and journalists had appeared at well-attended public meetings to denounce reciprocity. Tens of thousands of dollars had been spent on newspaper advertisements and pamphlets that attacked the proposed trade deal. Their basic message was simple and straightforward: reciprocity would destroy not only Canadian business, but Canada itself!

While the opposition continued to quote statistics to try to prove that Canada could never win in economic competition with the United States, its main appeal was to patriotism. Someone coined the slogan "NO TRUCK OR TRADE WITH THE YANKEES," and suddenly all the old flag-waving and loyalty slogans of the 1891 election were brought out of the Conservative cupboard. This time, the rallying cry was "The old flag, the old policy, and the old Empire." Once again it became a disloyal act to vote Liberal. Once again it became a pledge of support to the British Empire to vote Conservative. And the anti-reciprocity forces received unexpected, unintentional backing from indiscreet Americans. U.S. newspaper editorials talked of the annexation of Canada. Possibly the most damaging statement to Laurier's cause was made not by a Canadian Conservative, but by an American politician. Beauchamp

Edward VII died in May, 1910.

In August, 1911, this anti-Liberal cartoon appeared in the Toronto Daily News. *The tigers, whose stripes form the dread words RECIPROCITY and ANNEXATION, are looking around for their next meal. The "bones" of earlier victims are labelled with the names of territories absorbed by the United States in the course of the nineteenth century.*

Clark, speaker of the American House of Representatives, bluntly remarked: "I am for reciprocity because I hope to see the day when the American flag will float over every square foot of British North American possessions, clear to the North Pole."

As the Commons debated the proposed legislation in the early summer of 1911, Laurier still believed that most Canadians favored reciprocity. Ultimately, rather than decide the issue in Parliament, he gambled on winning by taking his case directly to the people. An election was set for September 21.

It was some time before the prime minister was able to appreciate the power of the forces pitted against him. Old friends and former allies were deserting him. One, Clifford Sifton, left the Liberal Party and joined the Conservatives. Eighteen Liberals, well-known in Toronto's financial community, publicly repudiated reciprocity. This "Revolt of the Eighteen" dealt a sharp, serious blow to Laurier. The defectors detailed their reasons for opposing Laurier in full-page advertisements in newspapers across the nation. (There was never any lack of money to pay for anti-reciprocity propaganda.) In the final week of the campaign, many Anglophone newspapers carried a full-page display of a telegram from Rudyard Kipling, the famous British imperialist poet. It began with the words, "It is her own soul that Canada risks today." Editorials ended with the warning "Britishers, stand firm!" The climax was reached on the day before the election. Numerous English-language newspapers featured front-page stories that condemned reciprocity. They were printed beneath a Union Jack and the Stars and Stripes separated by the caption "Under Which Flag?"

The most ironic twist of the election campaign was the unofficial alliance between the British-Canadian nationalist Robert Borden of the Conservative Party and the French-Canadian nationalist Bourassa of the Liberal Party. Despite the fact that Borden's basic argument was that a Conservative victory would strengthen the Canadian connection with the British Empire, Bourassa eagerly agreed to join him in the fight against Laurier. Almost completely ignoring the reciprocity issue, Bourassa concentrated his attack on the Naval Service Bill. In his own newspaper, *Le Devoir*, and in many campaign speeches, he told the people of Quebec that Laurier had given in to the British by creating a Canadian navy. He had become a traitor to his origins and to his fellow Québecois.

Laurier fought gamely in an election that was a confusing mixture of political and emotional prejudices. Seventy years old and exhausted by a heavy speaking schedule, he counterattacked furiously. But each of his efforts seemed to have less and less impact. For the first time as prime minister, he was openly jeered at when he spoke in Quebec. A few days before the voting took place, Laurier foresaw his defeat. As he wryly remarked,

> I am branded in Quebec as a traitor to the French, and in Ontario as a traitor to the English. In Quebec I am branded as a Jingo, and in Ontario as a Separatist. In Quebec I am attacked as an Imperialist, and in Ontario as an anti-Imperialist. I am neither. I am a Canadian.

The results were almost an exact reversal of the election won by Laurier in 1908. The Liberals took 87 seats and the Conservatives 134. Every constituency in British Columbia had gone Conservative. Even in the Maritime Provinces the government lost seats. In Ontario, where British-Canadian nationalists had rallied to the cause of the Empire and profited from the fear of the United States, the Conservatives gained 25 seats. In Quebec, with Bourassa's vital support, Borden had picked up 16 seats. Few Québecois had heeded the repeated warnings of the Montreal newspaper *La Presse:* "A vote for Bourassa is a vote for Borden, and a vote for Borden is a vote for imperialism with a vengeance." French-Canadian nationalists had helped elect the Conservative Party.

The election had set back, if not reversed, Laurier's patient attempts to create harmony within the nation. It was the high-water mark of British-Canadian nationalism, a point it reached at the expense of further isolating Quebec. That isolation would worsen six years later, when Anglophone-Francophone relations almost reached the breaking point during the First World War.

STUDY 6

1. Explain the Canadian reaction to the decision on the Alaska Panhandle boundary.
2. Use all the information you have gathered so far to write a summary of the main points and results of the Manitoba Schools Question.
3. Write a report on the settlement of the Canadian West under these headings:
   (a) the choice of Sifton as minister of the interior;
   (b) Sifton's vision of the development of the West;
   (c) the techniques used to attract immigrants;
   (d) the people — who they were, where they came from, where they settled, the problems they faced.
4. (a) How did railways contribute to the development of the mining industry?
   (b) Write a summary of mining and lumbering in Canada in the early twentieth century — location of resources, use of primary products, markets, etc.
5. (a) Explain in your own words the difference between primary and secondary industry.
   (b) Why is the development of secondary industry important to a nation's economy?
6. Review the Liberal and Conservative position on the tariff. Why do you think Laurier decided to continue Macdonald's National Policy? Account for the change in policy in 1910.
7. (a) Explain nationalism in your own words.
   (b) Discuss the special factors that affected Canadian nationalism.
   (c) Relate these to the controversy over the Autonomy Bills of 1905.
8. (a) What was the Imperial Federation Movement?
   (b) Explain the different Canadian attitudes toward participation in the Boer War.
   (c) How were these attitudes carried over into the debate on the Naval Service Bill?
9. What were the political and economic issues on which Laurier was defeated in the election of 1911? Which do you think were the most important and why?
10. Use the personalities and events in this chapter to describe the forces both inside and outside Canada that helped shape Canadian nationalism.

the test of War: 1914–1918

On election day in September, 1911, Conservative leader Robert Borden remained in his home constituency in Halifax watching the national results coming in by telegraph. Before the evening was over, he knew his party had won! Five days later, a throng of excited Conservatives greeted the new prime minister on his arrival in Ottawa. Marching behind blaring bands, they paraded through the streets of the capital on the start of a long night of celebration. Borden was the hero of the hour. He had led the Tories to their first election victory in two decades. For a party so used to winning elections under Sir John A. Macdonald, this triumph seemed long overdue.

ROBERT LAIRD BORDEN

Robert Laird Borden, 1854-1937

Victory was perhaps more vital to the Conservative leader than to his party. By 1911, his position as leader had become shaky. He had already lost two elections to the Liberals. Had he led his party to a third straight defeat, it would most likely have dropped him.

Robert Borden had not sought the Tory leadership. He had not even chosen politics as a career. As a young man in his native Nova Scotia he had been attracted to law and had worked his way up from law clerk to a partnership in a prominent Halifax firm of lawyers. He was just beginning to enjoy a comfortable life when Sir Charles Tupper, the Conservative leader, asked him to stand as a candidate in the election of 1896. After some prodding, Borden accepted, won the nomination as a candidate, and took the seat from his Liberal opponent. Four years later, he was again successful at the polls. When Tupper resigned in 1901, the Conservatives chose the somewhat reluctant Borden to succeed him.

Both friends and opponents recognized Borden as sincere and intelligent. He was, unquestionably, a man of principle. In parliamentary debate and on the campaign trail he relied more on facts and figures than on wit and passion. He lacked the flair and the color of Laurier, and he was stiffer and less fluid in movement and speech. But the electioneering in 1911 had exhausted most Canadians, mentally and emotionally. What they wanted was not inspired vision but sound leadership. Borden was determined to prove to his own party and to the country that he could provide this.

It was not an easy task. The tide of international trade was running against him. He took office just as the world economy was beginning to

Prime Minister Robert Borden (left) and (right) Mr. Winston Churchill, the First Lord of the Admiralty, leaving Admiralty House in London. This photograph was taken in the course of Borden's 1912 visit to Britain, when he took part in British cabinet discussions about the problems of imperial defence.

change direction, and unfortunately for Borden and Canada, the change was for the worse. By 1913, foreign demand for Canadian products had declined sharply. Investment funds dried up, factories cut back production, and there was unemployment in the land. After nearly twenty years of prosperity, Canada was heading into another depression. And as Borden and his cabinet groped for solutions to Canada's economic woes, international politics were producing an even more serious turn of events. During a hastily called conference in London in 1912, Borden learned just how serious the situation was: Europe stood on the brink of war.

Germany, the most powerful nation on the continent of Europe, had for several years been challenging Britain's supremacy on the high seas. To maintain trade with its empire and the rest of the world, Great Britain relied on controlling the seas. If Germany were ever able to equal Great Britain in naval strength, it could block the sea lanes of commerce and strangle British trade. Winston Churchill, the First Lord of the Admiralty, warned the 1912 conference that the German threat to match the British in battleship production was all too real. Unless Churchill could count on immediate support from the colonies, the Royal Navy might well lose the naval armaments race. This and other British fears about Germany impressed Borden, who returned to Canada hoping to persuade Parliament to act swiftly. In the House of Commons, he outlined the British position and then asked Parliament to approve the spending of $35 million in Great Britain to build three battleships that would be given to the British navy.

In the explosive debate on his Naval Aid Bill, the prime minister tried to convince the opposition that his proposal was a temporary measure to meet an emergency situation. He made it clear that Canadians would serve on these ships and that Canada would doubtless have the right to recall the ships at any time to form part of the Canadian navy. These assurances failed to persuade the opposition. The Liberals insisted that the money be spent on the construction of ships in Canadian shipyards. Borden did not hope to sway the Liberals, nor was he surprised by their line of argument. What he did fear was the amount of influence it might have upon his own Francophone Members of Parliament. How many of them would side with the Liberals against their own party? When the vote was taken, Borden was relieved. Only five Conservatives from Quebec had stood with the opposition. The rest of the party remained loyal to Borden, and the bill was passed.

In the Canadian Parliament, a bill has to pass both Commons and Senate and then be signed by the Governor General before it becomes law.

But the last word belonged to Wilfrid Laurier. The bill was passed by the Commons, but before it reached the Senate, Laurier made clear his unyielding opposition. Reject the Naval Aid Bill, he warned the Liberal Senators, or he would resign. They listened and obeyed. There followed months of passionate argument in the Senate and in the Commons, but no compromise was reached. Great Britain failed to receive the Canadian help it felt it needed, and two years after the defeat of the Naval Bill Canada went to war without any battleships.

THE LAMPS OF EUROPE GO OUT

Europe is the smallest of the continents. At the beginning of the twentieth century, many of its nations were the most technologically advanced in the world. The Agricultural and Industrial Revolutions had been born there, and many Europeans enjoyed their various benefits. For centuries, the arts, literature, education, philosophy, and science flourished in Europe as never before. And a few European nations experimented with systems of government that granted their citizens a considerable degree of personal freedom.

Despite their scientific and cultural progress, the nations of Europe had never managed to live side by side in peace. However, since 1815, the date that marked the end of nearly a quarter-century of armed strife, Europe had been surprisingly peaceful. There had been some wars, but none had lasted more than a few months. These wars had all been fought by professional warriors, usually at a safe distance from civilians in settled areas. There had, of course, been anguish, suffering, and death, but, as a general rule, those most affected wore the uniforms of the soldier and the sailor.

In 1914, all this changed. Most of Europe's nations combined advanced scientific knowledge with generations of pent-up hatred to wage one of the most vicious and prolonged wars that the world ever experienced. Whole populations were mobilized in the supreme effort to

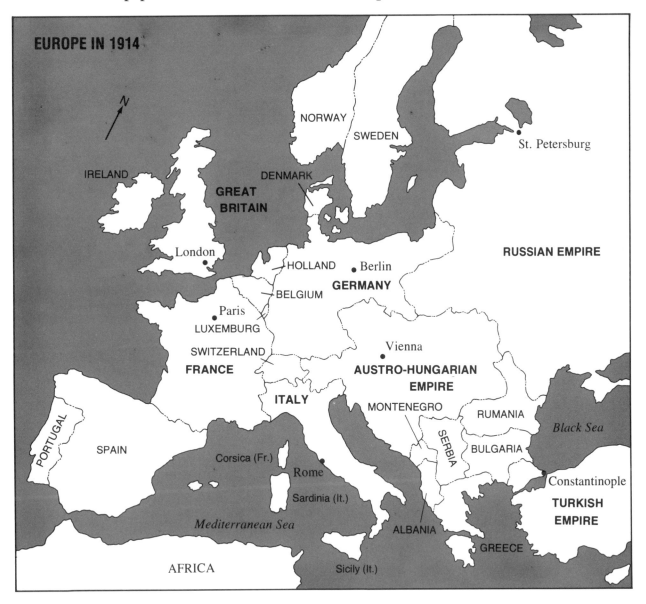

EUROPE IN 1914

destroy others. Military targets were no longer limited to enemy forces. They included unarmed men, women, and children. Weapons were more ingenious, more varied, and more deadly than in earlier wars: rapid firing machine guns, flamethrowers, and poison gases. By 1914, there was no longer any refuge from a hostile foe. Science had created the airplane, which could riddle anybody and everybody with bursts of gunfire or splatter them with bombs. Submarines were able to stalk and kill with stealth, sending entire shiploads of people to watery graves. The conflict that began in the late summer of 1914 was a war designed to annihilate, to wipe an enemy from the face of the earth.

Otto von Bismarck, the great German statesman who had cleverly arranged three brief wars in the nineteenth century to make his country the most powerful in Europe, had always lived in fear of "some damned foolish thing [happening] in the Balkans." Bismarck did not live long enough to realize the accuracy of his prophecy, but a "damned foolish thing" did happen in the Balkans, at Sarajevo, on June 28, 1914. It was the assassination of Franz Ferdinand, the heir to the throne of Austria-Hungary, by Gavrilo Princip, a teen-age student acting on behalf of a Serbian terrorist organization. After Princip's arrest, all of Europe watched and waited. Would Austria-Hungary take steps to punish Serbia? Would Russia, Serbia's ally, allow this to happen?

The Austro-Hungarian government remained strangely quiet for several weeks, raising hopes that the crisis might pass without further incident. But behind the scenes there was constant activity. The Austro-Hungarians were feverishly working out plans to invade Serbia. When they finally obtained the promise of German support in the event that Russia came to Serbia's aid, Austria-Hungary mobilized its army. Exactly one month after the assassination, Austro-Hungarian troops smashed through the thin line of Serbian forces guarding the border. War had begun.

Events followed swiftly. When Russia moved to protect Serbia, Germany declared war against Russia and its ally, France. By August 3, the leading powers of Europe had paired off into rival groups: Germany and Austria-Hungary versus Russia, France, and Serbia. After Italy had declared its neutrality, only Great Britain remained uncommitted. Then, on August 4, the German army invaded neutral Belgium. At noon that day, in the capital city of Berlin, the British Ambassador angrily reminded the German foreign minister that their two governments were pledged by a seventy-five-year-old treaty to guarantee the neutrality of Belgium. The German's reply was that the treaty was a mere "scrap of paper." That night, the British Admiralty sent a brief, coded wireless message to all warships of the Royal Navy: "Commence hostilities against Germany."

In those final hours before the British Empire went to war, Sir Edward Grey, the British foreign secretary, remarked to a friend, "The lamps are going out all over Europe; we shall not see them lit again in our

The name of the terrorist organization that hired Princip and two others to assassinate Archduke Ferdinand was the Black Hand.

In 1914, the Austro-Hungarian Empire included Austria, Hungary, and parts of Yugoslavia, Czechoslovakia, and Rumania.

Serbia, which was an independent kingdom in 1914, is now part of Yugoslavia.

lifetime." He was right. The struggle was to last almost five years, bringing tragedy and suffering to millions of people. When peace finally returned, many of Europe's ancient ruling families had been overthrown; the social order was changing; economic systems were being challenged. Indeed, the whole world was never the same again.

IN FLANDERS' FIELDS

For the nations of Europe, experienced in reading signs of trouble in the Balkans, the summer of 1914 was the lull before a storm. The only questions were: when would it break and how bad would it be? For Canadians, far from the scene, it was the holiday season. The war scare after the assassination of Franz Ferdinand had fizzled and burned out. Obviously, it was just another incident in the tangled affairs of European politics. Prime Minister Borden decided to get away from Ottawa for a

The Public Archives of Canada, PA-22593

On the grounds of Toronto's Canadian National Exhibition, visitors inspect the neat, tidy trenchworks, complete with underground dugout, built by the 35th Infantry Battalion. (The reality of the trenches is shown on page 205.)

201

while and take a holiday back home in Nova Scotia. His trip was short-lived. In response to British telegrams advising him of the rapidly growing conflict, he rushed back to Ottawa. On August 1 he called his cabinet together in emergency session.

When the British declaration of war was made public on the morning of August 5, Borden pledged Canada's total support for the mother country. As a colony, Canada was automatically at war, and many Canadians responded to the call of duty. They echoed Sir Wilfrid Laurier's ringing declaration:

> It will be seen by the world that Canada, a daughter of old England, intends to stand by her in this great conflict. When the call goes out, our answer goes out at once, 'Ready, Aye Ready.'

Canada was more enthusiastic for war than prepared for it: an army of 3000 men, a navy of two warships, and no air force. However, what was lacking in weapons was more than made up for by patriotic fervor. From Charlottetown to Victoria, men lined up at hastily organized recruiting stations, jostling each other to be among the first to sign up. They thought the war would be brief and they wanted a taste of action before the guns stopped firing.

After the defeat of the Naval Aid Bill, the Canadian government bought the *Niobe* and the *Rainbow*, two old warships, to patrol the Atlantic and Pacific coasts.

The entire situation was a joy and a challenge to Borden's minister of militia, Sam Hughes. He had tried teaching and journalism before being elected to Parliament as a Conservative from Ontario. His record as a volunteer in the Boer War had been brief and undistinguished, but this did not prevent him from promoting himself as an expert on military affairs. His energetic manner and his obvious desire to build a Canadian army impressed Borden, who had included him in his first cabinet. And the declaration of war set Hughes into rapid motion. By September, a military camp had been set up at Valcartier, just north of Quebec City. In the final days of the summer, thousands of recruits were jammed into this huge, sprawling, tent city, outfitted with uniforms and equipment, and rushed through a basic course of infantry training. On October 3, they boarded ships at Quebec City. Borden had promised Great Britain 25 000 men. When the ships carrying the First Canadian Division docked in England, 33 000 soldiers disembarked. During the coldest winter in years, British instructors put them through a gruelling training program on muddy Salisbury Plain.

In February, 1915, when the Canadians left for France, they were certain that nothing could be worse than English mud and English rain. How wrong they were! No training, no testing could have prepared them for the horrors they were to experience. No military leader, British, French or German, could have predicted the awful nature of the First World War. It was the most savage, the most murderous, and the most widespread conflict in modern history.

If the German plan had succeeded, the war would have been brief and decided in their favor. They were ready for it. Their master plan, named after its original creator, Count Alfred von Schlieffen, had been polished and refined every year since it was first drawn up in 1905. The Schlieffen Plan was based on the belief that Russia would be slow in mobilizing its enormous reserves of manpower. This would allow the German Army about six weeks to crush the French Army before turning east to meet the Russian attack.

The success of the Plan hinged on two factors: speed and the concentration of overwhelming German forces against the French Army. To reach the French by the shortest route involved violating Belgian neutrality, for across this small nation lay the most direct path to a quick victory. This plunge across tiny Belgium would also have the advantage of taking the French by surprise. They believed the Germans would be forced to go around Belgium to the south, where France and Germany shared a common border. Another vital factor was the route of the invading forces: they were to cross Belgium and northern France to the English Channel, race southwest along the coast, then wheel inland toward the capital city of Paris, the rail centre of France and the supply base of the French Army. Schlieffen had warned his staff officers time and time again: "Let the last man on the right brush the Channel with his sleeve." The German forces would take the shape of a giant claw that curled around the French Army and then squeezed the life out of it.

At first, the Plan went well. The Germans overran the brave but outnumbered, unprepared Belgians. Once on French soil, the invaders began their lunge to the coast. By early September, 600 000 German troops in their field-grey uniforms were moving in a vast arc across northern France. Just beyond them, in headlong retreat, were the French in their blue coats and red trousers and the khaki-clad British. Then, in the excitement and confusion of battle, the German commander on the far right forgot Schlieffen's stern warning. Instead of continuing all the way to the coast first, he wheeled his army southward toward Paris. This was a fatal move: he exposed his flank to enemy troops just beyond the cutting edge of the "claw." When observer airplanes reported the changing German movement, French and British commanders decided to regroup their forces for a thrust at the exposed German flank. The Franco-British counterattack took place near the Marne River about sixty-four kilometres north of Paris, and the shock of becoming the attacked instead of the attacker momentarily confused the Germans. They drew back with the Allied (the French and the British) forces in close pursuit. The "Miracle of the Marne" had ruined the Schlieffen Plan.

To the west of this battle lay a vast open plain that extended to the English Channel. And on the Channel coast were the ports of Dieppe, Boulogne, Calais, and Dunkirk, strategic bases from which the Germans could attack shipping or even invade Britain. To capture them, the Germans started a drive to reach the coast. For the next month, both sides engaged in a series of attempts to outflank each other as they

The British and German armies had adopted khaki or field-grey uniforms, which were less visible on the battlefield and so provided protective coloring. The French military refused to change the uniform worn since 1830 (when rifle fire carried only 200 paces, and armies fighting at this close range could not hope to hide behind dull colors). A former war minister of France declared, "Le pantalon rouge, c'est la France!"

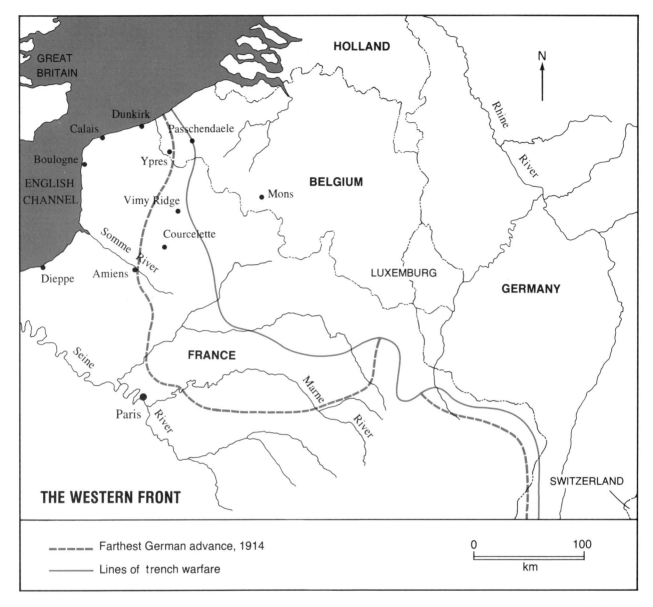

THE WESTERN FRONT

Legend:
- ----- Farthest German advance, 1914
- ——— Lines of trench warfare

Scale: 0 — 100 km

moved closer and closer to the English Channel. The race ended in a draw. By late October, exhaustion and freezing rains made it impossible for either side to launch a frontal assault. Rather than lose their positions, they decided to dig in. Before the arrival of the first snows, the rival armies had begun constructing two snake-like lines of trenches, several hundred kilometres long, that would twist and turn parallel to each other from the Belgian coast all the way to the Swiss border.

This brought an end to the first brief phase of the war on what came to be called the Western Front. It had featured great offensive thrusts by free-wheeling armies in a series of rapid movements over wide areas of territory. How different the second phase was! Each side became obsessed with an almost lunatic desire to maintain its trench lines. To yield

Soldiers used wooden duckboards to avoid sinking into mud that was sometimes knee-high. Dugouts were usually sandbagged structures built slightly above trench level, otherwise they became waterlogged. Keeping watch on the enemy was often done by telescope (right), which reduced the danger of being hit by sniper fire.

even a few square metres of soil was to suffer defeat. The battle cry became "Defend!," "Defend!," "Defend!" During the winter of 1914-1915, millions of sandbags, hundreds of thousands of metres of timber, and vast quantities of cement were transported to the front lines. Trenches were deepened and widened and then fortified with timber and sandbags. From narrow slits in grey concrete pillboxes, situated at irregular intervals along the winding lines of trenches, protruded the blunt mouths of machine guns, which spat out death at the rate of several hundred bullets a minute. Behind the front lines was a second or third row of trenches, a defence line to fall back on in the event of a successful enemy onslaught. Several kilometres farther back were the artillery positions — long rows of powerful cannon, their steel snouts raised menacingly and pointing towards the enemy.

A long way behind the battlefront were the various army headquarters, often located in large, comfortable French or Belgian châteaux. Here, fortified by fine food and excellent wines, the commanders talked and plotted strategy. Most of these officers knew little of or even cared about the hardships endured by the men in the trenches, who lived on hardtack, bully beef, tinned meat, and stale tea. They often had to sleep leaning against the sandbagged walls, their boots sunk in several millimetres of rain and mud. Even these conditions were almost acceptable to soldiers when they thought of the terrors that lay ahead of them when they climbed out of the trenches to attack. To reach enemy lines, the attackers had to make their way through "No Man's Land," an area pock-marked by shell craters brimming with stagnant water covered by slime. The churned-up earth was littered with bodies, parts of bodies, and pieces of shattered equipment. Those who escaped the lethal spray of machine gun and rifle fire as they picked their way across No Man's Land, stumbling, lurching, sliding and falling, found tangled webs of barbed wire barring their way to the enemy. The sights, sounds, and smells of that ghastly inferno stayed in the men's memories forever: a comrade crumpling into the muck, a bullet through his head; the deafening, death-dealing roar of hand grenades or mortar bombs; the fetid aroma of decaying human flesh. Trench warfare was a nightmare that lasted for four years. For many of those who experienced it, it lasted a lifetime.

Under British command, men of the First Canadian Division were posted in the front lines soon after their arrival in France. In their very

H.M.S. Dreadnought, *the British super-battleship that had greater speed and firepower than any other warship of its time. By 1914, Britain had built twenty-one of these vessels to Germany's thirteen. Despite the build-up of naval forces, there was only one major sea battle — Jutland — and both sides claimed victory.*

first engagement during the second Battle of Ypres they won a reputation for bravery and coolness under attack. Late in the afternoon of April 22, 1915, Canadians watched huge, olive-green clouds hovering near the ground and drifting slowly towards the French colonial troops on their left. When the fringes of the cloud reached these trenches, their occupants gasped in panic, clutching their throats. Some screamed "*Gaz, gaz*" and staggered out of the trenches in an attempt to escape the enveloping mist of death. Poison gas! And behind the choking clouds came hundreds of German troops. The Canadians, pressing cotton wads soaked in water over their mouths and noses, rushed to fill the gap that had opened in the French line. The battle raged through the night until the Germans gave up and pulled back. But the deadly chlorine gas and the enemy infantry returned the following day. Now strung out along a loosely linked line of trenches, the Canadians somehow hung on to their position for forty-eight hours until relieved by British troops.

The contribution of the Canadians at Ypres moved Sir John French, the British commander-in-chief, to cable Borden: "No words of mine can express the admiration I feel for their gallant conduct." But French's admiration had been dearly won: 6000 Canadians had been killed, wounded, or posted missing in just three days of fighting.

By early May, the Second Canadian Division had reached France to join their comrades. Together with the First Division it formed the Canadian Corps, under the command of a British officer, Lieutenant-General E. A. H. Alderson. The Canadian Corps was not involved in any major engagement until the following spring. Under a new commander, Lieutenant-General Sir Julian Byng, it was part of an attack mounted in June, 1916 and was driven back by murderous artillery fire. However, the Canadians regrouped and counterattacked until they had regained their objectives. In recapturing three small hills that barely rose above the level of the surrounding countryside, they suffered 8000 casualties.

The madness of war was plain for all to see in the summer of 1916 in what the Germans called "Der Blutbad" (the Bloodbath) and the British called the Battle of the Somme. On July 1, the British began their greatest offensive to that time. On that day, the first day of a summer-long battle, the slaughter of 57 000 British officers and men was a foretaste of the senseless, ugly future. In the months that followed, the high command on both sides ordered futile, frontal assaults time after time. These tactics revealed these commanders' lack of imagination and utter disregard for the lives of their troops: thousands of Britons and Germans were sent to their deaths on the blood-soaked terrain of the Somme.

In the numerous attacks and counterattacks that made up the Battle of the Somme, the Canadian Corps added a new laurel to its reputation for bravery. Lloyd George, the British prime minister, wrote in his *Memoirs* that in their assault and capture of Courcelette,

> The Canadians played a part of such distinction that thence forward they were marked out as storm troops; for the remainder of the war

The Third and Fourth Canadian divisions arrived between December 1915 and August 1916.

The battle was named after the Somme River, which flows through the area.

The Canadian cost in the near-suicidal missions at the Somme was 24 000 casualties.

207

William Longstaff's famous painting entitled "Vimy Ridge." The ghostly figures of Canadian soldiers drift across the ground now dominated by this huge marble memorial to Canada's war dead.

they were brought along to head the assault in one great battle after another. . . . Whenever the Germans found the Canadian Corps coming into the line, they prepared for the worst.

Easter Monday, April 9, 1917, was an unusually cold and miserable day in northern France. Rain, then sleet, and finally snow had been falling throughout the night. About 5:30 a.m., close to a thousand Canadian artillery guns began to lay a rolling barrage of shellfire on the heavily fortified German positions on Vimy Ridge, the barrage moving forward in leaps of about a hundred metres. Shortly after the first salvos started, the men of the Canadian Corps and members of a British brigade climbed out of their trenches and threaded their way across No Man's Land. The power and accuracy of the barrage combined to obliterate the enemy front-line trenches so that the Canadians passed them without knowing it. On they went to surprise a second line of defenders. Some managed to flee, but many surrendered to the first wave of Canadian assault troops.

Following the barrage ahead and enduring an ever-increasing enemy fire, the Canadians fought their way to the top of the ridge. This was a Canadian victory that would be remembered above all others long after the war had ended. In Canada, newspapers, magazines, and returning soldiers told and retold the story of the storming of Vimy Ridge. But Vimy did more than add to the reputation of the Canadian Corps. It served, at last, to convince the British that the Canadians should be led by one of their own. In June, Arthur Currie, whose Canadian brigade had held out for three days and three nights during the terrible poison-gas attack of 1915, was knighted and appointed commander-in-chief of the Canadian Corps.

Vimy had been a model victory. Months of careful planning and the brilliant use of artillery had resulted in an unusually small number of casualties for such a large operation. Unfortunately this success was not always repeated in the remaining engagements fought that year. In the first of these, Hill 70, the Canadians took their objective and held it against twenty-one enemy counterattacks. But when the Germans finally broke off action, about 9000 Canadians had been killed, wounded, or were missing. By 1917, many sections of northern France and southern Belgium — the Flanders of an earlier period of European history — had become so war-torn that there was little to suggest that human beings had once lived in these regions. The ground had been so pulverized and pitted by shelling that it resembled a moonscape. Protruding from muddy quagmires or slimy, water-filled shell holes were the limbs or trunks of men and horses. It was in just such a war-ravaged landscape that the second engagement took place, in an area called Passchendaele. Here, the Canadian Corps took the offensive on October 26, 1917. Brushing aside Currie's anguished plea for more time to prepare, the British ordered the Canadians into action. For ten dreadful days they slogged their way forward, ultimately driving the German defenders off the area's dominant feature, Passchendaele Ridge. Behind the Corps, drowned in shell holes or lying on hospital cots with severed limbs or bodies riddled with bullets or shrapnel, were more than 15 000 of its members. No other battle was so dearly won by Canadian troops.

In March, 1918, the final phase of the war opened with a dramatic German breakthrough. It was as if the clock had been turned all the way

The actual number of Canadian soldiers killed at Vimy Ridge was 3598.

Kneeling in front of King George V, the commander of the Canadian Corps receives the ceremonial sword tap on each shoulder that makes him a knight.

William Arthur Currie was a successful Vancouver Island businessman. He joined the militia in 1897 as a "Saturday-night soldier" and rose to command of an artillery regiment and, later, an infantry brigade. His brigade's fierce resistance during the Second Battle of Ypres moved even his German opponents to express admiration for the Canadians' discipline and courage in the face of chlorine gas attacks and intense artillery fire. Currie survived the war to become the commander of all Canadian occupation forces in the Rhineland. After his return home, he was appointed principal and, later, vice-chancellor of McGill University, Montreal.

Imperial War Museum, London

209

Left: The pilots and mechanics of a British fighter squadron "somewhere in France." The pilots of this war had no parachutes; on average, a flyer's life expectancy was as little as two or three weeks.

Right: By 1917, about a third of the pilots in British squadrons were Canadian. Several survived to become air "aces," the greatest being William Avery Bishop, here seen seated in the cockpit of his Nieuport Scout. In 1918, while on the staff of the British Air Ministry, "Billy" Bishop helped to create a flying force that, in time, became the Royal Canadian Air Force.

The United States entered the war on April 6, 1917, but the first American units did not arrive in France until early in 1918.

back to August, 1914. Once again, a solid grey mass of German infantry swarmed across France, driving the Allied troops ahead of them. However, when the invaders reached the River Marne for the second time, their great offensive ran out of steam. Short of supplies and weak in reserves, the Germans lacked the punch necessary to finish off their foes. Now the French, British, Canadians, and newly arrived Americans rallied for their counterthrust. And the Canadian Corps was in the vanguard of the assault. On August 8, "the Black Day of the German Army," the Canadians drove the enemy back several kilometres near the town of Amiens. By October, the Germans were in retreat along the entire length of the Western Front.

On November 11, 1918, the Canadian Corps had just made a triumphant entry into the Belgian city of Mons when the news reached the troops that the Germans had requested an end to hostilities! Mons was where the British and Germans had first clashed four long years before. And, for the Canadians, here it ended. On the eleventh hour of the eleventh day of the eleventh month, the armistice went into effect. Suddenly the fighting was over. No more waiting, shivering in water-filled trenches, to go "over the top." No more terrifying charges across No Man's Land. No more pain and death. Suddenly the unaccustomed chirp of birds could be heard in the shell-torn wastes of France and Belgium.

Although battles at sea and dogfights in the air contributed to the outcome of the war, it was the conflict in the trenches that earned

victory. That victory belongs to the ordinary foot soldier who endured the frightful agony of trench warfare, and some of these who survived to come back to Canada made sure that the credit for this victory would never be entirely forgotten. When the new Parliament Buildings were built in Ottawa after the war, a memorial chamber was built in the central structure, the Peace Tower. In the middle of this chamber is an altar on which lies a Book of Remembrance. Every day one of its pages is turned. In this book are inscribed the names of the 60 000 Canadian servicemen and servicewomen who lie buried somewhere in Flanders' fields.

POLITICAL BATTLE LINES

The outbreak of war made many people forget the intense bitterness during the 1911 election campaign and the debate on the Naval Aid Bill. *La Patrie*, a leading Francophone newspaper, was emphatic in its declaration of loyalty. "There are no longer French Canadians and English Canadians. Only one race now exists, united by the closest bonds in a common cause." Even Henri Bourassa, the leader of French-Canadian nationalism, maintained that it was the duty of Canada "to contribute within the bounds of her strength" to win the war.

Canada's initial strength was in manpower, and for almost two years the reservoir of eager volunteers appeared to be bottomless. Then, in early 1916, recruitment began to fall off. This decline was partly the result of competition from farmers and factory owners for able-bodied

Canadian and British soldiers chat beside a broken-down tank near Amiens, while a French artillery team, equipped with the more reliable horse, lumbers past. It was the use of large numbers of tanks late in 1918 that broke the stalemate on the Western Front. Unaffected by bullets and grenades, the tank forced its way through barbed wire and across trenches and routed the German Army.

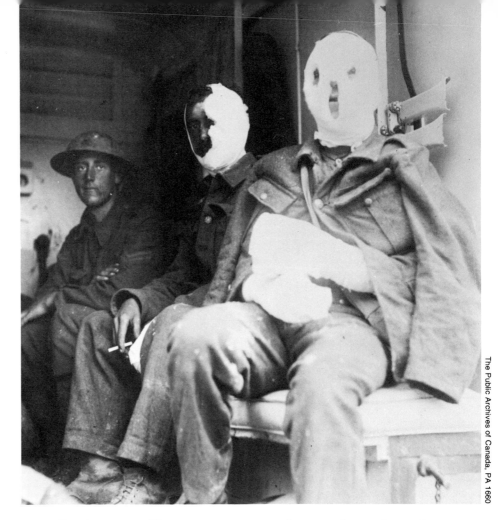

Canadians wounded at Passchendaele in 1917. Soldiers, sailors, and airmen were not the only ones killed or wounded in the war. Canadian nurses in field hospitals suffered their share of casualties. One was sent home a gas victim. "The soldiers who were gassed were brought to us," she explained. "You had to rip their clothes off, and everything reeked of gas. The fumes got down my throat." Another told of working in a tent on an airfield, with lanterns for operating lights, when there was a direct hit by a bomb. "Two of my classmates were killed," she said. "All they could find of one of the nurses was a wrist."

men. "Help Wanted" signs were everywhere. Piling wheat sheaves or packing shell cases may have been less heroic than serving in the armed forces, but the pay was better and the work was safer. By 1916, the glow of pride from Canadian victories in France was balanced by the shadow of pain and death: some of the victors had come home — without eyes or missing limbs. They told stories of the horrors of war that never appeared in newspaper accounts of successful Canadian encounters with the enemy.

At the same time that the number of volunteers at home was declining, the list of casualties overseas was increasing. To keep up troop strength, the government launched a series of recruiting drives. Patriotic Canadians enthusiastically supported the government campaign. At public rallies in theatres and arenas, politicians, community leaders, and clergymen urged the youth of the country to trade their overalls for khaki and their shovels for rifles. Newspaper editors repeatedly drew the attention of their readers to the glorious sacrifices being made by the boys at Ypres and the Somme. Why, they angrily demanded, were some boys in Prince Albert and Fredericton still at home? And what of other boys in Quebec City and Trois Rivières?

Recruitment figures showed that the smallest number of volunteers had come from Quebec. How could this have happened? During the first few months of the war young Québecois had responded to the call to arms. They had formed the only Francophone regiment, the Royal Twenty-Second, which became renowned for its gallantry and efficiency. Yet a larger proportion of Anglophone than Francophone Canadians had signed up to serve. Why was this? Despite the support of Quebec newspapers such as *La Patrie* and despite the fervent appeals for volunteers, the war had aroused less emotional response in Quebec than in the rest of Canada. As time passed, a growing number of Québecois came to believe that it was a struggle to save Great Britain, not Canada. They were willing to fight to the death to defend *Canadian* soil, but they were stubbornly opposed to dying in a land across the seas in a war which they believed posed no threat to Canada. A Quebec journalist ably expressed this attitude: "When an English Canadian pronounces the word patriotism he wishes to say love of Empire, while the French-speaking Canadian thinks only of Canada."

This regiment is popularly known as the "Vandoos," from their French name, "vingt-deuxième."

Many Anglophones scorned such ideas as treason or cowardice. Among them was the outspoken minister of militia who directed the recruiting program. Sam Hughes was both an ardent defender of the Empire and a militant opponent of Roman Catholics and Francophones. Hughes' refusal to consider the problems of young men who spoke only French also discouraged enlistment. English was the language of command in the training camps and on the field of battle. Had he been able to overcome his prejudices he could likely have put together more Francophone regiments. But, under his direction, recruiting teams conducted aggressive, frequently offensive, campaigns in the Province of Quebec. And the inclusion of Protestant ministers among the recruiters was regarded as an intentionally crude insult directed at the people of Quebec.

From the Francophone point of view, the timing of the recruiting campaign added insult to injury. There was a battle being fought in Canada over language rights. It had begun in Ontario in 1912 and by 1916 had spread to Manitoba. This threat was much more real to the Québecois than the conflict in Europe. The government of Ontario had passed a ruling that restricted the use of French to the junior grades of public schools (Regulation 17). The response of the Francophone minority in the province was openly hostile, especially in the Ottawa area, where angry members of that city's Catholic board of education refused to obey the law. The government of Ontario replaced them. The new members immediately put Regulation 17 into effect by firing two sisters, Beatrice and Diane Desloges, who had refused to accept the new language policy. When the substitute teachers hired to replace the Desloges sisters reached the school, they found the entrance barricaded by angry mothers waving long hatpins. Some days later, after the board of education had managed to remove the protesting parents, the

This recruiting poster was fairly low-key in its appeal, publicizing battles in which Canadian units had distinguished themselves particularly. As the war lengthened and victory, at times, seemed almost doubtful, posters became more brutally direct: "What will you answer when your children grow up and ask, 'Daddy, what did YOU do in the Great War?'"

Civilians, too, were prodded by poster propaganda to aid the war effort. One such poster, produced by the Essex County (Ontario) Recruiting Committee, proclaimed, "ESSEX MEN are not COWARDS but they must be shown. A few dollars from YOU WILL HELP US SHOW THEM!" The federal government, also, produced many an advertisement urging Canadians to "serve Canada" by buying "Victory Bonds."

214

teachers made their way into an empty school. The pupils had followed Beatrice and Diane to a school set up in a nearby Catholic church.

Francophones outside of Ontario were alarmed by Regulation 17. Could not other provincial governments also pass similar laws to limit the use of the French language? An answer came in 1916 when the government of Manitoba abolished all bilingual schools in that province. And so, when the recruiting campaign came to Quebec, Bourassa, no longer a supporter of the war, expressed the feelings of many when he thundered:

> In the name of religion, liberty, and faithfulness to the British flag, French Canadians are enjoined to go and fight the Prussians of Europe. Shall we let the Prussians of Ontario impose their domination like masters in the very heart of the Canadian Confederation under the shelter of the British flag and British institutions?

As the war of words between Quebec and the rest of Canada increased in tempo, the war of bullets continued to take the lives of Canadians in Flanders. By this time, however, the rate of enlistment had fallen off dramatically. During the month of March, 1917, while preparations were under way for the assault on Vimy, fewer than 5000 volunteers registered for military service. In that same month, one year earlier, there had been 20 000. The rapid decline in enlistment, not only in Quebec but across Canada, worried Borden and his cabinet. Unless something was done quickly, the Canadian Corps would soon fall below strength. The prime minister was also influenced by another factor. The mounting casualty rates among all Allied forces since 1914 made it clear that a supreme effort was necessary to win the war before the end of 1917. But victory required fighting men. In May 1917, after his return from an inspection tour of the Canadians in France, Borden decided that he must introduce conscription. To overcome the opposition he knew would be centred in Quebec, Borden approached Laurier with a proposition. Would the leader of the opposition give his support by joining Borden in a coalition government for the purpose of introducing conscription?

Conscription is a military draft in which civilians are required by law to serve in the armed forces.

The aging Laurier was in an awkward position. He had never wavered from his original stand on the war: he believed that Canada had an obligation to aid Great Britain. He strongly opposed Regulation 17, but he had repeatedly urged Québecois to enlist in the armed services. If he accepted Borden's proposal, he risked losing his position as the leader of Quebec to Bourassa. However, Laurier also feared that introducing conscription without a general vote on the matter could split the nation along ethnic lines. His fears were not groundless. The Grand Master of the Orange Lodge promised that if the people of Quebec refused to accept conscription, a quarter of a million Orangemen would gladly march into that province to help them change their minds. In the end, Laurier told Borden that he would be obliged to oppose conscription.

Laurier's refusal did not lessen Borden's desire to form a coalition government. If the leader of the opposition would not join him, perhaps some of his followers would. As talks between Borden and leading Liberals got under way, the prime minister introduced the Military Service Bill into the House of Commons in June, 1917. When, in July, it was passed and became law, it gave the government the right to call up men for military service.

That same summer, two other bills were introduced and passed to help a pro-conscription government to win the coming election. The Military Voters' Act granted the right to vote to all members of the armed forces regardless of age, sex, or length of residence in Canada. The Wartime Election Act gave the franchise to mothers, sisters, wives, and daughters of servicemen and servicewomen – women who, in all probability, would support the government. This legislation also took away the right to vote from anyone who had migrated to Canada from "enemy countries" after 1902 or who had become a naturalized Canadian since that year.

When Parliament recessed in late September, Borden had still not put conscription into effect. He was unwilling to do so until he had won an election on the issue. By October, he had convinced various Liberals, including Clifford Sifton and W. S. Fielding, to join him in forming a coalition party. This coalition, made up of Conservatives and pro-conscription, English-speaking Liberals, called itself the Unionist Party. Their opponents, led by Laurier, were anti-conscription Liberals, and most of them were Francophones. Laurier's party had lost its national character.

The electioneering of October and November, 1917 was even more bitter than that of 1911. Several Liberal newspapers deserted Laurier and backed conscription. Abuse was open and savage. Using such slogans as "A vote for Laurier is a vote for the Kaiser," the Unionists put their opponents on the defensive from the outset. The single issue of the campaign was conscription. The Unionists tried to convince the voters that this was the only fair method of providing men for the armed services: any opposition to this was branded as treason. Some of the fiercest recruiting speeches and the strongest support for Borden came from the Protestant clergy. Unionist politicians even promised not to draft farm laborers into the armed forces if they voted against the Laurier Liberals (a promise not kept after the election). The anti-conscriptionists were not much better, accusing Borden's party of war profiteering, of "raking in gold" while Canadians were being "raked by German shells." The physical violence directed against Unionist candidates in Quebec – occasional revolver shots and frequent volleys of stones and broken glass – was such that they had to have police escorts during the entire election campaign. When local authorities could not guarantee their safety, Unionist rallies just had to be cancelled.

Laurier tried to persuade Canadians that conscription was not necessary, that the war could be won by maintaining the system of voluntary enlistment. As Quebec newspapers supporting him pointed out, did Canada really *need* conscription? Did a need for reinforcements exist at all? The other Dominions — South Africa, Australia, and New Zealand — had voted against conscription. They did not mind if their soldiers fought as part of some British Army corps. Why did there have to be a distinctive Canadian Corps? Was the policy of maintaining a Canadian Corps the cause of conscription? Once again in its thoughts and its feelings, Quebec stood opposed to the rest of Canada.

The "Khaki Election" ended in a clear victory for the Unionists, who elected 115 Conservatives and 38 pro-conscription Liberals. A total of 82 anti-conscription Liberals were elected. Of these, 62 were from the Province of Quebec.

Was the Unionist victory worth the damage to national unity? In Quebec City in 1918, mobs, reacting to the high-handed manners and methods of conscription officers, went on a rampage and attacked the offices of pro-conscription newspapers. Troops called in to quell the rioters fired on them, killing four. The province was seething with hostility, and civil war seemed a real possibility. Opposition, both before and after the election, was not confined to Quebec, however.

One of the anti-conscription Liberals who were defeated was Mackenzie King.

The side of this Canadian army hut in Flanders is a sort of billboard asking soldiers to save scrap metal or invest in Victory Bonds. The poster that the soldier is looking at is a crude Unionist appeal for votes. "A vote against the Government means You are here for life. A vote for the Government means Another man is coming to take your place."

The Public Archives of Canada, PA 8518

Farmers from various parts of Canada strongly objected to conscription. On one occasion, about 5000 of them, mostly from Ontario, marched on Ottawa to demand exemptions for their sons. Two weeks before election day, Borden gave in to their pressure and agreed to exempt farmers' sons from the military call-up (and later felt he had to cancel these exemptions). But the government found it difficult to enforce the Military Service Act. Many men refused to report for duty. Draft dodgers from every province left home to hide in mines, lumber camps, and on farms to escape conscription. Of the 100 000 men drafted for military service, many were resentful recruits. Only about half of these, after a hurried training program, reached Flanders in time for the final Allied offensive in the summer of 1918.

Canadians learned a hard lesson from the conscription issue. It had ranged farmer against city-dweller, Anglophone against Francophone, soldier against civilian. It wrecked the Liberal Party and created in Quebec a profound distrust of the Conservative Party. It was all a sharp reminder that Canada's national existence depended on pleasing, not angering, many different regional outlooks. It was a fortunate thing that peace came before the strain on the bonds of national unity became too great.

WAR AND THE CANADIAN ECONOMY

Many farmers had opposed conscription for the same reason as Laurier. Many others had protested that conscription would take away their sons and hired labor at a time when replacements were unavailable. The war had stimulated the demand for agricultural produce, and farmers were earning money. And the potential for profit was there. Between 1913 and 1919, the amount of prairie land under cultivation increased by 80 per cent. Exports zoomed beyond the highest level reached before the war. The production of wheat and flour doubled; livestock more than trebled; meat rose nearly fifteen times. Between 1914 and 1918, Canada was able to supply Britain's population and the Allied armies in Flanders with most of the food they ate.

Agriculture was not the only sector of the economy to benefit from the slaughter in Europe. Both primary and secondary industries were swamped with orders. The most significant result of rising demand was the growth of secondary industry. Until 1914, most processing of raw materials had been done in American and British factories, which, in turn, sold their finished products to consumers in Canada. During the war, these factories were so busy making weapons that few were able to continue manufacturing for foreign markets. This gave some Canadians an opportunity to meet the domestic demand for manufactured products. With the profits from mining, pulp-and-paper, and other primary industries, businessmen built factories to produce consumer goods.

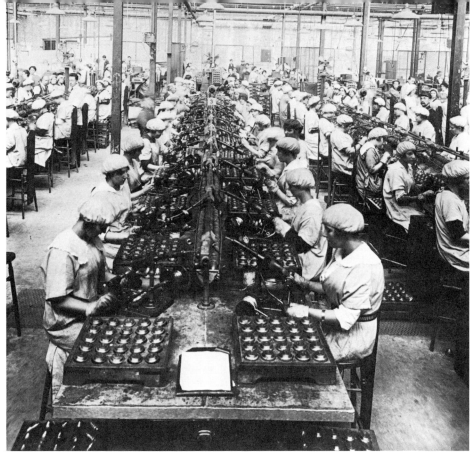

Women making shell fuses in the factory of the British Munitions Company at Verdun, Quebec. Canadian women played a major role in the manufacture of shells and high explosives. By the war's end, about 30 000 women had "done their bit" in dull, dusty, and sometimes dangerous work in munitions factories. Women also drove streetcars and ambulances and serviced machinery and equipment in railroad shops.

Other industrialists expanded existing factories to increase production for the war effort. Canadian workers were soon turning out shells, guns, airplanes, and ships for sale to the Allied powers.

Not all businessmen were satisfied by the wartime boom. Some, greedy for extra profits at the taxpayers' expense, manufactured shoddy products. Boots for the army were made of inferior materials: heels pulled off in muddy conditions, and the soles were worn out after one long route march. Tinned bully beef, a standard food ration in the trenches, was sometimes made from meat that had been officially condemned as unfit for human consumption. Government inspectors were bribed to turn a blind eye to shipments of inferior equipment or defective arms and ammunition. Another scandal was that of the Ross rifle. Sam Hughes, the minister of militia, liked it and insisted that it become the standard weapon of the Canadian infantryman. His opponents, however, said that it was too fine and delicate for use in combat conditions. They quoted instances of its becoming overheated and unworkable and drew grim pictures of Canadians, under attack, throwing away their jammed Ross rifles in maddened frustration and being reduced to fighting with bayonets.

One of the greatest scandals of the war involved the Shell Committee, headed by the controversial Sam Hughes. Its purpose was to award

Army blankets were made of shoddy material that kept out neither wind nor rain nor cold.

contracts to manufacturers to produce munitions for the British Army. By 1916, the Liberal opposition in Parliament had begun to concentrate on certain of the Committee's activities. The military-minded Hughes had insisted on giving some of his favorite members the honorary rank of colonel. This was foolish but less serious than the discovery that certain members had received large amounts of money from factory owners to whom they had awarded contracts. At no time did the opposition suggest that Hughes had personally profited from such deals, but he was responsible for the Committee and he had been careless in selecting persons who were eager to fill their own pockets. In the end, the axe fell on Hughes. In November 1916, Borden demanded and received his resignation. Nearly everyone, Liberals and Conservatives alike, sighed with relief at the departure of the short-tempered, dictatorial Sam Hughes.

In Ottawa, in 1917, Prime Minister Borden announces a Victory Loan campaign. The gigantic cost of supporting the armed forces and manufacturing war supplies was met largely through six Victory Loan campaigns. By 1919, $2 billion worth of Victory Bonds had been purchased by individuals, by insurance companies, and by banks.

THE REFORM MOVEMENT

For most people in Canada, the war was a time of hard work and personal sacrifice. Although an income tax was levied for the first time in Canadian history in 1917, the cost of war was paid for by business organizations and also by the average man and woman in the form of "Victory Loans." There were five such savings campaigns launched across the nation in the period 1914-1918 and they raised something like 85 per cent of the money needed to pay for the war effort. City workers gave up their holidays to help harvest crops. Businessmen paid the salaries of employees absent on active service in the war. Thousands of women knitted socks for the men in Flanders or made up food parcels for them or, when they were killed, visited the homes of their grief-stricken families to offer what comfort they could. Others took the place of men in fields and factories. Citizens planted "war gardens" of vegetables and put up with breadless and meatless days in the interests of conserving food supplies for dispatch to Europe.

Most Canadians believed that the war was being fought to wipe out the forces of tyranny in Europe. As a result, many reasoned that every source of evil at home should also be exterminated. One of the most popular targets of these reformers was alcohol.

There had always been prohibition organizations in Canada, but none had ever been powerful enough to convince governments to stop the sale and consumption of alcoholic beverages. The war gave them the opportunity and the argument they sought. Prohibition was linked to patriotism. Opponents of alcohol argued that cereal grains were needed

The best known prohibition organization was the Women's Christian Temperance Union (WCTU).

Archives of Ontario

In the Timiskaming district of Ontario, a raid on a "blind pig" (an illegal saloon) by provincial authorities results in the destruction of 160 kegs of liquor.

Members of the National Council of Women of Canada (NCWC) meet in 1898 in Ottawa. In the centre is Lady Aberdeen (the wife of the Governor General), a notable social reformer, a founder of the NCWC, and its first president. The NCWC worked for such reforms as the vote for women, the right of women to serve in the Senate, and the appointment of women to executive positions in government.

for bread, not booze. They appealed to the conscience of many Canadians who believed in the need for sacrifice. Thus, between 1915 and 1916, every provincial government except Quebec was swept away on a tide of anti-alcoholism. The sale of beer, wine, and liquor was forbidden by law. In 1917, the federal government responded to prohibitionist pressure by banning the importation of beverages with an alcoholic content of more than 2$^1/_2$ per cent.

One of the prominent opponents of alcohol was Nellie McClung, a popular Winnipeg writer and one of the first advocates of equality for women. Her opposition to alcohol was matched by her passionate demand for the right of women to vote. The war provided the circumstances needed by Mrs. McClung and others to show that women were fully capable of making political decisions: with so many men in the armed services, women had stepped in to fill their places in factories and on farms.

Suffragettes badgered provincial premiers with demands for the vote. There were public protest meetings and parades and petitions signed by thousands of women. Finally, the Province of Manitoba gave way. In

Quebec women won the right to vote in 1940.

The Public Archives of Canada, C 8482

January, 1916, the legislature of that province granted the franchise to women. Other provinces followed quickly; by 1922, all except Quebec had granted the right to vote.

The federal government soon followed the lead set by the provinces. The Elections Act of 1918 granted the right to vote in federal elections to all Canadian women. In 1920, they won the right to seek election to Parliament. This opened the door for women to hold political office. Edith Rogers was the first woman elected to a provincial legislature (Manitoba) in 1920. One year later, Nellie McClung won a seat in the Alberta legislature. That same year, Agnes McPhail became the first woman Member of Parliament.

*　　*　　*

The opponents of women's rights belonged to an era that had, unknowingly, received a death blow from the war. The old order had changed. The old values of class privilege, pre-established social roles, and automatic obedience to authority no longer held. The lamps of 1914 had been blown out by the winds of war. When they were relit in 1919, they illuminated a society ready to create a more democratic order in which men and women would have more freedom to question authority and to choose their own social roles.

STUDY 7

1. Describe Borden, the man and his career, up to 1911.
2. What were the reasons for the Naval Aid Bill and why was it defeated?
3. List the nations on each side in the First World War.
4. What was the Schlieffen Plan? Why did it fail? What was the result?
5. Describe the nature of the conflict in the second phase of the war.
6. List the major battles of the war and describe the Canadian participation in each.
7. What was the Canadian reaction and response in the early months of the war? For what reasons did recruitment fall off in 1916?
8. (a) What were the three bills passed in the summer of 1917? What was the aim of each?
   (b) Explain the attitudes (pro and con) of the political leaders and of the public toward conscription.
9. Discuss the questions raised on page 217 of the text. Write a paragraph summarizing your position on the conscription question.
10. (a) How did the Canadian economy benefit from the war?
    (b) Some people were more interested in "profiteering" than in profits. Explain.
11. What contributions were made by people on the home front?
12. What social and political changes came about during the war and in the early postwar period?
13. What do you think was Laurier's greatest achievement for Canada? Explain your choice.
14. How did Canada measure up — militarily, socially, politically, and economically — under the test of war?

a Restless Decade: 1919–1929

In the early morning darkness, several hundred heavily armed men filed silently out of Winnipeg police headquarters. Breaking up into several groups, they moved off quickly through the deserted streets. Before most Winnipeggers had eaten breakfast on that morning of June 17, 1919, the police had successfully carried out their raids. Taken from their beds, manacled, and then shoved into waiting cars, twelve men were swiftly whisked away to nearby Stoney Mountain Penitentiary. The charge laid against them was sedition — an attempt to overthrow the legally elected government.

For nearly five weeks since mid-May, Canada's third largest city had been paralyzed by a general strike. The bulk of Winnipeg's working force, some 35 000 men and women, had remained off their jobs. Virtually all business and commerce in the city had halted. The arrested men were leaders of the Strike Committee elected by the workers.

The mass walkout in Winnipeg had inspired workers in other Canadian cities to show support for the strikers. Within a matter of days, a series of sympathy strikes broke out in Vancouver, Edmonton, Calgary, and Toronto. Wild rumors of revolutionary plots followed the strikes. Fear of a mass uprising of Canadian workers flashed across the nation. Had labor gone mad?

THE UNION MOVEMENT

From the beginning of the Industrial Revolution in the eighteenth century, employers looked on the working man, woman, or child as one of the many resources used in the manufacturing process. Wages paid to

Courtesy Bureau of Mines, U.S. Department of the Interior

In the nineteenth century, Canadian industrialists and manufacturers made great use of child labor. Here, youngsters sort coal as it is carried past them on moving belts.

225

courtesy of B. J. Knight, Box 640, Ladysmith, B.C.

workers were one of several costs that employers had to add up in determining the price of a product. To keep costs low, employers paid laborers as little as possible. A worker either accepted the wage offered — and the number of hours in the working day, which was decided by the employer — or he or she had no job. The worker also had to accept working conditions that were often bad, if not dangerous. Employers were not required by law to assume responsibility for the safety and health of their employees. If they lost an eye or a limb while operating a machine, or became ill because of poor ventilation or dampness in the factory or workshop, there was no compensation.

An employer could fire or lay off workers without explanation and with little or no notice. Neither employer nor government provided any benefits. There were no health and accident insurance plans, no unemployment insurance schemes, no workmen's compensation boards, no pensions. With luck, a worker might find a good paying job with few risks. If not laid off and if healthy, he or she might be able to save a little money towards their old age. Few were able to do so. Dangerous working conditions, unsanitary homes and factories, poor diets, and inadequate medical attention took the lives of many workers at an early age in the eighteenth and nineteenth centuries. So workers gradually began to band together to form mutual-protection societies, which collected money to aid the widows and children of fellow workers who became the victims of disease and industrial accidents. It was not long before workers decided to approach employers to seek improved working conditions, shorter hours of work, higher wages, and the abolition of child labor. When employers refused to talk or to bargain with them, they resorted to their only weapon: the strike.

Employers had a powerful ally in government. Laws were passed to

The first evidence of union activity in Canada was recorded in the Nova Scotia legislature early in the 1800s: "Great members of journeymen workmen in the town of Halifax . . . by unlawful meetings and combinations, endeavored to regulate the rates of wages. . . ."

prevent the formation of workers' self-help organizations. In Britain, it was not until 1871 that the government passed an act that gave workers the legal right to form trade unions. From their beginnings in the pre-Confederation period, Canadian workers fought for the same right. But it was not until 1872, as the result of a strike of printers against George Brown's Toronto newspaper, *The Globe*, that they finally won it. When Brown had the union leaders arrested, jailed, and charged with criminal conspiracy, their trial publicized the fact that trade unions and their activities had never been given the protection of law. The prime minister was quick to come to their aid and embarrass his old political foe, Brown. Macdonald pushed through Parliament an act to legalize the status of unions. In future, no working person could be punished by law for joining a union.

Although Macdonald gave unions the right to exist, he made no attempt to eliminate the scandalous abuse of working people, especially children. Seventeen years after his government had passed the Trades Union Act, the Royal Commission on Capital and Labour revealed some frightening facts on children employed in factories. Boys labored from 6:30 a.m. to 6:15 p.m., with a brief break at noon, and put in a 66-hour week. In boot and shoe factories, girls were paid one cent for each pair they made and were fined four cents for any that were made badly. In cigar factories, children worked in buildings without ventilation or toilet facilities. As soon as they were old enough to claim an adult wage, they were fired.

Since government would not act against employers who allowed such exploitation, the struggle had to be waged by unions. One of the early unions, the Knights of Labor, started in the United States. At the height of its success, the Knights had about 700 000 members, 12 000 of them in Canadian "assemblies," as the local units were called. The workers who joined its assemblies were often the unskilled or semi-

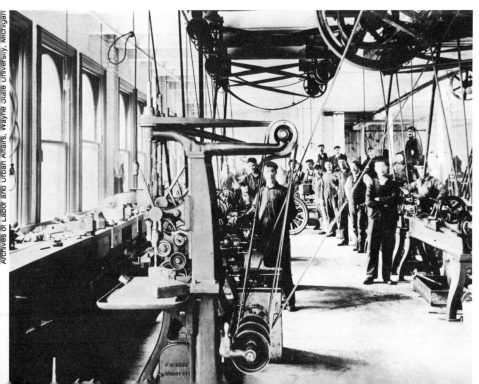

An early machine shop. In addition to the back-breaking work required in nineteenth-century and early twentieth-century plants, workers also labored in dangerous, unhealthy conditions. Lighting was often poor, dust filled the air, and unguarded moving belts caused many injuries.

227

skilled, who made up most of the force that labored on railroads, in building construction, and in factories. The attempts of the Knights to organize their members into assemblies of skilled workers were often unsuccessful. During the frequent periods of depression in the final quarter of the nineteenth century, there was heavy unemployment and low wages. Hungry men are usually too anxious to have a pay envelope in their pocket to risk being fired for trying to form a union. On the eve of the First World War, only about ten of every hundred Canadian workers belonged to a union.

In the 1970s, about 30 per cent of the Canadian labor force belonged to unions.

The best-organized workers were those in the skilled trades, such as printing and shoemaking, who formed craft unions. In 1886 many of these unions came together to set up Canada's first major labor organization, the Trades and Labour Congress (T.L.C.). Membership in the Congress was open to both craft unions and the Knights of Labor. The primary purpose of the T.L.C. was defined as,

> . . . the uniting of all labour organizations in order to work for the passage of new laws or amendments to existing laws, in the interests of those who have to earn their living, as well as to insure at the same time the well-being of the working class.

The T.L.C.'s aim was to obtain legislation favoring labor, particularly in the matter of shorter hours, safety regulations, fair-wage clauses in government contracts, and employer responsibilities.

Foote Collection, Archives of Manitoba

During the First World War, many men joined the armed forces and Canadian women took jobs in business and industry. After the war, many women stayed in the labor force. Here, in Manitoba in 1919, two women are employed as gas-station attendants.

Labor made gains during the war. Wages increased, working conditions improved, and by 1918 union membership had more than doubled to 400 000. But more than wages concerned labor leaders. They protested profiteering and rejected conscription. They believed that workingmen should not be forced to serve and die while employers remained safely at home and made excess business profits. Prime Minister Borden ignored their suggestion that profits from war production be "conscripted" to help pay the costs of the war effort. By 1918, the anger of labor leaders had mounted to near breaking point. Through bargaining with employers, unions had been able to raise wage levels, only to see them disappear due to a soaring leap in the cost of living: in four years, the price of many everyday items had increased by 40-60 per cent. They also foresaw other problems. The end of the war would bring an inevitable production slowdown in Canadian factories. Foreign manufacturers would switch from war supplies to peacetime products. As a result, Canadian exports would begin to decline, and men and women would be laid off. And where would be the jobs for the servicemen and servicewomen returning from overseas?

By June 1920, prices had reached a level double that of 1914.

The T.L.C. was an organization that always urged its members to conduct peaceful bargaining with employers. However, there had been strikes, some of them bloody and violent. Employers hired strikebreakers who tried to break up picket lines; the strikers retaliated, and pitched battles often took place before the police appeared. And there had been much suffering. Workers' families often lived on the verge of starvation during lengthy strikes, and men and women lost their property and went into debt. Yet most Canadian unions had shied away from massive confrontations with the police and with local authorities. A few labor leaders urged that unions form political parties to change the law and bring about reforms demanded by labor. But the T.L.C. preferred to follow the "Gompers' tradition." Samuel Gompers, a long-time president of the American Federation of Labor, had always insisted that wage increases and improved working conditions were best achieved through direct negotiations with employers. He was strongly opposed to forming permanent links with political parties.

The American Federation of Labor (A.F.L.) was, as its name implies, an association of unions, mostly craft. It was founded in 1886 and became one of the most powerful labor bodies in the United States. Many Canadian unions were members of the A.F.L.

During the annual convention of the T.L.C. at Quebec City in December, 1918, some delegates hotly attacked the Gompers' tradition. To support their position, they pointed to the success of the "Red Revolution" that had taken place in Russia in November, 1917. If, as they believed, the Communists had set up a government in the interests of the Russian working class, labor could gain power in the same way in Canada. The most outspoken advocates of forming a labor political party were delegates from western Canada. They demanded that the T.L.C. condemn the Borden government for "repressive" legislation it had passed forbidding strikes in war industries and on the railways. When neither proposal won much backing, the western radicals left the convention in a bitter frame of mind. Some of them vowed to form their own organization as a rival to the T.L.C.

In this official Soviet painting, Lenin is addressing a group of revolutionaries.

In 1903, Lenin became leader of the Bolsheviks, a group of socialists who followed the teachings of Karl Marx. Their aim was to overthrow Czarist rule in Russia by a revolution of industrial workers. The revolutionary movement gained strength on "Bloody Sunday," in 1905, when troops fired on a workers' march in St. Petersburg, killing or wounding hundreds of people. More strikes broke out, peasants and military groups revolted. Soviets (councils) of workers and soldiers were formed throughout Russia. On November 7 (October 25 by the old Russian calendar, hence the "October Revolution"), armed workers and servicemen, led by the Bolsheviks, seized key points in Petrograd (formerly St. Petersburg, now Leningrad). By November 15, the Bolsheviks controlled Moscow and formed a new Russian government headed by Lenin.

The convention of western labor, held in Calgary in March, 1919, was dramatically different from the T.L.C. convention in December. Calls for revolution rang through the conference hall as speaker after speaker rose to denounce the Canadian political and economic system. It was not fair, they charged, that a few people had so much wealth while most of the people had so little money. The system should be destroyed and power transferred to the workers of Canada. And there was one way that the workers could make their power felt — by a general strike, a complete stoppage of all work in a city, a province, or even throughout the entire nation. June 1 was the date set for a general strike, if approved by the mailed vote of those unable to attend the convention. They ended their conference by agreeing to work for the formation of a single union of all industrial workers, One Big Union (O.B.U.), which would gain control of the government through the weapon of the general strike.

Canadian newspapers reported the Calgary convention in close detail. For most working people who read the news reports, the terms "capitalism" and "communism" had little meaning. What was clear in their minds was that a tiny group of Canadian businessmen had made fortunes through war profiteering while working people were still barely making ends meet. If the political and economic system was to blame, it would have to be changed — and soon.

THE WINNIPEG GENERAL STRIKE, 1919

Against this background of urgent demands for political action and the increasing anger of Canadian labor, workers in the Winnipeg building and metal trades went out on strike at the beginning of May. The issues were higher wages and the right to engage in collective bargaining. Two weeks later, after conducting a vote of the city's union members to determine whether or not there should be a general strike, the Winnipeg Trades and Labour Council announced an overwhelming decision in favor of one. Business in Winnipeg halted as about 30 000 male and female workers walked off their jobs. Streetcars stopped running; banks and stores shut their doors; postmen stored away their mail bags; and telephone operators closed down their switchboards. A Strike Committee established by the workers set up its headquarters in the Labour Temple. Their aim was to ensure a peaceful strike by maintaining basic public services throughout the city. They urged policemen (who had voted to strike) to stay on the job. Firemen joined the strikers, but were replaced by volunteers. Milk and bread deliveries were resumed, and theatres and restaurants remained open. With all newspapers shut down, the Strike Committee published its own news journal, *The Western Labour News*.

At first, the mayor and city council of Winnipeg did nothing. Opponents of the strike, mostly business and professional people, were much quicker to respond. On May 16, they organized a Citizens' Committee of One Thousand with its office in the Board of Trade building. This group claimed that it existed to maintain public services, despite the Strike Committee's obvious efforts to do so. The real purpose of the Committee of One Thousand soon became evident. With large amounts of money raised from the business community, they began a propaganda campaign to break the strike. About one-third of the city's population were European-born, and much of the anti-strike propaganda was aimed at blaming them. In one of its public pronouncements, the Committee remarked,

> How much longer is the alien to run amuk, to insult our flag, take it by force from Canadian-born citizens in our streets, continue his threatening attitude toward law and order? . . .
>
> There are some 27 000 registered alien enemies in the Winnipeg District. The same "Reds" who are prominent leaders in this strike led them during the war to hamper and block, in every conceivable way, . . . reinforcements and supplies . . . going forward to the front.

The Committee brought in arms and ammunition for a volunteer defence militia enlisted from anti-strikers in the city. From the beginning, they remained in constant contact with the Borden government. The acting minister of justice, Arthur Meighen, and the minister of labor, Senator Gideon Robertson, arrived in Winnipeg on May 22. They were accompanied by a delegation from the Committee of One Thousand, which had travelled from Winnipeg to Fort William to meet them. These cabinet ministers remained a few days to assess the situation, then returned to Ottawa without attempting to meet and talk with the Strike

231

The Borden
government had also
outlawed certain
political organizations
and radical unions,
among them, the
International
Workers of the
World (I.W.W.). The
members of this
American union, who
were popularly
known as "Wobblies,"
tried to organize
workers ignored by
unions of skilled
tradesmen.

Committee. Several days later, the government rushed a bill through the House of Commons and the Senate in record time. It gave the Borden government the authority to deport, without explanation, anyone — including a British subject — born outside Canada.

The obvious support of the federal government stimulated Mayor Gray and his city council to act more boldly. They fired most of the Winnipeg police force, which had openly sympathized with the strikers. To replace them, they hired as "special constables" some university students, office clerks, and a few returning officers from the Canadian Corps, and the T. Eaton Company put its delivery-wagon horses at the disposal of these volunteer policemen. On June 10, in downtown Winnipeg, an argument started between two "specials" and a group of strikers. Heated argument led to some pushing and shoving. When several Royal North West Mounted Police (RNWMP) constables moved in to intervene, a fist fight began. The wild melee ended with several arrests but no serious injuries. It was the first occasion during the strike on which the peace had been broken.

Time was on the side of the anti-strikers. Despite financial support from unions in other parts of Canada, many strikers' families were suffering. Debts mounted, and food was scarce. And the increasing flow of propaganda leaflets issuing from the Board of Trade building was influencing many non-union workers who had supported the general strike. They were gradually drifting back to work. The anti-striker campaign changed the attitude of those Winnipeggers who had remained neutral. The Committee of One Thousand charged that the Strike Committee was controlled by dangerous foreign radicals, "aliens," "bohunks," and "foreigners." They were revolutionaries who were determined to wreck the Canadian parliamentary system and other British traditions. Huge advertisements appeared in the Winnipeg daily newspapers that urged the deportation of "the undesirable alien and land him back in the bilgewaters of European civilization from whence he sprung and to which he properly belongs." The Borden government, however, did not need much urging to take action. On his visit to the city in May, Justice Minister Meighen had believed the fears of the leaders of the Committee of One Thousand that the strike was simply the first stage of a national revolution. The order went out to bring in the leaders of the Strike Committee, which would end the whole affair.

The swift arrest of the dozen leading strikers in the early hours of June 17 crippled the strike, but did not end it. Four days later, a "Silent Parade" organized by ex-servicemen approached the Royal Alexandra Hotel in downtown Winnipeg to protest the arrests. (This demonstration had not been organized by the strikers, though many marched in it, in silence, as the parade leaders had requested.) They were met by a detachment of Royal North West Mounted Police, who quickened their pace as they advanced toward the mass of people filling Main Street.

The scene is Winnipeg, and the date is June 21, 1919. Before the day is over, a number of people will have been injured and two men will be dead. In this photograph, taken in front of the city hall, a group of men and boys, angered by the Mounted Police charge, try to topple a streetcar. A little later, they attempted to set it on fire.

Suddenly, with pistols drawn and clubs swinging, they charged into the throng. When the street was cleared some hours later, one man lay dead, another was dying, and thirty had been taken to hospital. That day, June 21, which later became known as "Bloody Saturday," effectively ended the strike, although strike officials did not formally accept defeat until July 3.

While a committee appointed by the Borden government set about investigating the causes of the Winnipeg General Strike, the trial of the strike leaders got under way. More arrests had been made, and the accused totalled fifteen. Before the trial began, charges were dropped against five. All of the remaining ten were Anglo-Saxons. They included two Protestant ministers, two Winnipeg aldermen, one member of the Manitoba legislature, and five respected local officials with several years of service in the labor movement. There was not a single foreign re- volutionary among them. The trials went on into 1920. One man was convicted on a charge of seditious conspiracy and received a sentence of two years in prison. Six others were sentenced to one year or less apiece. Three were acquitted.

The Robson Commission, which investigated the strike, later re- ported that there had been no attempt to overthrow the government. The strikers, the Commission concluded, were interested only in higher wages and union recognition, not in revolution.

Despite the findings of the Robson Commission, the House of Commons passed an amendment (to Section 98 of the Criminal Code) which outlawed any organization that might bring about "governmental, industrial or economic change" by force.

THE FARMERS PROTEST

Ontario Election,
1919
U.F.O.   43
Lib.   28
Cons.   26
Labor   12
Independent   2

Dissatisfaction and protest were not confined to western Canada. Despite its defeat in Winnipeg in June, organized labor scored a partial victory in Ontario several months later. In an October election in that province, a recently formed Labor Party won twelve seats. But this surprising success was overshadowed by the completely unexpected triumph of another party, the United Farmers of Ontario (U.F.O.). Going into the election, they had held a mere three seats. When the results were tallied, they had added forty more to their total. In November, 1919, their leader, E. C. Drury, was sworn in as premier of Ontario, the head of the first farmer-controlled government in Canadian history.

The U.F.O. victory climaxed a half-century of protest by Canada's agricultural community. There had been various attempts in the past to organize Canada's large agricultural community to wage a war of protest on a united front. All had failed. Because farmers lived far apart from one another, it was usually difficult to bring them together for meetings. And when they did meet, it was often just as difficult to draw up a policy and course of action acceptable to the majority. They were an independent lot who resisted mass organization. But they did agree on one thing: no other sector of the Canadian economy had received such shabby treatment as agriculture. Western farmers in particular felt that they were at the mercy of several powerful enemies. All of these were located in eastern Canada. They included the banks, which controlled credit and owned much farmland, and the CPR, which charged high freight rates. But it was the question of the tariff that formed a common bond of resentment among farmers in every region of Canada. In its desire to protect eastern manufacturers, Ottawa kept a tariff on cheap, imported farm machinery and many other goods needed by farmers. Yet farmers received absolutely no protection. They had to sell their products in a tariff-free international market that was highly competitive.

The Grain Growers' Guide, a lively, colorful newspaper that was read by most farmers, repeatedly harped on the need for a national farm organization. It pointed out that labor had long recognized the need to build a central organization to combat business interests. Only through unity could farmers find the same strength. In 1909, this step was finally taken with the formation of the Canadian Council of Agriculture. For the next several years, the Council tried repeatedly, but without success, to pressure the federal government to lower tariffs.

*For details on
conscription and
farmers, see p. 218.*

The introduction of conscription exhausted the patience of many farmers, who angrily demanded a series of reforms called the "New National Policy." Adopted by the Canadian Council of Agriculture in 1918, it insisted on lower tariffs, higher taxes for the wealthy, government ownership of railways, express and telegraph companies, votes for women, prohibition, and the abolition of the Senate. When neither the Conservatives nor the Liberals responded favourably to this New National Policy, various farm leaders began the formation of a national farmers' party. The stunning election victory of the United Farmers of Ontario in 1919 helped to convince many doubtful farmers that needed reforms would come only through direct political action.

NEW LEADERS

Among the already convinced was a prominent Manitoba farmer, Thomas A. Crerar. A former president of a farm co-operative called the United Grain Growers Company, Crerar had entered politics as a Liberal. In 1917, he accepted Borden's offer to become minister of agriculture in the Unionist government. When his persistent attempts to persuade his fellow cabinet members to lower tariffs were constantly rejected, he resigned in June, 1919. Then came the U.F.O. triumph in the autumn of that year. Early in 1920, he and ten other Members of Parliament announced the formation of the National Progressive Party. Their platform was the New National Policy.

The Progressives, full of fire for their cause and enthusiastically organizing their new political party, contrasted with the Liberals and Conservatives, who were stuck with the now aimless Unionist government. In 1917, the Conservatives had formed a coalition with pro-conscription Liberals. Since the end of the war, this Unionist government had staggered along as if it were suffering from a terminal illness. And, in part, it was. When the reasons for its existence (the war and

National Film Board Photothèque

Arthur Meighen, born and educated in Ontario, moved west in 1898 to study and practise law in Winnipeg and Portage la Prairie. As a member of Borden's wartime cabinet, Meighen helped produce several very complicated items of legislation, notably the acts by which the government of Canada acquired ownership of the bankrupt Canadian Northern, Grand Trunk, and Grand Trunk Pacific railways. Twice leader of the Conservative Party (1920-1926 and 1941) and twice prime minister (1920-1921 and 1926), Meighen was never an effective politician in the House of Commons.

235

conscription) disappeared, so, gradually, did many of its members. One by one, those Liberal Members of Parliament who, in 1917, had responded to Borden's appeal for national unity began to return to the other side of the House of Commons. In 1920, the name, Unionist, was dropped by the Conservative Party.

The loss of Liberal followers was not the only concern of the Conservatives. Their leader, Prime Minister Borden, old and tired, was anxious to leave politics. Yet, because he still commanded considerable respect throughout the nation, the party pleaded with him to stay on. Reluctantly, he agreed to remain until July 1, 1919.

Borden's final act as leader was to choose his successor as prime minister. When his first choice, Sir Thomas White, turned down the offer, Borden turned to Arthur Meighen, his minister of the interior.

Arthur Meighen, 1874-1960

Meighen had many obvious qualifications. He had served as a Member of Parliament from Manitoba since 1908 and had considerable government experience. As solicitor-general during the war, he had become Borden's parliamentary work horse, carrying the load of several cabinet ministers. He was both energetic and intelligent, and his rapid wit and superb command of the English language had made him the foremost debater in the House of Commons. But his wit worked against him, too, for he had a flaw that is fatal for a politician. In his judgment of parliamentary matters and opponents, he was rigidly absolute. Situations and individuals were either right or wrong, good or bad. He saw everything in black-and-white terms. Since there were no grey areas in between, this left no room for compromise. And this is where his wit worked against him. Instead of the political art of persuasion, he used venom-laden sarcasm to attack opponents who disagreed with him.

Meighen's belief in absolute principles, his energy and his verbal arrogance, made it almost impossible for him to perform well as party leader and prime minister. He had made too many enemies. He had become identified with the Military Service and Wartime Election acts, laws in which he believed with all his heart. As a result, he was never able to carry Quebec for the Conservative Party. He had made his anti-labor views obvious during the Winnipeg General Strike, and organized labor never forgave him. And because of his unshakable belief in the necessity of a high protective tariff, few farmers had a kind word to say about Arthur Meighen.

He had one other serious liability. He could not stomach the recently elected leader of the Liberal Party. "Speak up," he once taunted him and his fellow Liberals in the House of Commons. "Don't behave as your ancestors did ten thousand years ago." Meighen's method of handling this man would prove to be a particularly costly error of judgment.

William Lyon Mackenzie King, 1874-1950

The new Liberal leader was William Lyon Mackenzie King. He had been chosen at a leadership convention called after the death of Sir Wilfrid Laurier in February, 1919. Elected to Parliament in 1908, King became the first minister of labor in a federal government. After his

236

defeat in the 1911 election, he worked for the American multi-millionaire, John D. Rockefeller, Junior, as a labor-relations consultant. He returned to Canada to run as an anti-conscription Liberal in the 1917 election. When many of the party faithful turned their backs on Laurier, King remained loyal. Although he went down to defeat in that election, his backing of Laurier helped him in the years to come. In the seven general elections that he fought as Liberal leader, his party never failed to win Quebec.

If Meighen was direct and forthright, King was cautious and guarded. Some would say he was tricky. Where Meighen's careful selection of pointed and pertinent words communicated his ideas clearly and concisely, King's verbal wanderings often confused his audiences. He was a master of doubletalk. Was this deliberate or simply a reflection of his personality? The public never did find out. Unlike the clear black-and-white approach of Meighen, a misty greyness characterized King. Because there was little about the man to like or dislike, he remained inoffensive. By avoiding extreme positions on issues, he escaped antagonizing most people. He preferred caution to decision and delay to action. His political foes were seldom able to ruffle him and rarely able to force him to take a definite stand on an issue. He was usually able to hold firmly to a middle position on just about every matter.

Someone once said that during his frequent travels throughout Canada, he never met a single person who admitted to having voted for Mackenzie King. Yet when King retired in 1948, he had held office longer than any other Canadian prime minister.

A little over a year after he had replaced Borden as prime minister, Meighen called a federal election. Full of confidence, he entered the campaign stressing the need to maintain the protective tariff. Crerar, the Progressive leader, was equally firm in his opposition to the tariff.

William Lyon Mackenzie King on the campaign trail in Ontario. (Note the misspelling of his name on the election banner and the cutting reference to "Millionaire Meighen" on the hood of the automobile.)

It is said that while other boys grew up reading adventure stories, Mackenzie King was raised in his Berlin (now Kitchener), Ontario, home on tales about his rebel grandfather, William Lyon Mackenzie, and the Upper Canada Rebellion of 1837. The Liberal government under Mackenzie King passed reform legislation never even dreamed of by his grandfather.

Federal Election,
1921
Lib.   117
Prog.   64
Cons.   50
Lab.   3
Ind.   1

Farmers' parties won
elections in Alberta
(1921) and Manitoba
(1922).

Somewhere in between Meighen and Crerar was King. He neatly succeeded in being unclear in explaining the Liberal policy on the tariff.

The election of 1921 was the first since the war. It was also the first in which no party won a clear majority of seats in the House of Commons. The Liberals won 117 seats, the Progressives came second with 64, and the Conservatives trailed with 50. Where each party obtained its support revealed a disturbing fact about federal politics in Canada. In three provinces – Quebec, Nova Scotia, and Prince Edward Island – the Liberals won every seat. In those provinces and in three more – Manitoba, Saskatchewan, and Alberta – the Conservatives failed to elect a single member. Thirty-seven of the forty seats in the Prairie Provinces were taken by the Progressives. Nothing could have revealed more clearly the regional and cultural differences that divided postwar Canada.

The failure of any party to win wide national support created a most unusual situation in Parliament. How could a prime minister govern without a majority? King, as the leader of the party with the largest number of members, decided to try. He knew the danger he would have to face as the prime minister of a minority government. Should the opposition members ever combine, they could outvote him and force his resignation. Fortunately for King, the great policy differences that separated the Progressives and the Conservatives prevented such a combination. In this delicate position, he managed to remain in power for four years in a country that was rapidly changing.

A NEW AND DIFFERENT CANADA

The watershed of the twentieth century was the First World War. In the 1920s, a society emerged that was radically different from that of the pre-war era. It was an urban society with a mammoth appetite for consumer goods. This demand was met by mass production: manufacturers using assembly-line production methods. The decade of the 1920s was the dawn of the modern "mass" age. Mass production led to mass consumption with help from mass communication. Goods were made available to people in quantity and usually at low prices. This frequently resulted in a dull sameness, a loss of the originality that had characterized products fashioned by hand in an earlier age. But it supplied the masses with what they wanted – or with what mass advertising told them they wanted.

The Canadian census of 1921 showed that the number of people living in towns and cities had almost caught up to the number in rural areas. During the 1920s, annual immigration averaged 100 000, and most of the newcomers headed for cities to find work in factories. So did many native Canadians, who were lured not only by employment but by a more exciting way of life in the cities. Well before the end of the decade, Canada had become an urban society. The growth of cities and towns in

Henry Ford (1863-1947) pioneered the use of assembly-line methods to mass-produce an automobile (the "Model T") that the average person could afford. Here, the indoor section of the line moves the chassis along for the addition of various parts. The photograph on the next page illustrates a later, outdoor stage of an automobile's progress "down the line": the body drop station.

the 1920s reflected the shift from an agricultural to an industrial economy. Labor's fears had been realized. There was a postwar recession that lasted four years. When it ended in 1923, primary industry resumed the steady growth that it had been enjoying since the beginning of the century. Gold and copper at Rouyn and Val d'Or, Quebec, and silver and lead at Keno Hill in the Yukon sparked a new mining boom. With the development of the Arvida smelter in Quebec, Canada became the world's second largest producer of aluminum. The most impressive growth was in the pulp-and-paper industry, which was able to reduce costs because of cheap hydro-electric power. By 1929, Canadian exports of wood pulp equalled those of the rest of the world.

It was the development of inexpensive hydro-electric power that accounted for much of the success of secondary industry in this period. To meet the constantly mounting demand for consumer goods, new factories were being built. Radios, stoves, refrigerators, vacuum cleaners — all of them electrically-powered products — were rolling off assembly lines in increasing quantities. But not all regions of Canada enjoyed an equal share in the prosperity of the 1920s. It was confined mainly to the industrial heartland of Canadian manufacturing: Ontario, Quebec,

Canada's main exports continued to be raw materials and products from primary industry.

239

Henry Ford pioneered in the field of labor relations as well as in techniques of mass production. Early in 1914, he cut the working day in Ford plants from nine hours to eight and set the minimum wage for every employee over 21 years of age at $5 a day. (At that time, skilled workers in industry generally received $2.50 a day, unskilled workers $1.50 a day.) Ford further astonished his fellow industrialists by offering his employees a share in the profits. Their share in the first year was $10 million.

Henry Ford offered the Model T in any color the customer wanted, so long as it was black. This standardizing lowered costs but limited variety.

and, to a lesser extent, British Columbia. In the Maritime Provinces, growth was slow and unemployment remained high. And on the Prairies, despite bumper harvests, the price of wheat began to fall in 1925. The uneven economic growth of "have" and "have not" provinces intensified regional discontent, and increased the belief that the federal government favored certain regions over others.

There was another economic development that went largely unnoticed until many years later. The great economic expansion of the 1920s would never have taken place without huge amounts of money. Most of this finance capital that sank mine shafts, built factories, and laid down rail lines came from Americans who poured investment dollars into Canada. In the long run, Canadians would pay a heavy price for inviting American capital into this country. Even in the short run, some of the results were obvious. By the end of the decade, Americans owned 40 per cent of the Canadian machinery and chemical industries and 60 per cent of the electrical, rubber, and non-ferrous metal industries. They also owned almost all automobile manufacturing.

In his successful campaign for the presidency of the United States in 1928, Herbert Hoover commented: "The slogan of progress is changing from the full dinner pail to the full garage." In "the full garage," of course, was a car, sometimes two. The car craze was one of the main characteristics of the 1920s. For the well-to-do there were big, luxurious sedans such as the Packard, La Salle, and Pierce Arrow. However, the most popular car of the era was the Model T Ford, the "tin Lizzie," that could reach such high speeds as fifty-six kilometres per hour with its powerful twenty-horsepower motor. At a price of $395, it was within reach of most wage earners' budget. By 1930, one out of every two Canadian families owned an automobile.

Perhaps more than any other technological invention of the times, the internal-combustion engine transformed Canadian society. It changed the pace of life in cities. People were able to live in one part of town and work in another. By allowing cities to expand outward, it led to urban sprawl. It allowed business and commerce to expand. Goods and services could reach regions never served by railroads. The motor vehicle was a symbol of freedom for many. With an automobile it was no longer necessary to travel on fixed routes or follow fixed schedules.

Technology affected work and travel and also leisure. The electronic revolution produced the movies and radio and gave birth to one of the biggest industries of the era: the entertainment business. Although the first film to have a sound track, *The Jazz Singer*, was not produced until 1927, movies became the most popular form of entertainment of the 1920s. And it was not only the young who craved the escape from reality offered by the thousands of silent films churned out by the Hollywood studios. There were few Canadians who were not amazed by the swashbuckling adventures of Douglas Fairbanks or amused by the hilarious antics of Charlie Chaplin. These film "stars" and such others as Mary Pickford, Dorothy and Lillian Gish, Lon Chaney, and Rudolph Valentino became household names.

Spectator sports ranked a close second to movies. Baseball, rugby-football, and lacrosse had many fans, but in Canada the most popular sport far and away was hockey. Following its organization during the war, the National Hockey League grew quickly. By the late 1920s, there was a Canadian and an American division. The playoff series between the champion of each division received the Stanley Cup, a gift from Governor General Lord Stanley. Eventually it was no longer necessary for the keen hockey fan to leave home on a cold winter night to enjoy the favorite sport. By turning a dial on the latest technological miracle called radio, one could hear the voice of broadcasters such as the young Foster Hewitt reporting the play-by-play action. Radio brought more than hockey to the listener. It offered a variety of programs from grand opera to soap opera, from Shakespeare to local drama groups. One achievement which it shared with the automobile was to bring Canadians closer

At the price of only five or ten cents a show, movies quickly became part of "pop" culture. Movie fans followed the private lives of film stars. When Valentino died in 1926, crowds lined up for eleven blocks in New York City to pass his coffin. Women cried and swooned, overcome by grief.

Foster Hewitt made his first radio broadcast of a hockey game in 1923. It was an amateur game between the Toronto Parkdale Canoe Club and a team from Kitchener, Ontario.

In the 1920s, railroads bound the country together culturally as well as physically. The CPR owned a radio station, and the CNR operated a network of stations. Here, CNR staff "reproduce" a train using a bell (left), an "All aboard!" announcer (centre), a "toot" whistle (right), and a "clackety-clack" sound board (far right).

Canadian National

together. Through coast-to-coast radio Canadians began to learn more about the country and each other.

One of the important social changes of the era was in the role of women. During the First World War they had won the right to vote and proved their ability to handle many kinds of jobs once restricted to men. With the aid of modern technology, they took even bigger steps in the 1920s. The wider use of washing machines, refrigerators, and other electrical appliances eased household labors, and more women entered the work force.

Movies and television plays about the 1920s usually show women with bobbed hair and short skirts, dancing the "Charleston" or the "Black Bottom." This decade has often been referred to as the "Roaring Twenties" or the "Jazz Age." People wanted to forget the war, and so they let go and did all sorts of things in order to have a good time. There were many fads that attracted public attention: flagpole sitting, goldfish swallowing, and marathon dancing. And there was bathtub gin. The fervor of the anti-liquor crusade that swept Canada during the war vanished rapidly in the early 1920s as province after province repealed its prohibition law. Even when it was illegal to manufacture liquor for sale within a province, it could still be produced for export. The largest and richest market lay just south of the border, in the United States. But selling liquor to Americans was illegal, and often dangerous. Ever since 1919, it had been against American law to import and sell alcoholic beverages in the United States. However, smuggling was a highly profitable trade in which hundreds of dollars changed hands across the border.

It was difficult to enforce prohibition. There were hardly enough government agents and regular police to guard a border that meandered for more than 8000 kilometres along lakes and rivers, through prairies and over mountains. Much of the rum-running took place on the Great Lakes and along the Atlantic Coast. The captain of a Canadian boat laden with liquor would leave a port such as Windsor, Ontario, with papers indicating his destination as Mexico. Within a few hours, he had reached a quiet inlet on the American side of the Detroit River. There he would swiftly transfer his cargo to waiting trucks, silently draw anchor, and steal back to Windsor. Canadian customs officials rarely asked questions when he handed in his papers marked with a forged entry stamp suggesting he had delivered his cargo in Mexico. Since American and not Canadian law had been broken, Canadian officials did nothing. Smugglers often operated in packs. When they were spotted by an American coast guard cutter, they fled in different directions. If the cutter was able to catch one of the boats, the smugglers threw their cargo overboard. The liquor was in sacks tied together with rope and attached to a buoy. Bags of salt were also fastened to the buoy, and their weight carried the liquor to the bottom of the river or ocean. A few days later, when the salt had dissolved, the buoy and the liquor floated to the surface, to be picked up by the smugglers.

Prohibition in the United States was repealed in 1933.

Rum-running was a term applied to the smuggling of *any* liquor.

Photographs courtesy of The Windsor Star

The American government's decision in 1919 to prohibit the manufacture, transportation, or sale of intoxicating liquors was an opportunity for some Canadians to make smuggling a regular form of employment. However, even generally law-abiding Canadians welcomed Prohibition as a chance to make "easy money" every now and again. Here, a man and a woman demonstrate how this was done. In each case, the addition of a heavy topcoat will hide the portable drums and the bottles.

American protests at the illegal liquor trade went unheeded by the Mackenzie King government until a private investigation in 1925 conducted by a group of businessmen found evidence of corruption in the Canadian customs department. Its officials were working hand in glove with a nation-wide group of smugglers. When King was informed of their findings, the prime minister ignored them, but he knew that the charges of corruption would not be kept secret for too long. So, before the opposition had a chance to learn of the charges, King diverted everyone's attention by calling an election.

King asked the nation to return enough Liberals to provide him with a majority. The voters refused. The Liberals slipped to 101 seats, while the Conservatives leaped to 116. Behind them were the Progressives with only 24. Once again there was no majority party in the House of Commons. King decided on a gamble to retain power. By promising to introduce laws to suit the twenty-four Progressive Members of Parliament, he gained their support. For a time, he succeeded, and then the Conservatives discovered the charges of corruption in the customs department. Debate on the issue went on until the Conservatives

Federal Election, 1925

Cons.	116
Lib.	101
Prog.	24
Lab.	2
Ind.	2

243

General Sir Julian Byng was an immensely courageous British regular soldier who despised "softness" of any kind. In wartime France, when many generals preferred to live well behind the front line in comfortable houses staffed by many servants and several chefs, Byng lived "up front," and often ate soldiers' rations. Shortly after handing over command of the Canadian Corps to General Currie and returning to service with the British Army, he was given a peerage and became Viscount Byng of Vimy.

Lord Byng was Governor General of Canada from 1921 to 1926.

moved a vote of censure against the government. King realized that he could not win. The Progressives would surely vote with the Conservatives. To avoid defeat, King approached the Governor-General, Lord Byng, and asked him to dissolve Parliament and call an election. In fact, King asked three times for a dissolution, and three times his request was refused.

Normally, a Governor General accepts the prime minister's advice on the matter of the dissolution of Parliament. But in 1926 there were several awkward questions that made Governor General Byng hesitate. King's government was facing a vote of censure in the Commons, so should the government be allowed to escape that vote by calling an election? There had been an election a few months earlier, so was another one going to serve any useful purpose? Was it not possible that Arthur Meighen and the Conservatives might be able to form the next government, thus sparing the country the trouble and expense of an election? Did not Meighen have a constitutional right to *try* to govern with whatever Progressive support he could win in the House of Commons? The Governor General thought so and asked Meighen to form a government.

The Conservative leader held office for only three days. During a late night session, a sleepy Progressive Member of Parliament mistakenly cast his vote against the Conservatives. This single vote provided the majority that defeated the government. Having been defeated, now it was Meighen's turn to approach the Governor General with the same request King had made the previous weekend. This time Byng agreed to dismiss Parliament and issue the writs for an election.

Many experts on the constitution have debated the "King-Byng Crisis" over the years. Whether or not the Governor General acted improperly by granting Meighen what he had refused King is still a moot question. Of more importance is the fact that King made an enormous issue of it in the election, charging that a representative of the British monarchy had interfered in Canadian affairs. And, rightly or wrongly, many Canadians believed him. When the votes were counted, King had at last won his majority. The Liberals took 129 seats and the Conservatives 91. The faltering Progressives slid to 13.

THE STOCK MARKET CRASH

The following year, 1927, Canada celebrated its sixtieth anniversary, the Diamond Jubilee. The constitutional crisis was forgotten as the nation went on a spree of parties, parades, and pageants. Despite pockets of unemployment in various parts of the nation, the economy was booming. 1928 became 1929, and the stock market continued to climb. Values

The stock market is a place where stocks and bonds are bought and sold. The most important stock market in North America is the New York Stock Exchange.

Confederation Life Collection

On July 1, 1927, the sixtieth anniversary of Confederation was celebrated across the Dominion with parades, picnics, and bonfires. On Parliament Hill in Ottawa, a massed choir, flanked by army, navy, and air forces units, was the centrepiece of a special pageant. Overhead, a squadron of RCAF planes flew past in salute. It was led by the American flyer Charles Lindbergh, "Lucky Lindy," who had just returned from his historic solo flight across the Atlantic Ocean.

went up and up. The decade that had started so gloomily was apparently going to end joyously.

But beneath the surface of the Roaring Twenties there were several warning signals of the disaster to come. Many of the new mines, factories, machines, and equipment that were producing materials and goods had been financed on credit. The money to repay the loans was expected to come from selling the raw materials and manufactured products abroad. Canada's growing population provided a larger domestic market than ever before but, as always, the Canadian economy was dependent upon exports. Even before the end of the decade, a decline in Canada's foreign sales had begun. There were several reasons for this. Germany had been forced to pay the Allied powers for the losses and damages inflicted on them during the war. The staggering amount of these reparations forced Germany to raise money through loans in the United States. Now Germany had to pay both the reparations and the interest on its American loans. The enormous strain on the German

Left: This advertisement from a 1923 issue of Popular Radio *promised that the $85 Radiola RS was "light enough to carry with you. Powerful enough . . . to listen in from the farthest mountaintop camp to the big cities. . . . What a summer of fun it means!"*

Right: A 1920s refrigerator that is "as easy to operate as an electric fan, almost as portable . . . and unusually quiet."

Radio Corporation of Canada

Canadian General Electric Company Limited

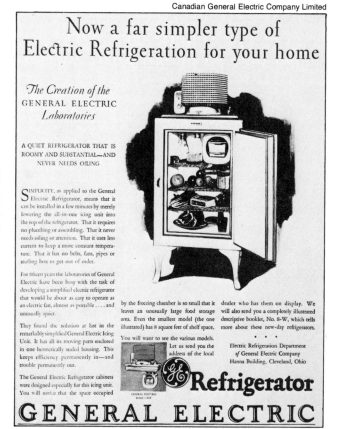

economy reduced its ability to pay for imported goods from foreign nations, including Canada. Tariffs also hindered the flow of international trade. As other European countries began to recover from the war, they gradually increased their tariff barriers to protect their own manufactured goods. The United States did the same. High tariffs made it difficult for Canadians to undersell their foreign competitors.

Another factor that ended the prosperity of the twenties was credit buying: many individual Canadians adopted the same financial methods as large industries. They owed much more than they earned, hoping that endless prosperity would allow them to pay all their bills at some future date. In the 1920s, there was a huge increase in the practice of "buying on time." Thousands of people bought houses, appliances, and cars for as little as 15-20 per cent cash down. And thousands of Canadians and Americans, from all classes and age groups, bought stocks and bonds "on margin." They paid a small percentage of the cost of stock and waited for it to rise in value. When it did, they paid what they owed from the money they made and pocketed the rest of the profit. But there were also thousands of Canadians and Americans who were not able to buy all those cars, stoves, and refrigerators, which kept piling up in car lots, warehouses, and factories because manufacturers would not cut their price. By 1929, the price of stocks and shares in American and Canadian companies had little or no relationship to these companies' *real* earning power. The entire North American economy was like a house of cards built on a shaky basis. Sooner or later, the entire structure would come tumbling down. And this is what happened late in 1929.

It started in September. A number of businessmen at last began to realize that something was wrong when prices were still going up and up while, at the same time, more goods were being produced than were being sold — at home or abroad. They slowly stopped buying stock, and the stock market began to falter. Then came the collapse as thousands of people rushed to sell the stocks they had only partly paid for. Prices began to fall on the New York, Toronto, and Montreal stock exchanges. On October 24, "Black Thursday," prices tumbled sharply. Panic seized stock owners, who tried to sell at any cost. Five days later, on October 29, there was a record-breaking day on the Toronto market: nearly one million shares were sold as their values continued to nose-dive. By November, the stock of the biggest and best companies had fallen in value by at least 50 per cent.

The stock-market "crash" ruined people who had invested their life savings in a wild investment binge in the late 1920s. It ruined small businesses that had mortgaged everything they owned to expand their operation. Banks, unable to collect debts, had to be closed down. Railroads went bankrupt. Large businesses were forced to operate part-time or with reduced staffs. The shock to the Canadian economy was devastating. Unfortunately, the Depression that would dominate the next decade was to bring even greater suffering.

Buying on margin is paying only a percentage of the price of the stock. The buyer owes the stockbroker the remainder of the price. To help prevent another stock market crash, the percentage required as down payment has been increased.

Many more banks failed in the U.S. than in Canada because they were individual operations. In Canada, with a system of branch banks, assets could be moved to branches, as needed, to cover loan payments, customer withdrawals, etc.

STUDY 8

1. List the social and economic conditions that led workers to form unions.
2. To aid your understanding of the labor movement in Canada, it would be helpful for you to check out and discuss the meaning of these terms: trade union, craft union, industrial union, strike, collective bargaining, workmen's compensation, compulsory arbitration, capitalism (or private or free enterprise), communism, socialism.
3. Trace the steps in the growth of the Canadian labor movement from 1870 to the end of the First World War.
4. With all the gains made during the war, why was labor angry and anxious?
5. What led to the formation of the O.B.U. and how did it differ from other unions?
6. Write a report on the Winnipeg General Strike using the following outline: origins, opposing forces, breaking the strike, the trial, the Robson Commission.
7. What were the farmers' protests? What did they hope to accomplish by the New National Policy?
8. Analyse the 1921 election under these headings: parties, policies, and leaders.
9. How was the society that emerged in the 1920s radically changed — socially, economically, technologically — from that of the prewar era?
10. Choose the change that has most radically affected your world and explain your choice.
11. How did American Prohibition lead to the Canadian election of 1925?
12. What was the "King-Byng" crisis all about?
13. List the causes of the Depression. How would you rank these as they applied to Canada?

from Riches to Rags: 1929–1939

Sand! Tiny, almost invisible particles of it forced a way through the narrowest of crevices and blanketed the furniture. Sand embedded itself in the bread and floated on the surface of the milk jug. It settled in the hair, crept into the ears, and penetrated the nostrils. It swept through farmyards, drowning them in granular seas that rose upward in frozen waves and threatened to engulf barns and outbuildings. It lapped at the walls of farmhouses and swirled into the fields to form weird, wind-whipped formations. Farmers scanned the skies, praying for the rain clouds that would transform their parched land into the rich breadbasket it had once been.

In the 1930s, large sections of southern Saskatchewan and Alberta resembled the Sahara Desert. Sand choked the young wheat shoots and smothered the clover and alfalfa. During these almost rainless years in

Manitoba Archives

In 1931, large parts of western Canada, notably southern Saskatchewan, were known as the "Dust Bowl." Prolonged drought dried out the ground, and the fertile topsoil was blown away. Then the wind picked up layers of sand and grit and spread these far and wide.

249

Prairie labor income
dropped from $508
million in 1929 to
$292 million in 1933.

western Canada, only a hardy plant called Russian Thistle seemed able to thrive. And grasshoppers. Without warning, swarms of these ravenous insects blackened the skies and then circled down to devour what crops there were. As farmers watched helpless, millions of grasshoppers reduced whole fields of grain to gnawed stubble in a matter of hours. It was so much like the plague of locusts in the Old Testament that some westerners were convinced that the Day of Judgment itself was not far off. The years of drought that followed the plague only strengthened their belief.

THE "DIRTY THIRTIES": THE GREAT DEPRESSION

Even before the grasshoppers and the drought, farmers had watched the price of wheat plummet from a high of $59 per tonne in the boom year of 1929 to a low of $14 three years later. And even at this ridiculously low price, they could not sell it: foreign wheat sales had sharply declined, and prairie storage bins were filled to the brim with the unsold harvests of 1930 and 1931. With little or no income, farm families were unable to buy adequate supplies of food and clothing. They faced mounting back payments on mortgages, household goods, and on farm equipment they had bought on credit during the years of plenty. A bailiff calling at a neighbor's farm to repossess a tractor or chesterfield suite or to announce the bank's foreclosure on the mortgage became a common sight. When families were no longer able to stomach another mouthful of gopher stew or to endure the shame of wearing clothes made from flour sacks, they packed their belongings and joined the dusty trail of the desperate heading for the cities and relief.

If mortgage payments
are owing past a
certain point, the
holder of the
mortgage can
foreclose (shorten the
mortgage period) and
take possession of the
property.

But instead of relief, they found even deeper misery. There were too few jobs and too many men and women looking for them. The unemployed included skilled and unskilled laborers, those with years of working experience and young graduates looking for their first job, tradesmen, technicians, professional people and, now, homeless farm families. Many of the jobless made daily rounds of the factories and offices, hoping for a break. Sometimes they were lucky enough to find a job shovelling coal, loading trucks, or washing dishes. More usually they were greeted by the all too familiar "No Help Wanted" sign that hung on most factory gates and office doors. So the thousands of jobless stood in line every day at public soup kitchens. "Brother, Can You Spare a Dime?" was a popular song in the "top ten" during the 1930s. It well described the desperate situation of those who took up positions at busy street corners, begging passers-by for enough money to buy a cup of coffee or a glass of beer. For many, the 1930s brought the most humiliating experiences of their lives. Canadians had been brought up to believe in "rugged individualism." Success was the result of hard work and careful savings; failure was the product of laziness and the poor management of money. It was disgraceful to be poor, and those who ac-

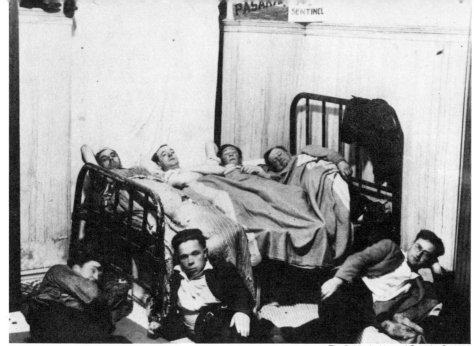

During the 1930s, many a "flophouse" (cheap hotel or rooming house) was the only shelter available to the unemployed. As a young reporter, Gordon Sinclair noted that, instead of living in one of Toronto's flophouses, many jobless men dug cave-homes for themselves in the tall banks of the Don Valley.

cepted handouts from charity organizations were usually looked down upon — or felt they were.

When the Depression began, there were few government agencies to help the unemployed, the sick, the orphaned, and the widowed. It was only when federal, provincial, and local governments realized the extent of unemployment and misery that they began to provide substantial forms of relief in the 1930s. But even this fell far short of people's needs. Married couples were usually better off than single men or women. They received food vouchers from relief agencies set up in most cities. The amount varied. In the Province of Saskatchewan, a family of five received a 44.5 kilogram (98-pound) bag of flour and vouchers for $10 worth of food per month. In a city like Toronto, a family of seven was allowed $1 per person per week. But, as someone remarked, even with bread selling at 5¢ a loaf, hamburger at 10¢ a pound, and jeans at $1.50 a pair, relief payments provided "not quite enough to live on, and a little too much to die on."

Single women could keep house for aging parents or share household duties with relatives. Married or single, it was a time when women could find jobs — if they were prepared to work long hours in factories for a few dollars a week. But life was much more difficult for men, particularly the unmarried. Some managed to make a slim living by peddling goods from door to door — apples, flour, silk stockings, waxes, polishes, and brushes and gadgets of all kinds. But, for most of them, there was nothing to do. They were lonely, bored, and frustrated. Summer and fall were the easiest times. Then, they could stroll downtown to sit on a park bench in the sun, perhaps share a game of checkers, or watch a sandlot baseball game. Winter was the worst season. For warmth and companionship they drifted into poolrooms, libraries, and even brokerage offices, where they could pick up newspapers left lying on a bench or thrown into a wastebasket. A court house was another popular place where a man could comfortably pass a few hours and have his mind taken off his misery. Murder cases — often as good as a movie — always attracted large crowds. Many men, however, were unable to tolerate the endless shuffling about a town or city. They took to the road, walking or hitch-hiking. Or they travelled across the country in railway freight cars, "riding the rails" as this illegal means of transportation was called, in an endless quest for work.

These years have been called the "Dirty Thirties," long years of near or total drought, of unemployment and breadlines; a decade of idleness, hunger, and poverty. They were the years of the Great Depression.

THE CONSERVATIVES RETURN TO POWER

The stock market crash of 1929 had been merely the opening roar of an economic storm of hurricane proportions. The steady decline in world trade that followed set the stage for a new kind of global conflict. It was economic warfare, and its weapons were tariffs. The fear that haunted every nation was that whatever money remained in circulation might be used to buy cheaper foreign goods. The best method of preventing this seemed to be to raise tariffs to keep out imported goods or at least make them much more expensive than domestically produced goods. Before long, every major trading nation had joined this economic free-for-all, jacking up its tariffs to record heights. The results were predictable: the international trade in goods fell to an all-time low.

In the long run, the tariff war harmed every nation, but to those that depended on foreign trade, the damage was immediate and disastrous. As a trading nation, Canada's economy was particularly vulnerable to world conditions. The nation depended heavily upon exports of such staples as wheat, newsprint, lumber, minerals, and fish. Throughout the 1920s, one out of every three dollars earned by Canadians had come from the sale of these products abroad. By 1933, the world prices of these commodities had fallen, on average, by 50 per cent: and within Canada, surpluses of these products only further depressed their prices. The shrinkage of foreign orders ruined Canadian exporters, who ended up hopelessly burdened by stockpiles of unsold raw materials or goods. Some simply closed down their businesses and went bankrupt. The more fortunate, who could afford to hang on, slashed production quotas and anxiously waited for a revival of world trade. Those who could not afford to wait, however, were the workers. Business shutdowns and production cutbacks caused massive layoffs. From a low of 2 per cent unemployment in 1928, the jobless rate shot up to 10 per cent in 1930 and kept climbing to a peak of just over 20 per cent in 1933. About one of every five men and women in the working force was unemployed. It was economic catastrophe on a scale never before known in Canadian history.

Canada's exports fell from a value in 1929 of $1 363 672 000 to $799 746 770 in 1931.

252

At first, people bravely tried to wish the Depression away. They hummed the hit tune "Happy Days Are Here Again" and reassured each other with the optimistic, but naive, statement that "Prosperity is just around the corner." But, as the breadlines lengthened and it became obvious that prosperity was a long way around that corner, people began to demand government action. Unfortunately, few politicians understood what to do about the worst economic conditions in Canadian history. Those bold enough to suggest remedies were labelled radicals. They frightened the Canadian voter, who behaved like the chicken caught in the snow storm. After balancing on one foot for a time, it then switched to the other. Neither position made the chicken warmer. During the 1930s, Canadians switched from one traditional political party to the other in the desperate hope that one or the other would lead them out of their economic misery. Unfortunately, neither did.

Mackenzie King was prime minister of Canada in 1929. On the day following the stock market crash, he remarked,

> While no doubt a number of people have suffered owing to the sharp decline in stocks, the soundness of Canadian securities generally is not affected. Business was never better, nor faith in Canada's future more justified.

During the next few months, when it became evident that things were not better, King denied that the unemployed had much to worry about. With supreme confidence, he called a summer election, fully expecting that he would win and continue as prime minister.

King did not think much of his Tory opponent, Richard Bedford Bennett, the Conservative leader who had replaced King's old enemy, Arthur Meighen, in 1927. Bennett was a New Brunswick lawyer who, like Meighen, had made his fortune in western Canada. Even more successful than Meighen, he became one of the top lawyers for the

Richard Bedford Bennett, 1870-1947

The Public Archives of Canada. PA 52437

Richard Bedford Bennett dressed in Windsor uniform, which was often worn when appearing before the monarch.

Bennett adored the institution of the monarchy and anything at all to do with royalty. He ultimately went to live in Britain and, in 1941, was created Viscount Bennett of Mickleham, Calgary, and Hopewell.

253

Canadian Pacific Railway. By channelling some of the money from his legal fees into real-estate investments, Bennett made himself a millionaire. Despite a well-defined plumpness (he frequently downed a box of chocolates in the course of an evening), Bennett was physically quite agile. His verbal agility was even more marked. "Bonfire" Bennett deserved the nickname he earned as a rapid-fire speaker. His ability to think and speak quickly on his feet stood him in good stead in the House of Commons.

Bennett's reputation for hard work, determination, and intelligence won him considerable support in the election of 1930. And if his speaking ability won him votes, an angry King speech also brought Bennett many votes. In the Commons shortly before the election, as Bennett and the Conservatives were attacking the prime minister for his failure to provide money to the provinces to support their relief programs, King suddenly lost his temper. First, he shocked the House by stating that ". . . we have no right to say that there is any national unemployment problem in this country." Then, after carefully listing the provinces, six of which were governed by Conservative administrations, he thundered,

> With respect to giving monies out of the federal treasury to any Tory government in this country for these alleged unemployment purposes, with these governments situated as they are today, with policies diametrically opposed to those of this Government, I would not give them a five-cent piece!

Amid cries of "Shame" from the opposition benches, King rose to say,

Accompanied by his sister, Mrs. W. Herridge, Prime Minister Bennett boards the CPR liner Empress of Australia *to journey to London, where an Imperial Conference was held in 1930. There, Bennett lectured his fellow delegates on the necessity for Commonwealth nations to raise their tariff rates on goods from other countries, although he favored reducing tariffs on goods being traded between Commonwealth countries. He then thoroughly annoyed his listeners by demanding that Canadian-made goods, and only Canadian-made goods, get extra-special tariff concessions.*

again: "May I repeat what I have said? With respect to giving monies out of the federal treasury to any Tory government in this country . . . I would not give them a five-cent piece."

That speech haunted King throughout the summer election of 1930. Wherever he went, there was always some heckler ready to screech out the burning words "five cents!" in the middle of the prime minister's speech. A majority of the voters went to the polls convinced that King had placed party politics above providing relief to the unemployed. They gave the Conservatives 137 seats, a comfortable majority of 46 over the Liberals. The chicken had switched to the other foot.

Because the world seemed turned upside down, perhaps it was not strange that the Canadian people elected a millionaire as their leader. Many voters believed that only a man who had achieved financial success could restore national prosperity. Doubtless Bennett believed this, too. The problem was that the conditions under which Bennett had made his fortune had vanished. Neither the new prime minister nor those Canadians who voted for him could guess the severity of this particular depression.

At first, Bennett treated the Depression as a typical "bust" part of the "bust and boom" business cycle. Had there not been bleak economic periods before, such as the ones before and after the First World War? He acted on his election promise to "blast a way" into world markets by the standard Conservative method of the protective tariff. When his opponents challenged him by arguing that international trade could recover only from lowering tariffs, Bennett had an answer. He recognized the folly of a tariff war and would be happy to enter into negotiations with any nation willing to lower its tariff barrier to Canadian goods. If this policy were successful, it would produce a series of trade treaties that would certainly stimulate Canada's export trade. But, for the present, he warned, unless Canada raised tariffs, foreign goods would undersell those made in Canada, and more workers would be laid off. By increasing tariffs, Bennett did provide protection for Canadian manufacturers producing for the domestic market. This salvaged the jobs of some Canadian workers, particularly in secondary industries in Ontario and Quebec. However, his trade negotiations to enter world markets were less satisfying. As host of a Commonwealth economic conference in Ottawa in 1932, Bennett tested his policy on Great Britain and the other Dominions. His success in arranging a series of treaties based on mutual tariff reductions between Canada and other Commonwealth countries did increase national exports to a certain extent. With other nations, he failed. By 1933, exports to the United States had dropped drastically. Unemployment in Canadian industries dependent on export sales continued to climb.

The rest of Bennett's efforts to bring back prosperity were hit-or-miss projects. To the urgent demands of the provinces that had been rejected by King in his damaging "five-cent" speech, Bennett responded in a

Federal Election, 1930	
Cons.	137
Lib.	88
United Farmers	10
Lib. Prog.	3
Lab.	2
Prog.	2
Ind. Lab.	1
Ind.	2

To make a "Bennett Buggy," you yanked out the engine, the battery, the generator, and as much other excess weight as possible.

positive manner. Parliament granted subsidies for relief programs set up by provincial governments. It also established its own public-works program to provide jobs building roads and constructing public buildings. To assist the farmers, Bennett's government bought up some of the wheat banked in storage. But none of these was enough. Unemployment continued to rise, and foreign trade continued to decline. The faint optimism of the first few months of the Depression gave way to anger, the bitter anger of a people unable to understand how a once prosperous nation could be so severely crippled. Nor could they understand the inability of the government to halt the economic slide. Bennett, as leader of the government, became the butt of many cruel jokes. A "Bennett Buggy" was an automobile drawn by a horse because the owner could not afford gas; a "Bennettburg" was a shantytown where hobos gathered; a "Bennett Barnyard" was an abandoned farm; and "Bennett Coffee" was a brew made from boiled wheat.

The Unemployment and Farm Relief Act was passed in 1931.

NEW LEADERS, NEW PARTIES

When it became obvious that the federal government was unable to get the economy going again, people turned to their provincial governments. Perhaps these could give some direction to a society that was drifting aimlessly. In Ontario, the boyish leader of the Liberal Party promised just that. He was Mitchell Hepburn, the boisterous, wise-cracking "onion farmer from Elgin County" whose vitality and confidence impressed voters. In 1934, they gave Hepburn and the Liberals, who had been in opposition for nearly thirty years, a landslide victory over the Conservatives.

Mitchell Hepburn, 1896-1953

During the election, Hepburn had promised to cut government spending and to eliminate costly frills. After firing several hundred civil servants, he staged a colorful display to prove that he could carry out his election promises. Before a near-capacity crowd in Toronto's Varsity

256

Stadium, he auctioned off forty-seven private limousines used by the former Conservative government. The car auction revealed that Hepburn was more showman than savior. Although he introduced some laws that raised agricultural prices and others that gave protection to trade unions, many of the promised changes for the people of Ontario never came into being. Instead, Hepburn eventually turned against trade unions and also directed much of his attention to a personal struggle against Mackenzie King.

In 1936, the people of Quebec also elected a new political leader, Maurice Duplessis, a lawyer who had created a new provincial party, the Union Nationale. His election victory drove out a corrupt Liberal administration that had held power for sixteen years. Rapid industrial development in Quebec since the beginning of the First World War had greatly increased the size of the work force. Most of the money for this expansion had come from American and British investors. Duplessis cleverly took advantage of the popular suspicion that the massive unemployment in Quebec resulted from the decision of these "foreign" factory and mine owners to take their money out of the province and close down their factories. He promised to take action against them.

Duplessis never did. During his period in office, the amount of foreign investment in Quebec actually increased. Publicly, he pretended to be the foe of the Anglophone businessmen who dominated Quebec's commerce and industry. Privately, he welcomed their money, which was steadily transforming a rural society into an industrial/urban one. The price of this, of course, was the suppression of any worker agitation for better wages and working conditions. With help from the Roman Catholic Church, which practically ran the educational system with the aid of provincial monies, Duplessis was able to deny Quebec workers many of the rights won by trade unions in other parts of Canada. To divert attention from all this, he identified Ottawa and the rest of

Maurice Duplessis, 1890-1959

In this publicity shot, Premier Maurice Duplessis of Quebec (left) holds a bunch of onions grown on the farm of Premier Mitchell Hepburn of Ontario (right).

Maurice Le Noblet Duplessis's Union Nationale Party was made up largely of provincial Conservatives, who had been out of office since the end of the First World War. In the name of "Quebec rights," they and their clever, tough-minded leader rejected all Ottawa plans that were based on treating all the provinces alike, from federal tax rebates to the project of a Trans-Canada Highway.

Mitchell Frederick Hepburn also promoted himself as a champion of "provincial rights," but proved to be more interested in joining forces with industrialists to battle unions and unionism.

The Public Archives of Canada, C 19518

Canada as the enemy of Quebec's language and literature, customs and religion, and himself as the savior of Francophone culture.

One province in which there was a sustained attempt to relieve the hardships of the people was British Columbia. An energetic provincial Liberal leader, Thomas Dufferin ("Duff") Pattullo, was elected in 1933 on a campaign slogan "Work and Wages" and promises to "distribute purchasing power" to everyone in B.C. He began by increasing relief payments. Next, he created jobs through public-works projects paid for by his government. To offset losses from the decline in exports, he paid subsidies to the mining and fishing industries. He passed laws establishing maximum hours and minimum wages for workers. However, the huge cost of this extensive program sent him to Ottawa to plead for financial assistance from the federal government. When Bennett refused to provide all the needed money, Pattullo was unable to carry out all of the reforms he had planned.

Perhaps the worst suffering during the Depression was on the Prairies, where a one-crop economy caused an endless spiral of debt. The cost of producing wheat — which was being sown and reaped in reduced amounts all through the Depression years — far exceeded its selling price. The farm family's income was slashed by almost 75 per cent, which, in turn created a ripple effect. For example, the farmer could not pay the storekeeper and the manufacturer of agricultural machinery and tools. So industry suffered because of the farmer's inability to pay for goods: factories closed, workers lost their jobs, and so on. With a drastic fall in the total of wheat being shipped east and goods being transported west, railway revenues dropped, sometimes by as much as 50 per cent, and railwaymen were laid off.

In the 1930s, one out of every two Canadians in the labor force was a farmer or worked on a farm.

Not surprisingly, the most radical of the new parties were born in western Canada.

William Aberhart,
1878-1943

The founder of the Social Credit Party, William Aberhart, was a Calgary school principal. To thousands of his fellow Albertans he was better known as "Bible Bill" Aberhart, lay preacher and president of the Prophetic Bible Institute. They faithfully tuned in to his radio program every Sunday night to hear his dynamic, evangelical sermons. They accepted his version of Heaven and Hell, and when he suddenly began to talk about economics and politics, they listened and believed. Like many westerners, Aberhart blamed eastern banks and insurance companies for much of the economic mess. He claimed that they controlled the amount of money in circulation: this amount was pitifully inadequate; the result was economic stagnation, a lack of money flow. The solution Aberhart proposed was that the government of Alberta put more money in circulation by giving every man, woman, and child in the province a "social dividend" of $25 a month. If each person spent the $25, the economy could be revived. Money in circulation would stimulate demand for goods. Factories would return to production, and workers would be called back to their jobs.

The Public Archives of Canada, C 9339

Unconcerned by critics who ridiculed his "funny-money" theories, Aberhart organized the Social Credit Party. Most Albertans took him seriously. In the 1935 provincial election, called shortly after the founding of the party, they gave Aberhart and his new party a huge majority in the Alberta legislature. It was a position that he and his successors were to maintain for thirty-six years, until they were defeated by the provincial Conservatives in the 1971 election.

In 1932, at the same time that Aberhart was developing his political and economic theories, another political movement was taking shape. The party that was formed was a federation (union) of farm workers, laborers, and various other groups that shared a common interest and purpose:

> The establishment in Canada of a co-operative commonwealth in which the basic principle regulating production, distribution, and exchange, will be the supplying of human needs instead of the making of profits.

From this statement of purpose, it was clear that the new party, the Co-operative Commonwealth Federation (C.C.F.), wanted to change the economic basis of the Canadian society. Other political parties — federal or provincial — agreed that the best system of government was one that encouraged *private enterprise*. Under this system, certain individuals own and operate their own companies, which employ workers to produce materials and goods. These are sold at a profit, some of which is used to expand the business, thus providing more jobs for more workers to produce more materials and goods. What the C.C.F. wanted to do was to establish a different system — *socialism* — in which more

259

James Woodsworth (centre) and the other members of the first caucus (a meeting of parliamentary members of a political party) of the C.C.F. On the far left is "Tommy" Douglas, a future premier of Saskatchewan and the first socialist to head a government in North America. Second from the right is Woodsworth's daughter, Grace MacInnis, who also had a parliamentary career, with the New Democratic Party, which succeeded the C.C.F.

The C.C.F. was re-formed as the New Democratic Party in 1961.

companies are owned and operated by government and fewer by private enterprise.

At the first national convention of the C.C.F., held in 1933 in Regina, Saskatchewan, the party announced a planned program of socialism for Canada. This program, known as the "Regina Manifesto," called for "a planned, socialized economic order." The federal government would own and operate key industries, industries that were essential to the nation: banks and insurance companies; public utilities (gas, hydro, telephones); public transportation and communication (railways, highways, and airlines); primary industries based on natural resources (lumber, mining, and steel). Manufacturing industries that were not essential could be privately owned, but profits, prices, and working conditions would be regulated by government. All medical and health services, including hospitals, doctors, and dentists, would be government-operated. There would be unemployment insurance for the jobless, old age pensions for the elderly, and family allowances to help provide for children's needs. The money to pay for the services would come from the profits from government-owned industries and from increased income and inheritance taxes.

J. S. Woodsworth, 1874-1942

The convention delegates chose James Shaver Woodsworth to lead the party. Woodsworth, a Methodist minister, spent several years working with immigrants in the All Peoples' Mission in Winnipeg. He eventually resigned from the Methodist Church, partly because he disliked the Church's whole-hearted endorsement of the war, partly because he felt many Church members ignored the social and economic needs of their fellow Canadians. He was a dock worker in Vancouver for a time and then worked for a farmers' party in Alberta. During the Winnipeg General Strike, he was arrested for printing "dangerous statements" in the *Western Labour News*, a newspaper he edited. (The charges against him were dropped when he showed his embarrassed accusers that one of these was a quotation from the Old Testament.) In 1921 he was elected to the Commons as a labor member for the riding of Winnipeg North Centre, a riding he represented until his death in 1942. Woodsworth had an immense sympathy for the average man and woman. He once wrote,

> I cannot keep out of my mind the pictures of plain homes, in some of which there is a desperate struggle for existence. What is Ottawa to them? In some ways, the Government has been removed too far away from the people.

Woodsworth's life-long ambition was to bring the farmers and the urban workers together to form a mighty reform movement of "Canadian Socialism." However, the tendency of many Canadians to link the C.C.F. with the Communist movement hampered Woodsworth's party throughout the 1930s. He was considered a dangerous "Red," dedicated to the destruction of the Canadian way of life, whereas he was really a socialist who believed that Christian principles and government enterprise could be combined to produce a just society. Through his persistent support of the downtrodden and the poor, he ultimately earned the respect of all parties. Indeed, upon his death in 1942, he was called the "conscience of the House of Commons."

Party membership was also limited because most labor unions, influenced by the Gompers tradition of no links with political parties, did not join.

It was understandable that many Canadians confused the C.C.F. with the Communist Party. On the surface, they appeared alike. They pursued similar aims: government ownership of industry and a planned economy. But the two differed entirely on the means of achieving those aims. The C.C.F. were social democrats — they believed in working within the democratic system to establish a socialist government. The Communists were committed to seizing power through violent revolution.

The Communist Party of Canada was formed in 1921, the oldest and the smallest of the new radical political groups. It attracted few converts during the booming 1920s, but as the Depression deepened, party membership grew. So did the fear of communism. A series of violent strikes led by Communist organizers gave rise to rumors of plots to overthrow the government. Were these the first steps on the road to revolution? Prime Minister Bennett and George Henry, the Conservative premier of Ontario, agreed that it was better to act than to wait and see. In August, 1931, a squad of police raided the party's national

It was first called the Workers' Party of Canada. The name was changed in 1924.

headquarters in Toronto and arrested the party leader, Tim Buck, an immigrant machinist from England, along with several other members. They were tried and convicted under Section 98 of the Criminal Code, which forbade membership in an unlawful association. Thousands of Canadians who had no sympathy with Buck and his political beliefs protested against this law. To ban a political party and jail its members and supporters was contradictory to the principle of freedom of speech which is essential to democracy.

THE ON-TO-OTTAWA TREK

One of the miracles of the Depression was the way in which most Canadians patiently endured the suffering and humiliation of hunger and poverty. Still, public officials were fearful that anger and bitterness might one day explode. The young men who drifted from town to town in search of work had little to lose. They might be tempted to use violence to get rid of their frustrations. As the number of these "hobos" or "knights of the road" rapidly increased, uneasy public officials in various Canadian cities complained to the federal government. They were already stretching skimpy relief budgets to support local residents. How could they be expected to provide food and shelter for the wandering jobless? And what would happen if these ragged, tattered drifters came under the influence of Communist agitators?

The federal government finally responded by setting up a number of relief camps across the country. It was significant that they were put under the control of Major-General A. G. L. McNaughton, Chief of the General Staff of the Canadian Army. The government was determined to keep watchful eyes on a potentially dangerous group.

The experience of living in relief camps did nothing to ease the feelings of humiliation and despair. The strict military regulations and

The Single Men's Association parades to a service in a Toronto church during the Depression. During these years, the burden of hardships fell mainly on three major groups in Canada: farm families, the unemployed, and, particularly, young men looking for their first job.

The Public Archives of Canada, C 29397

prison-like atmosphere made the men feel like criminals. Camp administrators treated them as if they were themselves responsible for their jobless situation. The men resented being treated like lazy bums. What they wanted above all was a real job — any job — that would restore their dignity and self-respect. What they got in the camps, in return for doing such work as raking leaves or cutting wood, was a bed, food, and 20¢ per day. As far as they were concerned, the camps were further evidence of the government's total failure to take action against the forces that had created the Depression. Many of them spent nearly three years hopelessly wandering in and out of relief camps. In a letter to the *Vancouver Sun* in 1935, one man described their frustrations.

We walk around the streets [of the local town] at night to kill time, so we can sleep in late the next day.

What do we see while putting in the hours? What do we think about?

We see a great many people going to shows, to this and that. Young couples who seem to be enjoying themselves, well-dressed and acting as if the world isn't so bad after all. People who have homes and kids and all the rest of it. People who seem to have faith in the future.

We think that something is wrong, We can't do as they do. We must go around lonely and dejected. No home life to enjoy, shut off from all social existence. . . . Are we criminals unwanted by society? Are we lunatics who are to be shunned? What's wrong with us? . . .

We see . . . we think. We see Red . . . and we think Red. Can you blame us? Would you like to have us lie down like a bunch of spineless whelps and be contented as slaves? Is that all our grandfathers toiled for? Canada . . . young nation . . . letting her youth go to hell! . . . How can you sleep at nights while thousands of us are idle in brain and body, in want and privation? . . . What fools our mothers were to bear us. 'Tis to be hoped that there will be a stop made to bringing kids into this hopeless world if all they are to [be] offered is a relief camp! We who should be the pride of the nation are the derelicts! . . .

I leave it to you. Where do we go from here?

At least one thousand of them decided to go to Ottawa to complain directly to the prime minister. They left Vancouver in early June, 1935, travelling in empty freight cars, picking up more campers along the route. When they reached Regina, they were met by a detachment of RCMP, who had been ordered to stop them. Bennett had decided to break up the On-to-Ottawa Trek. He would, however, talk to a representative delegation. When the Regina city council learned that the prime minister was willing to meet with the Trek leaders in Ottawa, it nervously agreed to provide food and shelter for the remaining men.

The trekkers change trains en route to Ottawa. At the town of Golden, B.C., they were greeted by trestle tables heaped with slices of bread and all sorts of makeshift cooking vessels filled with, one trekker wrote, "simmering, bubbling, thick, heaven-smelling beef stew. Over one fire (and this is the gospel truth) was suspended a full-size bathtub, also full to the brim with beef stew."

They also demanded that relief camps be taken out of the control of the department of national defence.

The delegation of eight, led by Arthur H. "Slim" Evans, a Communist, arrived in the nation's capital, after travelling at government expense in a passenger car of the Canadian National Railways. The meeting was a farce. The delegation's demands included a 50¢ per hour minimum wage and guaranteed work for all the campers. When the prime minister made it clear that he had no intention of granting their demands, the meeting dissolved into a shouting match. Bennett charged that Evans was a criminal, and Evans replied that the prime minister was a liar. The row blazed on until an exasperated Bennett stood up and remarked, "I have nothing more to say. Good morning, gentlemen. We have been glad to listen to you." Evans and his group of seven stormed out of the Parliament Buildings. He later told reporters that nothing, including the police, would prevent him from leading his followers to Ottawa to confront the government.

Once back in Regina, Evans called a mass meeting for Dominion Day. As the trekkers gathered in Market Square in the early evening, a force of RCMP and city police closed in. Some shoving began, then the police charged. For the next four hours, the area was a bloody battlefield from which the sounds of smashing glass, ambulance sirens, and gunfire echoed down the streets leading away from the square. When the police finally gained control, about one hundred people had been injured, and one of them, a city detective, had been bludgeoned to death. Four days later, fifteen hundred trekkers climbed aboard a special train that took them westward, back to their relief camps. Evans and eight others stayed behind in jail. They were later tried and sentenced to prison.

The riot in Regina reinforced the belief of some Canadians that communist and socialist radicals were dangerous elements who were using the Depression for their own end. But there were others who charged that "Big Business" was also using the Depression in a way that was perhaps more damaging to Canadian society. Indeed, the most sensational criticism of business was yet to come — from Bennett's own cabinet!

THE BENNETT "NEW DEAL"

Henry ("Harry") Herbert Stevens had been a Conservative Member of Parliament for Vancouver since his election in 1911. He and Bennett had gone to Ottawa that same year as members of Borden's government. When Bennett formed his cabinet in 1930, his choice for minister of trade and commerce was the efficient, dependably true-blue Stevens. In January, 1934, Harry Stevens went to Toronto to address several hundred delegates attending a convention of boot and shoe manufacturers. The following day, his remarks made the headlines of most Canadian newspapers. In a carefully prepared speech, which contained detailed statistics, the minister of trade and commerce, in effect, declared war on large department and chain stores. He accused them of beating down the prices that small manufacturers charged for consumer goods. This, in turn, forced these manufacturers to pay their employees pitifully small wages for long hours of work. But the big stores continued to charge the same prices for the same goods; instead of charging less, they pocketed the extra cost. As a result, while sweatshop conditions were spreading in many factories, department and chain stores were reaping huge profits.

In the furniture industry, for example, most employees earned $13 a week or less; maximum wage for youths 18-19 years of age was $3 weekly.

The charge that there was a huge gap between the cost and the price of many goods shocked Canadians. At a time when tens of thousands of the nation's population were on the verge of starvation, a group of businessmen was making more money than ever before.

Two days later in Ottawa, Bennett and Stevens met to talk. Bennett was under pressure from many businessmen who had contributed money to the Conservative Party's election fund. Stevens' charges were damaging. When the prime minister asked his cabinet colleague to avoid repeating his accusations in the future, Stevens wrote out a letter

Two famous French-Canadian nationalists, the controversial Maurice Duplessis (right) and the equally controversial, long-time mayor of Montreal, Camillien Houde, enjoy each other's company.

The impact of the Depression on Quebec was much the same as in other provinces: mass unemployment, falling incomes, bread lines, and the flight of farm families to the cities. However, one big difference was the quick, angry acceptance of Quebec nationalist propaganda claiming that the capitalist system was responsible for the catastrophe. Coupled with antagonism towards English-speaking management in commerce and industry, nationalistic ideas began to spread rapidly through the province. "Quebec for the Québecois" became a highly popular slogan in the 1930s.

of resignation. Strangely, Bennett not only refused to accept the resignation, but completely reversed his position by appointing Stevens the chairman of a parliamentary committee to carry out further investigations into the costs and prices of Canadian goods. In the course of the next four months, the Royal Commission on Price Spreads (the Stevens Report) collected mounds of evidence that clearly backed up its chairman's original charges. For example, the weekly earnings of workers in Quebec textile mills were as low as $3; the work week in some Ontario factories was as high as seventy-two hours.

Eventually Stevens and Bennett had a falling-out. The minister of trade and commerce resigned not only from the cabinet but from the party, his main reason being that nothing was done about the Stevens Report. He formed his own Reconstruction Party, which he hoped would gain the support of small manufacturers and store owners and workers in the "sweatshop" industries.

Did the Stevens Report have any effect on Bennett's thinking? It certainly provided convincing criticism of an economic system which, as prime minister, Bennett had been defending since 1930. It revealed that the rich had been growing richer — and at the expense of those who could least afford it. Stevens had wanted Bennett's government to take action by regulating prices and wages. In this way, workers would receive a decent wage and manufacturers a fair price, and department stores would still make a reasonable profit. Yet, Bennett hesitated. To take such action would be to break faith with one of the most hallowed principles of the free-enterprise system: government interferes as little as possible with the operation of business. And Bennett genuinely believed that Canada had been built on this principle. It was for much the same reason that Bennett had rejected demands from various quarters that the federal government provide jobs for the unemployed. To Bennett — and many other politicians — this was an industry responsibility. Once business got back on its feet again, there would be as many jobs as there had been in the 1920s. Unfortunately, this showed no signs of happening. In 1935, unemployment was still at a high level; thousands of people continued to leave the "dust bowl" of the prairies for the already overcrowded cities; there was constant turmoil in the relief camps.

At the beginning of 1935, Bennett was beginning his fifth year as prime minister. He would soon have to call an election, and what accomplishments could he claim since his government entered office in 1930? The traditional policies in which he had placed so much faith had been tragic failures. What new policies could he propose? At this point, Bennett was influenced by his brother-in-law, William Herridge, the Canadian ambassador in Washington. Herridge described to Bennett in considerable detail and with much praise the "New Deal" program of the recently elected president of the United States, Franklin D. Roosevelt. Although big-business leaders in the U.S. loudly criticized Roosevelt for using government rules and regulations to prop up the American economy, his program was achieving results. Thousands of men and women were going back to work in jobs created by the government in Washington.

Roosevelt's New Deal legislation had been introduced to save the private-enterprise system, not to destroy it. Bennett also wanted to save the free-enterprise system. Perhaps the only way to do this was through

Photo by Bill Braden, DIAND Public Affairs, Yellowknife

Float planes on Great Slave Lake near Yellowknife, Northwest Territories.

During the Depression, many men turned their backs on civilization and headed into the northern wilderness. Some learned how to trap and skin fur-bearing animals and made a good living at it. Prospecting was a popular occupation, and one or two individuals actually made a fortune. Perhaps the most famous example was Gilbert LaBine, who located a rich vein of uranium ore on the shore of Great Bear Lake, N.W.T.

reform. In January 1935, he announced his intention of introducing several reform measures in the next session of Parliament. The program, which he called a "Canadian New Deal," would include laws to regulate business practices, control the export trade, establish an eight-hour work day, and provide a minimum wage. He also promised to eliminate child labor and to set up a comprehensive scheme of unemployment insurance.

Bennett publicized his new political beliefs in a series of six radio broadcasts. An incredulous nation listened to a Conservative prime minister preaching nothing less than socialism.

> The day of the robber barons is over. This is the end of an economic era. Capitalism [the private-enterprise system] will never again work in the old way. The only system that can work hereafter is the system guided and controlled by the state.

(His own party members were even more stunned than the general public. He had consulted none of them before going "on the air.") This about-face by a millionaire who typified big business, a politician who had followed traditional economic thinking, confused Canadians. The man who had once boasted that it was a great advantage to start life in poverty was now saying things like "Canada on the dole is like a young and vigorous man in the poorhouse. The dole is condemnation, final and complete, of our economic system. If we cannot abolish the dole, we should abolish the system." True to his word, Bennett introduced the new laws, which were passed in Parliament. He then called an election for October.

However sincere Bennett may have been, the voters asked themselves the obvious question. Why did he wait so long to introduce these anti-Depression measures? Many voters could not believe that Bennett was sincere in his election-year promises of drastic social and economic reform. And their rejection of him was crushing. The voters swept the Liberals, under Mackenzie King, into power with 117 seats in the House of Commons. The Conservatives won only 39 seats. The Social Credit Party won 17, the C.C.F. 7, Stevens' Reconstruction Party 1 (his own), and the Communist Party none.

Stevens rejoined the Conservative Party in 1938.

THE ROWELL-SIROIS REPORT

In a moment of crisis, the people of Canada had turned again to King and the Liberal Party. The chicken had again switched feet. By a strange coincidence, Mackenzie King's first day back in office as prime minister was October 24, 1935. On the same day six years earlier, "Black Thursday," stock market prices had taken a spectacular plunge. King, prime minister at the time, had revealed little understanding of the catastrophe that had begun in those terrible October days. Had he learned anything since?

Newfoundland fishermen spreading cod to dry in the sun, a method of curing that is at least four hundred years old.

The Depression hit Newfoundland with particular force because of the island's great dependence on exporting the products of its fisheries. Incomes fell so drastically that, in 1934, Great Britain assumed responsibility for the government of Newfoundland and took over its public debt.

The Liberals' 1935 election slogan "King or Chaos" prompted someone to joke after the election that their victory had given the people of Canada both. But this was not true. In his five years in opposition, King had become more sensitive to the human misery and economic stagnation in Canada. Unlike Bennett, he was not willing to bank everything on some hastily prepared reform program. He was far too cautious for that. In any case, King knew that there were two factors preventing him from taking action right away. The first was the world economy. Until international trade began to flow again as it had in the 1920s, there would be severe unemployment in Canada. The second related to the Canadian constitution and the powers of the federal and provincial governments.

In their desire to create a federal system of government that would function without conflict between Ottawa and the provinces, the Fathers of Confederation had carefully defined the powers of the federal and provincial governments in the British North America Act. Despite their careful efforts, there had been numerous conflicts between the two

For details on federal-provincial conflicts, see Chapter 4.

Credit for the development of commercial flying in Canada belongs to two small groups of people: "bush pilots" and their mechanics and a few businessmen who backed early attempts at air transport with their own money. One of the latter, James Richardson of Winnipeg, helped establish Western Canada Airways. In March, 1930, this company introduced the Prairie Air Mail Service between Winnipeg, Regina, Saskatoon, Calgary, and Edmonton.

levels of government, which had had to be settled by the Privy Council in Britain. Since the 1880s, most constitutional decisions had favored the provinces. By the time of the Depression, they had become almost as powerful as the government of Canada — except in the matter of raising money. They lacked the taxation powers necessary to raise large sums of money. So they had to turn to Ottawa for funds. Yet federal-provincial rivalries made the federal government unwilling to provide money to provincial governments. King's "five-cent" speech in 1929 was an example of this. Another was Bennett's refusal to grant money for the "Work and Wages" program of Pattullo's government in British Columbia in the 1930s.

Constitutional matters related to the separation of powers were not always decided in favor of the provinces. When the Aberhart administration in Alberta produced laws based on Social Credit theories, some of them were disallowed by the King government. Others were declared *ultra vires* by the highest constitutional authority, the Judicial Committee of the Privy Council in London, England. However, whichever government — federal or provincial — won a particular case, it was obvious that the separation of powers in the BNA Act was not producing the desired result: a smoothly functioning federal system of government. And the constitutional question reached a critical point in 1937

270

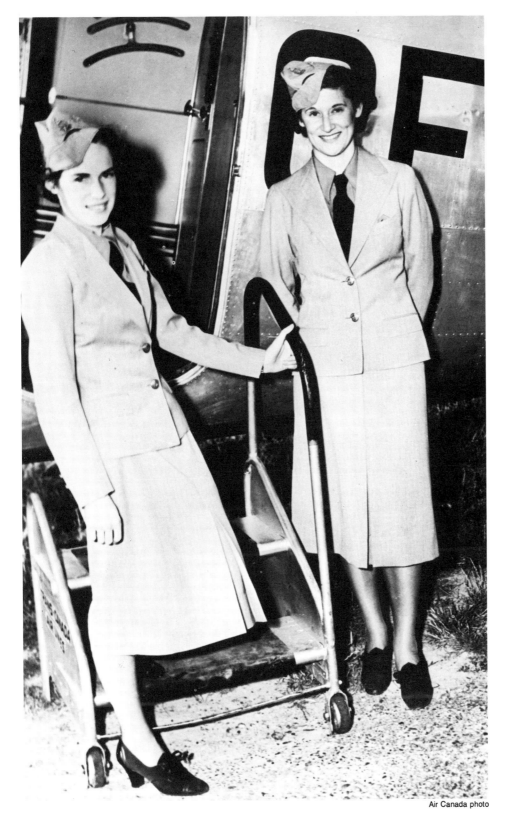

Air Canada photo

Trans-Canada Air Lines (TCA) stewardesses Pat Eccleston (left) and Lucile Garner Grant (right). Stewardesses served tea, coffee, and box lunches and handed out oxygen masks, which the passengers had to put on every time the unpressurized planes flew above 3000 metres. Lucile Grant, the first woman employed by TCA, remarked that there was so much airsickness in those days that "few people could even think of food." Stewardesses were sometimes left behind so that the plane could carry extra fuel to battle strong headwinds.

Established in 1937 by act of Parliament as a subsidiary of Canadian National Railways, TCA (now Air Canada) started out as a Vancouver-Seattle (USA) service. A Vancouver-Montreal service was introduced in 1939. (An overnight service, it took 14 hours eastbound and up to 17 hours westbound.) A further two years passed before transcontinental service was established between Vancouver and Halifax.

271

In 1938, in the Centre Block of the Parliament Buildings, Prime Minister W. L. Mackenzie King unveiled a tablet honoring those Alberta women who led the "Persons Campaign," the struggle by Emily Murphy and her associates to gain for women the right to become Senators. Among those present on this occasion were Nellie McClung (far right) and Senators Fallis and Wilson (back row).

The Public Archives of Canada, C 54523

when the Judicial Committee of the Privy Council handed down its decision on Bennett's "New Deal" legislation. The court ruled that all but one of the laws passed in the 1935 session of Parliament were *ultra vires*. King realized that unless some changes were made in the division of financial powers between federal and provincial governments, there could indeed be chaos in Canada.

Typically, his decision was based on caution. He appointed a Royal Commission headed by Newton W. Rowell, Chief Justice of Ontario, and later by Joseph Sirois, a prominent Quebec lawyer, to investigate "the economic and financial basis of Confederation" and to make recommendations designed to alter federal-provincial relations to meet existing conditions.

The result was the Rowell-Sirois Report, a three-volume summary of extensive enquiry and research that took three years to complete. From the thousands of pages of its detailed findings and analysis came three basic recommendations:

1. The federal government should assume all the debts of the provinces. In return, the provinces should surrender to the federal government their right to levy personal income tax, corporate income tax, and succession duties.

2. The federal government should pay to the provinces "adjustment grants," which would vary according to the needs of each province. This would insure a minimum standard of social services throughout the nation.

3. The federal government should be completely responsible for unemployment relief.

The worst effects of the Depression had vanished when the Report reached King's hands in 1940. The following year, he arranged a federal-provincial conference to discuss the recommendations. It was a complete failure. Unwilling to surrender any of their powers to Ottawa, the premiers of Ontario, British Columbia, and Alberta refused to co-operate with King.

But the Rowell-Sirois Report had not been prepared in vain. As a clear indication that Ottawa accepted the responsibility to provide for the social and economic security of the Canadian people, the King government established a system of federal unemployment insurance in 1940. The Great Depression left scars on the lives of many Canadians. But at least the experience of that terrible time produced the idea that the state had to look after the social and economic welfare of its citizens. It was in the Depression that the basis was laid for the welfare-state system that would gradually emerge in the next thirty years.

INVASION FROM THE UNITED STATES

The hesitant, gradual response of the King government to the Depression contrasted with the rapid American reaction. Shortly after taking office in 1933, the administration of Franklin D. Roosevelt had introduced unemployment insurance and numerous other social-security measures. Canadians were aware of this. In the name he gave to his 1935 legislative program, Bennett had made it obvious that he had copied the ideas of the American New Deal. But this was only part of a general, unspoken and unwritten "deal" between Canadians and Americans. As neighbors speaking the same language and sharing similar political traditions, as trading partners doing most of their business with each other, Canadians and Americans were bound together by close cultural and economic ties. These bonds became tighter as the American way of life, mass-produced and mass-communicated, peacefully invaded Canada.

This invasion took various forms. Hollywood movies provided an avenue of escape from the dreariness and frustrations of the Depression. For a 10¢ ticket, you were transported to the world of make-believe, to *A Night in Casablanca* with the Marx Brothers or to glamorous Brazil with Fred Astaire and Ginger Rogers in *Flying Down to Rio*. Audiences shivered as Bela Lugosi stalked a victim in *Dracula* and sighed when Clark Gable kissed Claudette Colbert in *It Happened One Night*. Reality, often ugly, cold, and menacing, met them when they walked out of the theatre, but for ten cents they could always escape again. They came back as often as they could afford it. By the mid-1930s, few places in Canada lacked a movie theatre.

Everybody listened to the radio. During the day, as they ironed or washed the dishes, women tuned in to afternoon soap operas like *"Ma" Perkins* and *Mary Noble, Backstage Wife*. In the late afternoon and early

The National Film Board was created in 1939. The aim of NFB films is "to interpret Canada to Canadians and to other nations."

273

These were a few "home brew" personalities that Canadians listened to on radio in the 1930s. In the front row in this broadcasting studio are, left to right, Don Messer, Marg Osborne, and Charlie Chamberlin.

evening, kids listened to *Jack Armstrong, the All-American Boy, The Green Hornet,* and *The Lone Ranger.* On Sunday nights, the entire family gathered around the radio to hear two of the favorite comedians of the 1930s, Jack Benny and Fred Allen. And on Saturday night Canadians danced to the band music of the Dorsey brothers, Duke Ellington, and Benny Goodman, "the King of Swing." They followed American sports on radio and discussed how many home runs Babe Ruth would hit that year or whether Joe Louis, "the Brown Bomber," could lick Max Schmeling, the German champion, in their famous 1938 rematch.

The popularity of American radio worried some Canadians, who succeeded in persuading Prime Minister Bennett to establish a national network called the Canadian Radio Broadcasting Corporation. Four years later, in 1936, Mackenzie King reorganized it as the Canadian Broadcasting Corporation (CBC). Just as the transcontinental railway had tied the nation together with transportation links, so the CBC would unite it with bonds of communication. In this role, the CBC was able to provide an outlet for Canadian performers and to establish a news service to keep Canadians informed on national and international events. The CBC received considerable publicity in April 1936. When news came that a collapsed mine shaft at Moose River, Nova Scotia, had trapped three miners, J. Frank Willis, a radio reporter, rushed to the scene. For the next three days, Willis remained at the site, conducting interviews and reporting on the rescue efforts. Every radio station in Canada and hundreds in the United States carried the tense, hourly reports until two of the men were brought up alive sixty-nine hours later.

The broadcasts were carried on all 58 Canadian radio stations and on 650 U.S. stations.

Willis' coverage of the Moose River Mine disaster was one of the great radio "scoops" of the decade. It established the quality of CBC reporting and emphasized the value of a Canadian radio network.

Canadians may have rejected Laurier's proposed reciprocity treaty with the United States in 1911, but they certainly did not reject Canadian-American trade. It not only continued, but it grew. By the end of the First World War, the United States had replaced Great Britain as Canada's main trading partner. When Bennett's high-tariff policies caused a sudden decline in trade, American corporations resorted to a technique they had used against Macdonald's National Policy. They simply "leaped over" the tariff "wall" by establishing branch plants in Canada. Although this provided jobs for Canadian workers, it also led to a gradual American takeover of Canadian industry and resources. That pattern began long before the Depression and went on long afterwards until, in the 1950s and 1960s, the nation suddenly became aware that a large percentage of Canadian businesses was owned or controlled by Americans.

Percentage of Foreign Investment in Canada

	1900	1945
U.S.	14	70
U.K.	85	25
Other	1	5

During the Depression, American unions followed American companies into Canada, as they had in the past. The American Federation of Labor (A.F.L.), which had begun to organize Canadian workers back in the 1880s, was well established in Canada. From time to time there had been some opposition to this "foreign interference" in the affairs of Canadian labor but this had never gained much public attention. In 1937, in Ontario, it became a serious issue.

The Congress of Industrial Organizations (C.I.O.), an American federation of unions in the mass-production industries, had sent several agents to Ontario to try to establish C.I.O. unions in Canadian factories. They were beginning to have some success at the General Motors plant in Oshawa when the workers voted to strike in protest against low wages, long hours, and their employer's refusal to pay overtime rates. General Motors refused to negotiate with a C.I.O. union. At this point, the peppery premier of Ontario, Mitchell Hepburn, intervened in the strike to "keep the agitators out." Like many industrialists in Ontario, Hepburn claimed that the C.I.O. had become a nest of Communist troublemakers. As he put it, "This is part of a Communist plot to smash our economy, and we will not tolerate it." There were some Communists in the C.I.O., as there were in most unions in the 1930s. But the C.I.O. was dominated by its president, the fiery John L. Lewis, who opposed communism. Whether or not they were Communists, they definitely were Americans, or as Hepburn once termed them, "foreign malcontents."

The C.I.O. was a federation of industrial unions; the A.F.L., of trade and craft unions. In 1955, the two federations united to form the A.F.L.-C.I.O.

Hepburn requested the services of about one hundred members of the RCMP, but changed his mind after an argument with Mackenzie King and sent them back to Ottawa. To assist the Ontario Provincial Police, he formed a force of several hundred special policemen, which his enemies named "Hepburn's Hussars." Most of them were university students and war veterans. Actually, no police were needed. There was no violence at any time, and the strikers were under strict orders from their union leaders to picket peacefully. But Hepburn wanted to prevent any success by the Americans and was willing to go to great lengths

Industrial disputes between employers and employees did not end in the Dirty Thirties. In the 1940s, there were strikes protesting wartime wage controls in the steel, aircraft, and mining industries. And there were postwar strikes in the automobile industry to protest the retention of wartime controls. Here, in a 1945 strike (in Oshawa, Ontario), Canadian war veterans parade to protest the use of fellow ex-servicemen as strike police.

to do so. In his anger, he fired his attorney general, Arthur Roebuck, and his minister of labor, David Croll, who were known to be pro-labor. Both resigned, and Croll bluntly told Hepburn in his letter of resignation that he preferred to walk with the strikers than to ride with General Motors.

The strike ended after sixteen days. The union won its demands, and Hepburn and General Motors publicly boasted that they had broken the C.I.O. in Ontario. They claimed that agreement had been reached with the workers themselves and not with the American union. In response, the union president insisted that the contract had been signed by men who recognized themselves as members of the C.I.O. Both sides claimed victory, but time was on the side of the C.I.O. Within the next few years, its influence would spread throughout Canada and claim many members. Eventually, American unions would be as common in Canada as American-owned businesses.

*   *   *

In the 1930s, Canada had been crippled by severe economic difficulties. Beyond the nation's borders, other nations were enduring much the same problems. But, in this same decade, much more dangerous events began to take place. Far across the Pacific Ocean, an aggressive Japan began its conquest of Asia. Across the Atlantic Ocean, in Europe, Germany and Italy set out to terrorize some of their weak neighbors. For Canada, the shock of the Depression was about to be forgotten in the even more terrible experience of the Second World War.

STUDY 9

1. Describe the social and economic conditions suffered by city people and country people during the "Dirty Thirties." In what ways was each group worse off than the other? Better off?
2. How and why were tariffs used as weapons to wage economic warfare in the 1930s? Why was Canada particularly threatened by these weapons?
3. Explain why Bennett won the election in 1930. What policies and programs did he put forward to remedy the ills of the Depression? How effective were they?
4. Describe the efforts of Ontario, Quebec, British Columbia, and Alberta to combat the Depression under the following headings: leaders, policies, results.
5. The C.C.F. claimed to provide a better alternative for the chicken than hopping from one foot to the other. Write a brief report on the C.C.F. Party: reasons for formation, membership, aims, program.
6. Sketch the events that led to the Regina riot of 1935.
7. What led Bennett to introduce his "Canadian New Deal"? Describe the program. What reasons can you think of to explain why the voters did not buy Bennett's program?
8. Why did King appoint the Rowell-Sirois Commission? What were its main recommendations?
9. Describe the extent of the American cultural and economic invasion of Canada during the 1930s. In your opinion, is the "takeover" greater or less today? Why do you think so? Should Canadians do anything about this situation? If so, what; if not, why not?
10. What were the issues in the Oshawa strike in 1937? Who won?
11. Canadian nationalism is a two-edged sword: sometimes it works *for* national unity and sometimes *against* it. Discuss Canadian nationalism and national unity from the following points of view: French- and English-Canadian relations; Canada-Great Britain relations; and Canada-U.S. relations.

CHAPTER 10

A Second World War: 1939–1945

The Canadian summer of 1939 was beautiful. The brilliant sunshine that emerged from behind the black clouds of the thirties seemed like a good omen, a bright foretaste of the forties. There were still some patches of cloudy sky here and there in that final summer of the Great Depression. Thousands of men and women remained out of work, and governments continued to pay out large sums of money for relief. But times were slightly better. The recovery from that dreadful year of 1933, when industrial production slumped to its lowest level, was getting easier. Factory gates had been opening wider. And many farmers had returned to the prairies, which had been made fertile again by the return of normal rainfall. For the first time in years, people had a little extra money in their pockets. It was not much, but it was enough to afford a little fun that would erase a few of the bitter memories of the recent past. Summer resorts were busy, movie theatres were full, and the happy crowds at the nation's largest sideshow, the Canadian National Exhibition, were bigger than ever.

On September 1, 1939, the storm clouds returned, and skies were black over all of Canada. News reports on the radio and headlines in the paper that morning were shocking. At daybreak, German armed forces, supported by waves of fighter planes and dive bombers, had broken across the Polish border. Two days later, France and Great Britain declared war on Germany. After twenty years of uneasy peace, the nations of Europe had again decided to settle their quarrels on the battlefield.

FROM COLONY TO NATION

As it had done in the First World War, Canada joined the conflict. But this time, the Canadian Parliament made the decision to do so. Entry into the war was not automatic as it had been in 1914, when Canada was a colony and dutifully followed Britain into war. During the interval between the wars, Canada had become an independent nation.

The achievements of the Canadian armed forces in the First World War had fertilized the seeds of nationalism. Prime Minister Robert Borden had sensed this and used his country's war effort to persuade Britain to grant Canada a greater degree of independence. He began by insisting that a Canadian should lead Canadian troops. The British

In the summer of 1939, King George VI and Queen Elizabeth toured Canada. In this photograph, taken on the steps of the Centre Block of the Parliament Buildings, the monarch salutes a march past of army, navy, and air force personnel.

The entrance archway of the Centre Block is decorated with shields bearing each province's coat of arms. Note the shield left blank in anticipation of the day (March 31, 1949) when Newfoundland would join the Dominion.

The Public Archives of Canada, C 17440

gave way by replacing Byng, the British commander of the Canadian Corps, with Arthur Currie. Borden's forceful demands that Canada and the other Dominions share in devising general war strategy led to the formation of the Imperial War Cabinet, which was made up of the British prime minister and the Dominion prime ministers. When the victorious powers met in Paris in 1919 to draw up the peace treaties, Borden fought for the right of Canada and the other Dominions to sign the treaties as sovereign nations. Despite American and French objections that Canada was merely a British colony, Borden won his point.

Although the Dominions were all asked to provide troop support, they had not been fully consulted before the crisis broke. Canada and South Africa particularly felt that this was a British problem that did not affect them. The Chanak incident pointed up the difficulty of a single imperial foreign policy.

The announcement of plans for Canada's own separate diplomatic representation in the U.S. was made in Parliament in 1920.

In 1949, Canada won the right to amend the BNA Act except for certain specific matters affecting Parliament and provincial legislatures.

The contribution of the Dominions to victory had been crucial. Next to the major powers, they had supplied the greatest number of fighting men and had suffered the greatest casualties. Canada, a country of nine million that mourned 60 000 dead in Flanders' fields, had lost more men than the United States, a nation with ten times its population.

Prime Minister Mackenzie King expressed this growing sense of nationalism in 1922 when Great Britain, on the verge of war with Turkey at a place called Chanak, demanded a Canadian pledge of assistance if war broke out. King refused to commit Canada without the approval of Parliament. This set an important precedent. Canada no longer felt obligated to support Britain's wars; acting according to its own best interests, Canada would form its own foreign policy. King then took another step to assert Canada's control of its own affairs. He informed the British government that Canada, on its own, without Britain's co-signature, intended to sign a pact with the United States. He brushed aside the suggestion that the British ambassador in Washington should sign the treaty. The Halibut Fisheries Treaty of 1923 was the first international trade agreement made by Canada acting independently of Great Britain. Four years later, Vincent Massey was appointed Canadian ambassador to the United States. The embassy opened by Massey in Washington was the first of many that Canada would establish in various nations as it assumed complete responsibility for its own affairs and interests abroad.

The Canadian movement toward independence influenced the reshaping of the British Empire. The British themselves, already feeling the winds of change, began to redefine the relationship that bound the members of their global community. The essence of this new relationship was contained in a report made by Lord Balfour, a former British prime minister, at the 1926 Imperial Conference. Canada and the other Dominions would now be recognized as

> autonomous communities within the British Empire, equal in status, in no way subordinate one to another in any respect of their domestic or external affairs, though united by a common allegiance to the Crown and freely associated as members of the British Commonwealth of Nations.

The Balfour Report was a statement of policy that recognized the independence of the Dominions. Five years later, in 1931, the Statute of Westminster put into law the principle laid down by Balfour. The British Commonwealth of Nations replaced the British Empire. As a member of the British Commonwealth, Canada was legally free to make its own laws without any fear of British interference. There were only two powers still held by Great Britain. The Judicial Committee of the Privy Council remained the highest court of appeal for nations in the Commonwealth, and amendments to the Canadian constitution still had to be approved by the British Parliament.

Perhaps the most influential man at the Paris Peace Conference in 1919 was the American president, Woodrow Wilson. He believed that war could be prevented if "a general association of nations" could meet regularly to discuss their problems and preserve peace and order in the world. This was the basis for the League of Nations, which was formed in 1919, with headquarters in Geneva, Switzerland. The success of the League depended on the willingness of its member nations to accept the principle of collective security: an attack on one member was an attack on all. Whenever any member was threatened, all of the others would come to its aid. In the Charter of the League of Nations, the terms of collective security were spelled out in Articles X and XVI. Article X called on each member nation to provide military support for any nation that was attacked by a League member. Article XVI defined economic sanctions and other non-military methods of punishing aggressor nations.

Canada joined the League with mixed motives. Membership added prestige to its new status as an independent nation. But Canada wanted status without responsibility. As a new nation trying to free itself from British attachments, Canada was not really prepared to become involved in European affairs. Borden believed in international co-operation but doubted the wisdom of Article X as a policy for achieving collective security. And King saw no need whatsoever for binding overseas commitments. The Canadian delegate to the League summed up his country's position: "We live in a fireproof house far from inflammable materials. A vast ocean separates us from Europe." There was also the reassuring certainty that neither Great Britain nor the United States would stand aside if Canada were attacked.

American foreign policy in the postwar period influenced Canadian thinking. Despite President Wilson's pleas, the United States refused to join the League of Nations. After the war, Americans wanted nothing more to do with European politics. They shut the door on the outside world and became absorbed in their own affairs. Although Canada did join the League (and even accepted the presidency of the international organization in 1925), it took little active interest in League affairs. Like Americans, Canadians preferred to isolate themselves from the world.

The 1920s were peaceful years. To the surprise of many sceptics, the League of Nations solved several disputes that arose among some of its members. These were small nations, but their willingness to accept intervention in their affairs gave hope to those who believed the League could maintain world peace. Then came the Depression and the decline in world trade. Nation after nation erected mammoth tariff walls and turned inward, refusing to consider the problems of others. Co-operation gave way to suspicion — and then to aggression. The strong began to prey on the weak.

Economic sanctions include such actions as a total trade boycott, restricted trade on certain goods, etc.

Canadian officials also served on League committees dealing with such matters as drug trafficking, international labor relations, and disarmament.

In 1931, Japan invaded China's northeastern province of Manchuria. This was the first step towards acquiring a great new Asian empire, which would supply Japan with raw materials and also markets for its manufactures. Unable to resist the powerful aggressor, China appealed to the League. This was the first major test of the League, and it backed away from direct action. The League appointed an investigating committee, which took a full year to make its report. China was distant and its affairs unimportant. No nation came to China's aid. Japan occupied Manchuria and then made plans for the conquest of the rest of China. When the League finally did announce that it refused to recognize Manchuria as Japanese territory, the Japanese responded by withdrawing from the world organization and continuing their attacks on China. The League, in its collective insecurity, did nothing.

The League's reaction to Japanese aggression interested Benito Mussolini, the Italian dictator. He and his black-shirted followers, the Fascists, had come to power in the 1920s. By the early 1930s Mussolini was looking for an easy excuse to expand his armed forces and also distract the attention of Italians from their generally low standard of living. He found one in Abyssinia (now Ethiopia), a small, underdeveloped African nation, reputedly rich in natural resources. While Italian dive bombers and tanks massacred Ethiopians armed with spears and antiquated rifles, the Abyssinian government asked the League for assistance. The proud bearing of Emperor Hailie Selassie as he tried to speak over the crude hissing of the Italian delegates moved the League Assembly. It quickly passed a resolution declaring Italy an aggressor and appointed a committee to draw up sanctions. The Canadian delegate, Dr. Walter Riddell, proposed that the sanctions include an embargo on oil. Without oil, Mussolini's war machine would grind to a halt. But

UPI Photo

A trio of Ethiopian tribesmen are forced by law to give the fascist salute to a huge poster of Mussolini. (Il Duce wears his characteristic bullfrog expression.) To his Fascist Party, the Ethiopian campaign was an ideal opportunity to enjoy military glory while suffering few of the agonies of a real war.

In 1937, Japan began to wage all-out war on China, a course of action that was blandly described by Tokyo officials as the "China Incident." In this photograph, the flag of the "nation of the rising sun" is carried by Japanese soldiers into what is left of the Chinese town of Tsungyang.

neither Great Britain nor France was willing to go that far. Nor was Canada; Mackenzie King refused to back Riddell. The failure of support from other nations killed the resolution. Suddenly the enthusiasm for stopping Mussolini's forces died. The League did nothing. As Italian troops, using flame-throwers and mustard gas, were destroying the last units of the Abyssinian army, Hailie Selassie warned the League Assembly that "God and history will remember your judgment."

The most dangerous test came from Adolf Hitler, Chancellor of Germany, who actually dealt the League its final and fatal blow. As leader of the Nazi Party, Hitler had come to power in 1933 with promises to end unemployment and avenge Germany for the harsh terms of the Treaty of Versailles, which had crippled and humiliated the nation. Once in office, Hitler revealed his contempt for world opinion. He withdrew Germany from the League of Nations and broke the Treaty

In addition to payments of money, reparations included replacement of goods and property lost or damaged in the war — ships, coal, livestock, etc.

283

of Versailles in a series of bold moves. According to the Treaty, Germany was forbidden to manufacture any major weapons of war or to increase its army beyond 100 000 men. And the Rhineland, a German province bordering Belgium and France, had been declared a demilitarized zone. Hitler defiantly broke all these terms. In 1935, he ordered a massive rearmament (which sharply reduced unemployment), introduced conscription, and announced the creation of a German air force and navy. In 1936, he sent armed troops into the Rhineland in what he called a "symbolic occupation."

Why had all these events taken place? What had caused the rise of the dictatorships? Why did the democracies do nothing to check these aggressions? A world war and a worldwide depression had drained and exhausted the energy of the industrialized nations. People felt defeated and demoralized, ready to give up some of their freedoms to a strong leader (like Mussolini or Hitler) who promised them jobs and economic security. Thus Germany and Italy became dictatorships. In another dictatorship, the Soviet Union, the people were suffering a series of purges imposed by Joseph Stalin to get rid of "enemies of the state." In dictatorships, with strong central governments, it is much easier to find "solutions" to political and economic problems, and to impose them. Sometimes these solutions, though violent, are confined within the state; sometimes they lead to military aggression. The democracies, struggling with domestic economic problems and remembering the horrible events and effects of the First World War, desperately tried to avert another international conflict. They watched the rise of dictatorships, fearful, yet anxious to do almost anything to appease the dictators. (This willingness to sacrifice almost any principle to avoid war was known as "appeasement.") Of the two types of dictatorship — communist and fascist — the Western democracies thought communism was the greater threat. Fascist dictators like Hitler and Mussolini, and later Franco in Spain, knew this and took advantage of it. It made them more aggressive. When they were appeased, both their appetite for power and their boldness increased.

In July, 1936, General Francisco Franco led a military revolt against the legally elected Spanish government. Franco's supporters, known as Rebels or Nationalists, included most Spanish servicemen, the industrialists and large landholders, many officials of the Roman Catholic Church, and the Falange (the Spanish Fascist movement). Ranged against them were the Loyalists or Republicans, most of whom were men and women in the working classes and members of the liberal, socialist, and communist parties. The revolt became a war, the most bloody civil war of the twentieth century. But Spaniards were not to settle their own quarrels without outside help. Within a month of the outbreak, German airplanes and pilots and Italian mechanized army units joined the Nationalist forces. In October, fighter planes and tanks arrived from the Soviet Union to aid the Loyalist forces. The Spanish

Civil War became front-page news around the world. What had begun as a civil war was soon viewed by most outsiders as a titanic struggle between fascism and communism.

Canadians were more interested in the Spanish conflict than in any other foreign event of the decade. Many Canadian Catholics, especially in Quebec, were terrified of communism. Believing, wrongly, that the Loyalist forces were directed from Moscow, they became strong backers of Franco. When Spanish Loyalist representatives (including a Roman Catholic priest) came to Canada to win support for their cause, they were met by abuse in Quebec. Adrian Arcand, the Canadian fascist leader, and his Silver Shirt bullies used violence to break up pro-Loyalist meetings in Montreal. Many liberals, C.C.F.ers, communists, working-class people, and intellectuals opposed Franco. A Canada-wide organization, the Committee to Aid Spanish Democracy, raised money to send medical supplies to the Republican government. At least twelve hundred men left Canada to join the Mackenzie-Papineau Battalion in Spain. They were part of the International Brigades, a volunteer army from more than sixty nations that fought on the Loyalist side. The most famous Canadian to go to Spain was the Montreal surgeon, Dr. Norman

The worldwide response to the struggle in Spain attracted thousands of youthful idealists to fight for the Loyalist cause. George Orwell and Ernest Hemingway have written about their experiences in the war. Among the Canadians who fought for the Loyalists were Hugh Garner, Ted Allan, and Tim Buck.

Standing in front of the German eagle and the swastika, the symbol of his Nazi party, Adolf Hitler is saluted by his followers. Hitler led a party that was extremely nationalistic, anti-Communist, and anti-Jewish. Using a mixture of lavish promises, massive propaganda, and planned violence, the Nazis managed to dominate the German Reichstag (Parliament), which enabled Hitler to be appointed Chancellor (leader) of Germany.

Ullstein

Bethune. Bethune's mobile blood-transfusion service, the first in history, saved the lives of hundreds of Loyalist soldiers. Prime Minister Mackenzie King viewed the Spanish Civil War as a possible threat to Canadian unity. He was very aware of French Catholic support for Franco. In 1937, Parliament passed the Foreign Enlistment Act, which prohibited any Canadian from joining the conflict in Spain. By that time, however, most of the Canadians who were willing to fight in Spain had already crossed the Atlantic.

The two powers that might have stopped the intervention of Germany, Italy, and the Soviet Union were Great Britain and France. But both were afraid that if they took action, they would antagonize the dictators and cause greater violence. As a result, they brought together representatives from more than twenty-five nations to discuss the Spanish Civil War and the fear of its spreading. Eventually they drew up the Non-Intervention Agreement by which foreign nations, including the three intervening powers, agreed to stay out of the Spanish conflict. It was a total sham. While Great Britain and France stood aside, German, Italian, and Soviet arms continued to arrive in Spain. Once again the desire of the democracies to appease the dictators had increased the spread of violence.

At the height of the Spanish Civil War in July 1937, Germany and Japan signed the Anti-Comintern Pact. Japan gave up its pretence of wanting only Manchuria and launched a full-scale invasion of China. Newspapers reported the horrible atrocities committed by the Japanese army, but Western governments did nothing. There were many expressions of regret in Canada, but the only Canadian to take part in this war was Dr. Bethune. He joined the Chinese Communist Eighth Route Army as medical director. Eighteen months later, in November, 1939, he died in China from a wound he suffered while performing battlefield surgery.

China was too remote from North America to concern most Canadians. Europe was closer, and the situation there was growing worse every month. Hitler had long dreamed of uniting all the German-speaking peoples of Europe into a "Greater Germany" that would dominate central Europe. In March 1938, Hitler's armies marched unopposed into neighboring Austria and declared it part of Germany. No nation came to the aid of little Austria. Hitler turned next to nearby Czechoslovakia, where a large number of German-speaking people lived in an area called the Sudetenland. When the Nazi leader claimed the Sudetenland belonged to Germany, the British prime minister, Neville Chamberlain, visited Hitler twice to discuss the issue. At Munich, Germany, in September 1938, Hitler met with Mussolini, Chamberlain, and Prime Minister Daladier of France. (No Czech leader was invited to attend this meeting.) He promised that he wanted no more territory in Europe, and this served to satisfy the appeasers. They signed an agreement giving him the right to annex Czech territory.

This alliance, later enlarged to include Italy, was directed against the Soviet Union.

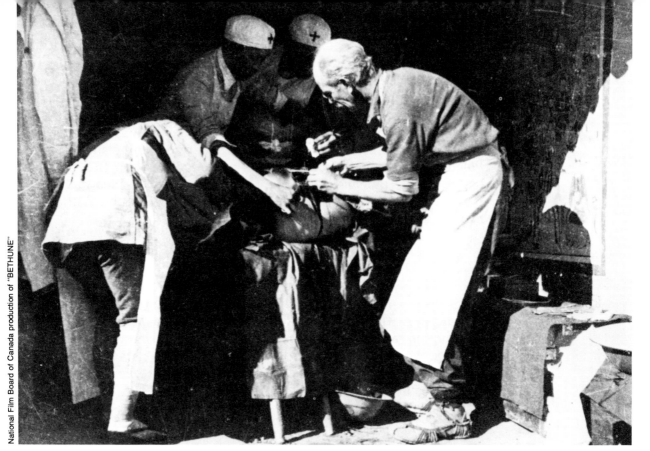

Bethune's battlefield surgery in China was performed in makeshift operating theatres, in this case, a Buddhist temple. He never had adequate medical equipment and supplies, and the absence of surgical gloves led to his death from an infected finger. This photograph, one of the best known in modern China, was used in the design of a stamp issued by the Chinese government in memory of "Comrade Norman Bethune."

When Chamberlain reached England waving a copy of the Munich agreement, which he proudly described as a guarantee "of peace in our time," the British people were delighted and relieved. So were Canadians, and Mackenzie King wired Chamberlain: "The heart of Canada is rejoicing tonight at the success which has crowned your unremitting efforts for peace." But "Munich" became a synonym for appeasement, and convinced Hitler that he had nothing to fear from the democracies. He later said, "Our enemies are little worms. I saw them at Munich." In March 1939, German troops occupied the rest of Czechoslovakia without any protest from Great Britain and France. (A few weeks later, Mussolini seized the little Balkan state of Albania.) Hitler next turned, as everyone expected he would, in the direction of Poland, to regain territory Germany had lost by the Treaty of Versailles. He demanded the return of the former German city of Danzig, which the now-useless League of Nations governed as an international city.

Two weeks later, fighting stopped in Madrid; Franco had triumphed in Spain.

It was at this point that Britain and France finally snapped out of their paralysis. They announed that they would fight to defend Poland. This unexpected show of strength by the democracies caused Hitler to pause.

Tension slowly eased — until the world heard a completely unexpected announcement on August 22. Nazi Germany and Communist Russia had just signed a non-aggression pact. Hitler now had nothing to fear on Poland's eastern border. On the western border, nothing stood in his way except the promised action of the weak democracies. Hitler decided to call their bluff. On September 1, German troops and planes attacked Poland. This time the democracies responded. When the Germans ignored their demand to pull back from Poland, France and Great Britain declared war, on September 3, 1939. The Second World War had begun.

THE BATTLEFRONT

On September 10, 1939, the Canadian government declared war on Germany. In the House of Commons debate on the issue, only one Member of Parliament took a stand against Canadian involvement. He was J. S. Woodsworth, the leader of the C.C.F. and a life-long pacifist. After demanding that his vote of opposition to the declaration of war go on record, he spoke again:

> I must thank the House for the great courtesy it has shown me. I rejoice that it is possible to say these things in a Canadian Parliament under British institutions. It would not be possible in Germany, I recognize that. . . . I want to maintain the very essence of our British institutions of real liberty. I believe that the only way to do it is by an appeal to the moral forces which are still resident among our people, and not by another resort to brute force.

By 1944, the Royal Canadian Navy had nearly 100 000 personnel and 900 ships, third in rank among the navies of the world. The RCAF reached a total of 200 000 service people, and the Canadian Army 650 000. From a population of fewer than 12 million, nearly one million served in the Canadian armed forces.

The brave decision of Woodsworth to stand, alone, for his anti-war beliefs won the respect of some Canadians. But most believed that the brute force of Nazism was running roughshod over moral force. To save itself, Canada would also have to resort to brute force. Unfortunately, in 1939, Canada had little more than moral force to offer. Its total armed force was composed of just over 10 000 men and women, a small group of tanks, a few airplanes and ships, and some outmoded weapons.

After the German invasion of Poland, with its devastating technique of "blitzkrieg" (lightning war), the brave but outfought and underarmed Poles were forced to surrender within three weeks. They had had little chance to resist. As they turned to face the Nazi onslaught from the west, they were attacked by Russian forces from the east. By the end of September, Poland had been divided between the two conquering powers. Hitler then pulled the bulk of his forces back to Germany. He made no attempt to invade France; nor did the French and British take the offensive against Germany. The first Canadian army units, which arrived in training camps in England just before Christmas, spent a dull winter of waiting. On the continent of Europe there was virtually no

Canadian troops bound for Great Britain watch as their ship eases away from the dock at Halifax. The first army units to reach Britain sailed up the river Clyde in December, 1939. Scottish bystanders soon learned the nationality of those on the troopships. Simulating the school yells learned at home, they spelled out, in unison, C-A-N-A-D-A, and then roared a mighty "CANADA!"

fighting as French and German troops stayed safely barricaded behind their respective frontiers, taking occasional shots at each other.

This "phony war" or "sitzkrieg" dragged on until the spring of 1940. Then, in early April, using the same successful blitzkrieg tactics that had worked against Poland, the Germans overran Norway and Denmark within a few weeks. Next, they invaded Holland, Belgium, Luxembourg, and France. Their panzer (armored) units threw back the defending British and French armies, which were forced to turn and head for the English Channel and safety. At the beginning of June, nearly 350 000 French and British soldiers were evacuated across the Channel from the French seaport town of Dunkirk. And though he growled, "Wars are not won by evacuations," Winston Churchill knew that it was a miracle. By holding off the advancing Germans until the evacuation was completed, French and British units had saved men who would some day come back to wrest western Europe from Hitler's grasp.

With the surrender of France, Britain was the next target. For the next three months, the summer of 1940, the German Luftwaffe (air force) tried to eliminate British air strength in preparation for Operation Sea Lion, the invasion of Britain by water. Hundreds of German

Winston Churchill replaced Neville Chamberlain as prime minister in May 1940.

Women in the armed forces drove trucks, deciphered messages in code, and operated radar equipment. The largest force of servicewomen in the Second World War was the Canadian Women's Army Corps, which eventually numbered 21 000 officers and other ranks. Of these, about 3000 served overseas.

Canadian War Museum

The error was twofold: the military and industrial might of the Soviet Union now entered the war on the side of the Allies, and Germany found itself fighting on two fronts — the same situation that had been a major factor in its defeat in the First World War.

bombers came across the English Channel to dump tonnes of bombs on Britain's airfields. The Hurricanes and Spitfires of the Royal Air Force and the Royal Canadian Air Force flew up to do battle with the Luftwaffe, scattering the German fighter escorts and gunning down the bombers. By mid-September, the scale of German losses forced Hitler to call off the battle. It was a victory won by the "gallant few," a group of several hundred young men, most of them in their early twenties. Winston Churchill paid a fitting tribute to their magnificent effort: "Never in the field of human conduct was so much owed by so many to so few." The victory was purely defensive, however; Great Britain lacked the strength to strike back at the Nazi power in Europe, which continued to expand with the conquest of Yugoslavia and Greece.

Then, at the very height of his power, Hitler made a vital error. On the morning of June 22, 1941, nearly three million German soldiers and airmen, supported by the most advanced military weapons yet produced, slashed into northern, central, and southern Russia. Swooping Stuka dive bombers and fast-moving panzer tanks threw Russian armies and civilians into headlong retreat. Within months, hundreds of thousands of prisoners had been taken, and the two great cities of Leningrad and Moscow lay under siege. It was not until the arrival of the Russian winter's ice and snow that the German offensive slowed down, giving the Soviet armies a chance to regroup and establish defence lines. What had appeared to be another swift German conquest bogged down into a deadly, four-year struggle.

For Great Britain, Canada, and the other Dominions, the German invasion of the Soviet Union gave them the opportunity to build up their armaments and their forces to liberate a Nazi-dominated Europe. In that time they acquired a formidable ally. The United States of America had remained neutral since the outbreak of war. President Franklin D. Roosevelt revealed his sympathies by extending military aid to Great Britain, but a strong isolationist sentiment among the American people prevented direct participation. Only direct aggression against the United States could draw that nation into the war. This happened with savage swiftness on Sunday, December 7, 1941, when Japanese naval aircraft attacked the American naval base of Pearl Harbor in the Hawaiian Islands. The air strike had been designed to knock out the U.S. Pacific Fleet so that Japan could carry out a campaign of conquest in Southeast Asia without opposition. The attack on Pearl Harbor was largely successful, but it brought into the war, on the side of the Allies, the most powerful nation in the world.

The United States possessed the material resources, the money, and the manpower to wage total war. But it took time to mobilize these and

This military aid was a lend-lease program under which Great Britain leased materiel from the U.S. under the guise that it was to be returned at the end of the war. Lend-lease solved the problems of U.S. neutrality and British lack of funds to pay for the materiel.

The corvette was the vessel that handled the bulk of Atlantic convoy duties. Much like a whaling ship in design and construction, it was highly manoeuvrable and could survive the worst weather. Packed aboard (in conditions of considerable discomfort) were a crew of ninety men, submarine-detection equipment, and a large load of depth charges. Canada built and manned about 150 of these tiny but tough warships.

UNION OF SOVIET SOCIALIST REPUBLICS

Alaska

Aleutian Is.

CHINA

Pacific Ocean

Tokyo JAPAN

Chunking

Greatest extent of
Japanese expansion

Midway Is.

INDIA

Mariana Is.

Hawaiian Is.

Philippine Is.

Caroline Is.

Marshall Is.

Dutch East Indies

Indian Ocean

Solomon Is.

AUSTRALIA

0   1000 km

NEW ZEALAND

GREATEST EXTENT OF AXIS EXPANSION: 1942

Greenland

Iceland

GREAT
BRITAIN

GERMANY

USSR

Moscow

London

Berlin

FRANCE

Paris

ITALY

Rome

CANADA

Ottawa

UNITED
STATES
OF AMERICA

Washington, D.C.

MEXICO

Atlantic Ocean

AFRICA

N

SOUTH AMERICA

Pacific Ocean

Atlantic Ocean

Under Allied control

Under German-Italian control

Under Japanese control

Neutral

293

In mid 1942, public and military opinion demanded offensive action against Hitler-occupied Europe. In Britain, the Canadian soldiers, led by General A. G. L. McNaughton, were eager to fight. Thus, on August 19, a raid was made on the French vacation resort of Dieppe by 5000 Canadian and 1000 British troops. Its object was to test the strength of German coastal defences and gain experience in landing men, tanks, and other equipment on a hostile shore. In the heroic attempt to seize Dieppe, 900 Canadians were killed, 500 wounded, and nearly 2000 taken prisoner. But some historians say that the heavy losses in the Dieppe experience made possible the relatively low casualties of the 1944 invasion of France.

turn them against Japan and Germany. Meanwhile Japan marched into eastern and southeastern Asia with the same success that Germany had had in Europe. They drove deep into China, occupied Dutch and French colonies, and came very close to invading India and Australia. They easily captured the supposedly impregnable British fortress of Singapore and fell on the tiny British outpost of Hong Kong, overpowering it on Christmas Day 1941. Among the defending forces at Hong Kong was a contingent of Canadian troops that had been hastily sent to the Asian colony at the urgent request of Great Britain. After their surrender, they spent the remainder of the war in Japanese concentration camps.

The year 1942 was the high-water mark of the three Axis powers, Japan, Germany, and Italy. On every front, the Allies were in retreat or on the defensive. Not until October did the Allies have a major victory to celebrate. At El Alamein in North Africa, British, Australian, and New Zealand troops, "the Desert Rats," inflicted a decisive defeat on the German Afrika Korps led by the famous "Desert Fox," General Irwin Rommel. It was the beginning of the end for the Germans (and Italians) in Africa.

294

In 1943, Prime Minister Churchill of Great Britain (far right), President Roosevelt of the United States (centre), and their military advisers met for a conference in Quebec City. The two Allied leaders pose here for a publicity shot in company with Prime Minister King (far left), Governor General the Earl of Athlone, and his wife, Princess Alice.

In July 1943, the First Canadian Army Corps, led by Lieutenant-General H. D. C. Crerar, took part in the Allied invasion of the Italian island of Sicily. They were the first Canadian troops to win victory in battle during the Second World War. By September, Sicily had been taken and an even tougher campaign had begun — the invasion of the Italian mainland. When the Italian government surrendered that same month, Hitler sent in German troops to stiffen resistance. And this they

When not making publicity photographs and films to promote the sale of war bonds in Canada, Messrs. Wayne and Shuster would turn up in France to put on a show for the troops.

295

On an airfield in Italy, Allied airmen try to save a parked aircraft that has been shot up by German fighter planes in the course of a low-level attack.

certainly did. Fighting was vicious and progress slow, although Allied troops ultimately forced the Germans to retreat the entire length of the Italian peninsula. Canadians distinguished themselves throughout the war in Italy, particularly in the savage house-to-house combat that resulted in their capture of the town of Ortona in December 1943.

The Italian campaign dragged on into 1945, sapping German military strength. Meanwhile, the main Allied offensive was being organized:

The railway yards at Munster, Germany, the target of many attacks — at night and in daylight — by bombers of the Royal Air Force, the Royal Canadian Air Force, and the United States Army Air Force.

In almost any high school in Canada, the roll of honor of those who served in the Second World War contains many RCAF listings. In Bomber Command alone, 16 000 Canadian aircrew members died on active service.

Operation Overlord, the invasion of Europe by combined American, British, and Canadian forces. It began on "D-Day," June 6, 1944, on the beaches of Normandy, and it took the Germans by surprise. Once ashore and some distance inland, Canadian troops ran into strong German resistance at Caen and Falaise but finally won these battles. With the exception of a determined German counterattack in the Ardennes region of northern France later that year, the Allies remained on the offensive from their initial landings at Normandy. In the fall of 1944, the Canadians were given the difficult task of clearing the Germans out of Belgium's Scheldt Estuary. They succeeded and freed the huge port of Antwerp, to which reinforcements and supplies were brought from England. Early in 1945, the Allies crossed the German border. On May 8, V-E Day, Germany accepted terms of unconditional surrender.

The Pacific Theatre remained, and the blood spilled there was mostly American and Japanese. Island by island, U.S. naval, air, and land forces had to fight hard for every bit of ground in a struggle that inflicted heavy casualties on both sides. In July 1945, U.S. President Harry S. Truman made one of the most fateful decisions of the war. First, he sent a message to the Japanese government advising surrender by August 3 or else "the alternative for Japan is prompt and utter destruction." There was no reply from the enemy.

Franklin Roosevelt died on April 12, 1945.

The Japanese industrial city of Nagasaki, where thousands of people were cremated by the second atomic bomb used in the Second World War. Shock waves generated by the blast carried death up to sixteen kilometres from "ground zero," the point immediately beneath the mid-air explosion. Unknown to the dazed survivors, radiation levels were still deadly for days after the explosion, which resulted in large numbers of cases of radiation poisoning.

Official United States Air Force Photograph

Then, early on the morning of August 6, a lone U.S. B-20 bomber, the "Enola Gay," headed for the Japanese city of Hiroshima. At 8:15 a.m., the plane dropped a single bomb. When it exploded in mid air, there was a stupendous flash of light, and a massive, mushroom-shaped cloud slowly rose into the atmosphere. The intense heat generated by the first atomic bomb ever used in war created a radio-active holocaust that killed thousands and flattened half of Hiroshima. Three days later, another atomic bomb was dropped on the city of Nagasaki, with similar results. Five days later, Japan sued for peace and signed terms of surrender on September 2. With their signing, the Second World War ended.

THE HOME FRONT

Canada was second only to the United States as a supplier of financial aid and war supplies to the various Allied powers. The fiasco of Sam Hughes and supply contracts in the First World War was a valuable lesson: the same mistakes were not repeated. Under the control of C. D. Howe, the minister of munitions and supply, wartime production was quickly organized and smoothly co-ordinated. Howe awarded contracts to industries with the understanding that payment would be made on a cost-plus-10-per-cent basis. Some Canadians felt that there should be no profits in wartime, arguing that if the government could draft a man or woman into the army at $1.50 a day, it should use its powers to regulate industry and conscript wealth. Ultimately, public and business accepted the "cost plus" arrangement. There seemed to be no better way to get on with the job of winning the war.

The result was the greatest production boom in Canadian history to that time. Factories and yards turned out everything from bullets to ships. Airplanes and corvettes, tanks and trucks, rifles and howitzers, radar and signals equipment poured off assembly lines for use not only by Canadians but also by British and other Allied forces. Agricultural

A special celebration attended the production of the half-millionth unit of motorized equipment produced in Canada during the Second World War. Here, Clarence Decatur Howe, the Minister of Munitions and Supply, ceremonially starts up the vehicle for delivery to some armed-forces unit.

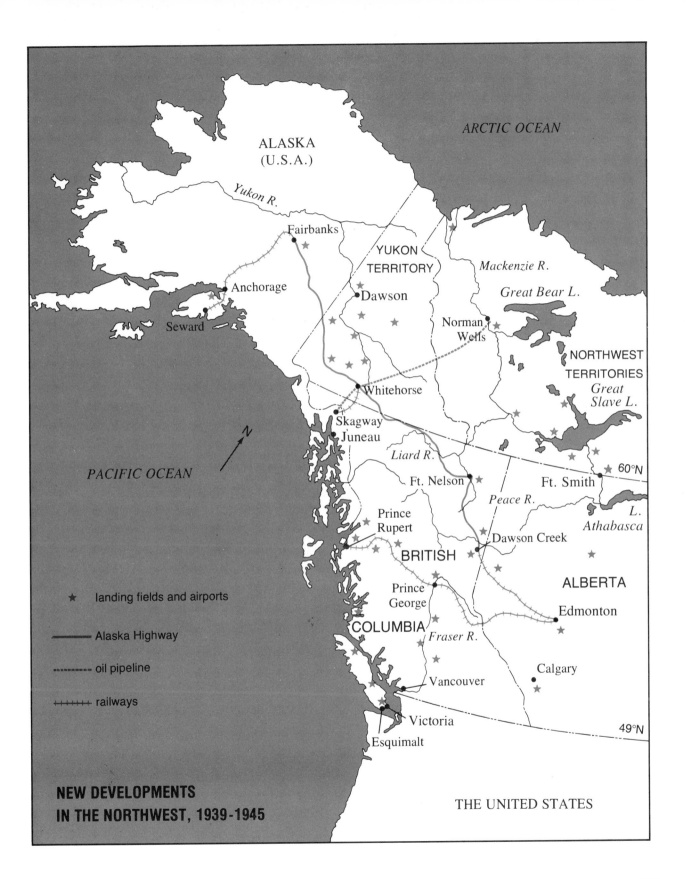

ARCTIC OCEAN

ALASKA
(U.S.A.)

Yukon R.

Fairbanks ★

YUKON
TERRITORY

Mackenzie R.

Great Bear L.

Anchorage

★ Dawson

Seward

Norman
Wells ★

NORTHWEST
TERRITORIES

*Great
Slave L.*

Whitehorse

Skagway
Juneau

Liard R.

60°N

PACIFIC OCEAN

Ft. Nelson ★

Ft. Smith ★

Peace R.

Dawson Creek ★

L.
Athabasca

Prince
Rupert ★

BRITISH ★

ALBERTA

★ landing fields and airports

Prince
George

Edmonton

—— Alaska Highway

COLUMBIA

Fraser R.

- - - - oil pipeline

Calgary

++++++ railways

Vancouver

Victoria

THE UNITED STATES

49°N

Esquimalt

**NEW DEVELOPMENTS
IN THE NORTHWEST, 1939-1945**

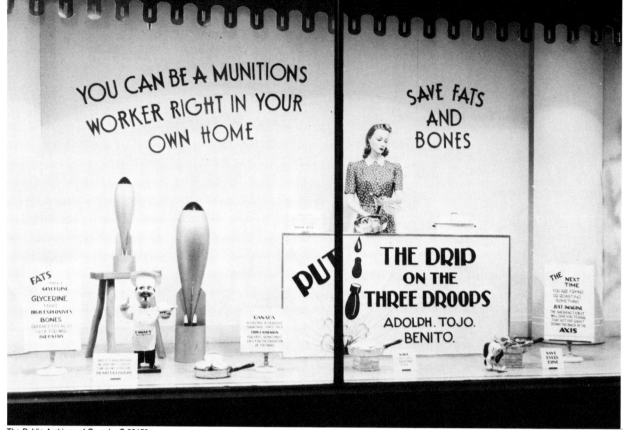

The Public Archives of Canada, C 29458

Posters on billboards and displays in store windows encouraged Canadians to help win the war by saving scrap metals, fats, and bones. Scrap could be turned into bomb casings. Glycerine could be extracted from fats to make high explosives. And both fat and glue could be extracted from bones. (The three "droops" were Hitler, Tojo, the Japanese leader, and Mussolini.)

Malaya, the main source for natural rubber, was occupied by the Japanese. This made the discovery of a method of producing synthetic rubber, by scientists at the National Research Council in Ottawa, of vital importance in keeping the wheels of war turning.

produce increased by almost 40 per cent during the war, and Canadian meat, grains, and numerous food products were shipped to Allied forces around the world. The war particularly spurred the growth of secondary industry. Many primary industries found their foreign markets cut off, and many importers were unable to obtain finished products from abroad. One result was the establishment of many new industries. Some of the largest were for the manufacture of electronic equipment and diesel engines. By the end of the war, the value of products from secondary industry was greater than that from primary products.

The war brought about close military and economic co-operation with the United States. In 1940, at Ogdensburg, New York, Prime Minister King and President Roosevelt signed a document that committed Canada and the United States to a permanent military partnership in defence of the entire North American continent. By the Hyde Park Agreement negotiated between Prime Minister King and President Roosevelt a year later, the two nations avoided unnecessary duplication of products for war use. Meeting at Hyde Park, Roosevelt's private estate on the Hudson River, they worked out a scheme whereby they

300

would complement their war production, each purchasing certain requirements from the other. Thus, Canadians bought such items as machine tools and aircraft engines from the United States, while Americans placed large orders with Canada's small arms and ammunition industry. Coupled with heavy American investments of money in Canada during the war, the Hyde Park agreement emphasized the ever-increasing trading connection between the two countries. (Some critics of Mackenzie King maintain that this was the beginnings of today's American domination of Canada's economic affairs.)

The total cost of war production was about $20 billion. Unlike the Borden government, King and his cabinet leaned more heavily on personal income and corporation taxes to raise this money. Almost half came from these taxes. The rest came from Victory Bonds, which were purchased almost equally by individuals and by insurance and trust companies. To allow the federal government the tax monies needed to finance the war, the provinces entered into "tax-rental" agreements by which they surrendered to Ottawa their right to levy income and corporation taxes. In return, they received increased subsidies from federal revenues. (Two years earlier, this arrangement had been one of the main recommendations of the Rowell-Sirois Report.) The 1942 tax-rental agreement was the first of a series of such agreements between Ottawa and the provinces, a development that went a long way towards re-establishing Ottawa's leadership in Canadian affairs.

For recommendations of the Rowell-Sirois Report, see pp. 272-273.

In 1942 and 1943, a 2400-kilometre highway was constructed from Dawson Creek, British Columbia, to Fairbanks, Alaska, with several sideroads leading to military airfields and emergency landing strips. A joint venture by the Canadian and American governments, the Alaska Highway was constructed to provide speedy transportation of men and materials to Alaska to counter a possible Japanese invasion.

The Public Archives of Canada, C 25739

Of course, the war increased the power of the federal government in other ways. In 1940, Parliament passed the War Measures Act, which gave the federal government authority far beyond its constitutional limits. Under this Act, the cabinet could issue, without the prior approval of the House of Commons, emergency orders of any kind at any time. These orders were used, for instance, to direct civilians into war work, to restrict the use of lumber, leather, steel, and oil to war production, to impose prices on goods and services (including rents), to freeze wages, and to ration certain consumer goods. It was under this Act that the federal government set up a Wartime Prices and Trade Board. (In the First World War, without any such controls, some prices had risen by as much as 60 per cent: in the Second World War, prices rose, on average, about 20 per cent.) It became almost impossible to buy a new car, tires, and certain other commodities during the war. But people in Canada suffered little. Gasoline, sugar, and butter were rationed, and people carried booklets with ration coupons. However, if you had a sweet tooth, it was usually possible to swap a few butter

Another Canada-U.S. war venture to offset any Japanese attack on Alaska was the construction in 1944 of a 950-kilometre, small-diameter, pipeline from Imperial Oil's Norman Wells oilfield in the Northwest Territories to Whitehorse in the Yukon Territory. By 1945, about a million barrels of oil had been pumped over the Mackenzie Mountains into the Yukon, processed at Whitehorse into fuel oil and gasoline in a refinery imported (at great expense) from Texas, and then supplied to troops and air force personnel along the Alaska Highway. The final cost of the Canol Pipeline (Canadian Oil Project) was somewhere around $134 million.

Like Americans on the west coast of the United States, British Columbians were worried by the possibility of a Japanese invasion. The result was one of the most shameful actions even taken by a Canadian government. In 1941-1942, Canada's entire Japanese population — about 23 000 people — were treated as enemies. Their few properties were confiscated and sold. Regardless of how long they had lived in Canada or whether or not they were citizens, Japanese Canadians were herded into prison camps in British Columbia and Ontario or made to work on prairie farms. Families were often broken up, men going to one camp, women and children to another.

coupons with a neighbor for some sugar coupons. And almost everybody had money during the war. It was an irony of fate that wartime in Canada meant full employment and overtime. Lunch pails were full, and investors had little to complain about. The Second World War killed the Depression.

POLITICS AND NATIONAL UNITY

In September 1939, Prime Minister Mackenzie King had one special fear. Could the nation pass through another war without a repetition of the conscription crisis of 1917, which had turned Quebec and the rest of Canada against each other? Borden and Laurier had failed to avoid a wartime split between Francophone and Anglophone. King felt he simply had to guide a united Canada through the conflict or, he thought,

*For details on the
conscription issue
during the First
World War, see
Chapter 7.*

in the end there would be no Canada. Thus, when the decision to declare war had been made, King stated emphatically that his cabinet would not introduce conscription. In his own words, he promised that:

> The present government believes that conscription of men for overseas service will not be a necessary or an effective step. Let me say that so long as this Government may be in power, no such measure will be enacted.

King never admitted any regret in making this pledge, although his words returned to haunt him through the political battles of the war years.

Within a month, his pledge was challenged. The premier of Quebec, Maurice Duplessis, saw conscription as an issue that he could use to win re-election in his province. In October, 1939, he called an election and charged that King and the Liberal government would use the war to take away the rights of Francophones and weaken the powers of the Province of Quebec. One of those ways would be by forcing Québecois to fight overseas in the Canadian armed forces.

The use of conscription as an issue in the Quebec election terrified King, but Ernest Lapointe, minister of justice in the Liberal cabinet and King's lieutenant in Quebec, was convinced that he knew how to defeat Duplessis' challenge. He and two other federal ministers from Quebec campaigned on behalf of Adelard Godbout, Duplessis' Liberal opponent. Lapointe and his colleagues put their case bluntly before the people of Quebec. Since the three men were absolutely opposed to conscription, the people of Quebec could remain assured that it would never be passed as long as they remained in the cabinet. They strengthened their case by threatening to resign if Duplessis were elected. Naturally, if they resigned, Quebec would have no one to speak up for its interests in the federal cabinet. Lapointe's gamble was successful. The election was a severe defeat for Duplessis and a sweet victory for a worried Mackenzie King. For the next five years, the Liberal Party of Quebec was in office and co-operated with Ottawa in furthering the national war effort.

In January 1940, King was challenged by another provincial premier, this time by a fellow Liberal, Mitchell Hepburn of Ontario. Hepburn loathed King and sensed an opportunity to embarrass the Liberal Party into replacing King with a stronger war leader. He introduced in the Ontario legislature a resolution condemning King for his timid handling of Canada's role in the war. King's answer caught Hepburn — and just about everyone else — off guard. In 1940, King needed an excuse for an election, and Hepburn had given it to him. Announcing that he could not hope to govern wartime Canada without the confidence of the people, he called a federal election. The results revealed that most Canadians supported him. The 178 seats won by the Liberals represented the largest parliamentary majority since Confederation. King had won a second wartime victory for national unity.

After the election, an act was passed that gave the government the right to conscript men for home service only, as a defence force. Quebec accepted the conscription of a separate army for domestic defence — the so-called "Zombies" — and the rest of the country tolerated this costly compromise. However, demands within and without the Liberal Party to send larger numbers of troops overseas began to exert pressure on King. He reacted, as usual, with caution. In April, 1942, he held a Canada-wide plebiscite that asked the voters whether or not they favored *releasing* the Liberal government from its pledge not to introduce conscription. Throughout the country, 64 per cent voted for allowing King to do as he saw fit. But in Ontario and Manitoba, the vote was 80 per cent in favor of giving the government this free hand. And in Quebec

CANADA IN 1945

it was 72 per cent against releasing the government. Although the voters were not asked to state whether they favored or opposed conscription, there was little doubt that those who favored releasing King from his pledge wanted him to introduce conscription. King solved his problem by a carefully confused public statement that, as a result of the plebiscite, his policy would be "conscription if necessary, but not necessarily conscription."

For the next two years King followed his usual course: he delayed. When manpower became a serious problem after the terrible losses in Italy and in the fighting that followed D-Day, King again came under pressure. Replacements were needed for the final Allied assault on Germany. Colonel James Layton Ralston, his minister of defence, led the many Liberals who demanded that the home-defence conscripts be sent overseas. King's answer was to dismiss Ralston from the cabinet and replace him with General A. G. L. McNaughton, the former commander of the Canadian Army overseas. The new minister, who was popular among the Canadian soldiers, believed that the gaps in the army divisions could be filled without resorting to conscription. He confidently conducted a recruiting campaign among the home conscripts – and these men proved him wrong. About 550 signed up for overseas service. Clearly, only conscription could provide the needed men.

There was no more time left for delay. In November, 1944, King reluctantly introduced a bill to conscript 16 000 of the home-defence force for active service overseas. When the bill passed Parliament by a vote of 143-70, one influential cabinet minister from Quebec resigned because he had long opposed conscription and could not accept it. But fortunately for King, an important Francophone colleague stood by him. Louis St. Laurent, a much-respected corporation lawyer who, in 1941, had replaced the late Ernest Lapoint as King's lieutenant in Quebec,

On VE (Victory in Europe) Day, Prime Minister Mackenzie King (left), and his cabinet colleague, Louis St. Laurent (right) were attending the conference in San Francisco, California, that founded the United Nations Organization. They are seen here broadcasting to Canadians the news of the surrender of Nazi Germany.

gave the bill his full support. In the words of historian Bruce Hutchison,

> Canada had at last found its first Quebec statesman prepared to defy
> the deepest French-Canadian emotion, to accept the most hated
> symbol of the conquest, to put the whole nation above its parts.

The majority of Québecois, together with those members of the Liberal Party from Quebec, grudgingly went along with St. Laurent and the conscription order.

Eventually about 13 000 home conscripts were sent to Europe to join the Canadian Army. Opponents of King charge that his desire to retain power compelled him to delay action in order to avoid losing support in Quebec. Those who defend him point out that while there was controversy over conscription, as there had been in 1917, it never reached the same crisis level and did not cut as deeply. When the war ended, Canadian unity had received only a surface wound, not the severe gash it had suffered a generation earlier.

As prime minister, King was very much the descendant of John A. Macdonald, Wilfrid Laurier, and Robert Borden. Like them, his great aim was the avoidance, at any cost, of a split between English-speaking and French-speaking Canadians. As Macdonald had sought out Georges Etienne Cartier and, later, Hector Langevin, to be the Conservative Party's voice in Quebec, so King called on Ernest Lapointe and, later, Louis St. Laurent, to fill the same role for the Liberal Party. Like Laurier and Borden, King strengthened Canadian independence by loosening ties with Great Britain. However, unlike Macdonald (in the case of Louis Riel) or Laurier and Borden (in the matter of conscription), King, in the period 1939-1945, warded off deep racial wounds that again would have fractured Canadian unity.

Fervent patriot though King was, some of his policies resulted in a growing Canadian military and economic dependence upon the United States. And that dependence would create many difficulties and problems for Canada and Canadians in the years following the Second World War.

*   *   *

In 1945, Canada was almost halfway into the century that Laurier had said would be "the century of Canada." Although the full hope of Laurier's prophecy had not been realized, still, much had been accomplished. The nation had grown from a Confederation of four provinces in 1867 to a Dominion of nine provinces and two territories stretching from sea to sea. The economy, initially based on agriculture — fur, fish, timber, wheat — had expanded and diversified with the development of primary and secondary industries — mining, pulp and paper, manufacturing. The population had increased with the flood of immigrants who settled the "last best West" and added their customs, talents, and traditions to the French-English heritage to produce our Canadian multicultural society. Macdonald's vision of a strong and independent nation in the northern half of the continent had become a reality.

The fulfilment of that vision had not been easy. The nation had been tested by two world wars and the Great Depression of the thirties; its federal basis had been challenged by constitutional controversy; its national unity had been strained by cultural division and regional differences. Canada had survived these stresses and had achieved nationhood.

In the struggle, some problems had been solved, some remained, and some new ones had arisen. Politically, the nation had achieved independence from Great Britain, but economically it had grown dependent on the United States. For Canada, which must export or die, the delicate balance between politics and economics would have to be carefully maintained. To preserve national unity, a definition of nationalism would have to be worked out that recognized the bilingual-bicultural basis of Canada and also expressed the multicultural diversity of the Canadian people. For Canada, these would be the challenges in the second half of the twentieth century: to preserve political and economic independence and to strive for a nationalism that would embrace both its French-English heritage and its multicultural and regional diversity in a unique national unity.

STUDY 10

1. By what actions did Canada show a growing sense of nationalism that was finally recognized by the Statute of Westminster?
2. (a) What was the purpose of the League of Nations?
   (b) By what methods did the League expect to achieve this aim?
   (c) What tests did the League face, from its formation in 1919 to its final failure?
   (d) Explain why the League failed each of these tests.
3. Keeping in mind the political climate at the time, how do you explain the worldwide response to the Spanish Civil War on the part of both governments and ordinary people? How did the Canadian reaction fit into the general world response?
4. What factors help to explain the Western democracies' policy of appeasement? What finally led them to change this policy?
5. (a) Trace the trail of Axis victories from the outbreak of war to 1942. What were the bright spots for the Allies during this period?
   (b) List the events after the tide turned in favor of the Allies.
6. What do you think was the most significant event — military, political, technological, etc. — of the Second World War? Explain your choice.
7. Outline and evaluate Canada's contribution to the war effort in armed forces and materiel.
8. How was the Canada of 1945 different from the Canada of 1918, with respect to (a) the economy, (b) national sovereignty, and (c) national unity?
9. Mackenzie King stayed in power longer than any other prime minister. What personal qualities and what social, political, and economic conditions made it possible for him to do so?
10. In your own words, how far has Canada come on the road to nationhood, how far do we still have to go, and what direction do you think we should follow?

INDEX OF PEOPLE AND PLACES

ACKNOWLEDGMENTS

Cover photograph by Bill Brooks. Maps and diagrams by Frank Zsigo.

Gage Educational Publishing Limited wishes to thank the National Film Board Photothèque for permission to reproduce the photograph by Ted Grant on page 1 and Bill Brooks for permission to reproduce the photograph on page 167. Gage also wishes to thank the Harriet Irving Library and *The Vancouver Sun* for permission to quote, on page 263, an excerpt from a letter sent to *The Vancouver Sun* in May, 1935.